P9-APA-418

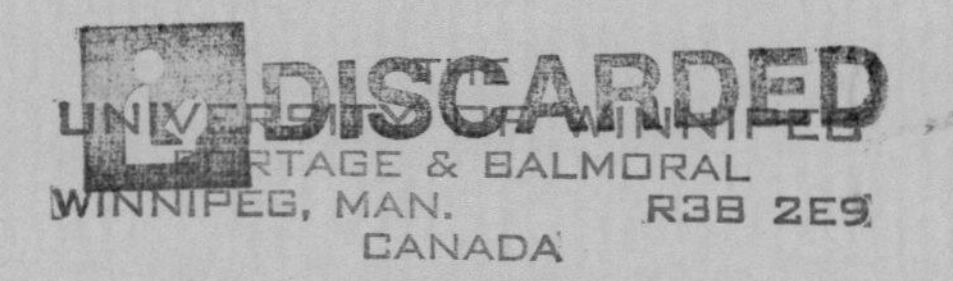
DISCARDED
PORTAGE & BALMORAL
WINNIPEG, MAN. R3B 2E9
CANADA

THOMAS HARDY

The Poetry of Perception

TOM PAULIN

First published 1975 by
THE MACMILLAN PRESS LTD
London and Basingstoke
Associated companies in New York
Dublin Melbourne Johannesburg and Madras

SBN 333 16915 8

Printed in Great Britain by
WESTERN PRINTING SERVICES LTD
Bristol

For Giti

Contents

Let us fix our attention out of ourselves as much as possible: Let us chace our imagination to the heavens, or to the utmost limits of the universe; we never really advance a step beyond ourselves, nor can conceive any kind of existence, but those perceptions, which have appear'd in that narrow compass. This is the universe of the imagination, nor have we any idea but what is there produc'd.

David Hume, *A Treatise of Human Nature*

Under that despotism of the eye (the emancipation from which Pythagoras by his numeral, and Plato by his musical, symbols, and both by geometric discipline, aimed at, as the first *propaideuma* of the mind) – under this strong sensuous influence, we are restless because invisible things are not the objects of vision; and metaphysical systems, for the most part, become popular, not for their truth, but in proportion as they attribute to causes a susceptibility of being seen, if only our visual organs were sufficiently powerful.

S. T. Coleridge, *Biographia Literaria*

Preface

It's sometimes said that the reason why there are so few books about Hardy's poetry is that the poems are so various that no one has found a consistent way of approaching them – a lever to shift them with. My approach is through his stress on sight and the numerous issues which are implicit in it, but I have by no means confined my discussion of the poems to his positivism. This is mainly because I wanted to give as full and flexible an account of his poetry as possible, and also because I wanted to redeem and develop the postgraduate thesis which is at the basis of this book. Here, I must stress that I haven't simply resprayed six chapters and a thousand rusty footnotes – I have revised, expanded, ruthlessly cut and totally rewritten my original discussion, and I have added a great deal of new material.

The discussions of Hardy's poetry which I found most valuable are Donald Davie's *Thomas Hardy and British Poetry* (though I've often disagreed with it) and also his great essay, 'Hardy's Virgilian Purples', in the special Hardy issue of *Agenda* he edited. Samuel Hynes's *The Pattern of Hardy's Poetry* is the only good full-length discussion of the poems I've read, though again I often disagree with it, and two reference works – F. B. Pinion's *A Hardy Companion* and J. O. Bailey's *The Poetry of Thomas Hardy: A Handbook and Commentary* – are invaluable.

I owe great debts of gratitude for their help and encouragement to Dennis Burden, Dorothy Bednarowska, R. N. R. Peers and the staff of the Dorset County Museum, Merryn Williams, Samuel Hynes, T. M. Farmiloe, David Williams and James Gibson for his help over the Eweleaze illustration. And I'm particularly indebted to Peter Messent for checking the manuscript and making many necessary corrections and valuable suggestions.

The author and publishers are grateful to the following for permission to quote copyright material: to Faber & Faber Ltd for 'This be the Verse' from *High Windows* by Philip Larkin, and for 'The Hunched' from *The Happier Life* by Douglas Dunn; to Geoffrey Grigson for 'Objects' from *A Skull in Salop* and for 'Scullion' and 'Dead Poets' from *Discoveries of Bones and Stones*; to Michael B. Yeats, Miss Anne Yeats and the Macmillan Publishing Co. Inc. for 'Paudeen' from *The Collected*

Poems of W. B. Yeats (copyright 1916 by the Macmillan Publishing Co. Inc., renewed 1944 by Bertha Georgie Yeats); and to Charles Tomlinson for 'Winter Encounters' from *Seeing is Believing*.

The notes at the back of the book, which are not essential to an understanding of the text, include the sources of the less accessible quotations. These notes are keyed by the page number and the opening words of the quotation or phrase to which they refer.

January 1975 T.P.

Introduction

In an introductory note to *Discoveries of Bones and Stones* Geoffrey Grigson states:

> Objects are mean, or nothing; yet can all the same, if they are discovered by the right objectifier, elicit and exert benediction. On this account all perceptional artists (can there be artists of any other kind?) now find themselves in an exceptional dilemma between difficulties and temptations, or ways out, the worst temptation being to abandon everything for looseness, or easiness, untautened, unexquisite in means.

As Grigson implies in one of the best poems in the volume – 'In View of the Fleet' – Hardy is a perceptional artist, a poet who 'notices things'. Coincidentally, I've called this book about Hardy *The Poetry of Perception*, though in writing it I've begun to wonder whether the word 'perception', with its connotations of a dry and deadening positivism, fully covers a body of work which, although it is agnostic and humanist in spirit, never finally settles for the impossibility of 'vision'. Hardy's best volume (the collection that contains 'During Wind and Rain') is called *Moments of Vision* and although he says in the penultimate poem in the *Collected Poems* that

> We are getting to the end of visioning
> The impossible within this universe,

and though the example he gives of this visionary impossibility refers to human, social progress and not religious faith, the religious question is left, if not open, at least ajar. His last, aptly titled poem, 'He Resolves to Say No More', imperiously offers a characteristic combination of religious reference and scientific-humanist application:

> And if my vision range beyond
> The blinkered sight of souls in bond,
> – By truth made free –
> I'll let all be,
> And show to no man what I see.

As he says in the grumpy 'Apology' with which he prefaced *Late Lyrics and Earlier*, 'belief in witches of Endor is displacing the Darwinian theory and "the truth that shall make you free" '. The quotation from St John, 'And ye shall know the truth and the truth shall make you free', is linked with Darwin here, not with Christian belief, and it would be wrong to argue that what he is refusing to show us is a vision which cannot be understood in terms of nineteenth and early twentieth-century science. Still, right up to the end he refuses to tell – refuses, in other words, to abandon his position somewhere between the 'Rationalists' and the 'Revelationists or Mystics' who, for him, 'err' in opposite directions, the former 'as far in the direction of logicality as their opponents away from it'. What Hardy wanted was a compromise: the Anglican service with God and theology left out. He liked hymns and old churches and he knew his bible, and he didn't want to abandon the cultural values that go with them. Also, as he told William Archer, he found the 'material world...so uninteresting' and was 'most anxious to believe in what, roughly speaking, we may call the supernatural.' However, he was unable to find any evidence for it. 'People accuse me', he told Archer, 'of scepticism, materialism, and so forth; but, if the accusation is just at all, it is quite against my will.' He would give ten years of his life, he said, 'to see a ghost – an authentic, indubitable spectre'. But later in the conversation he quotes the principle in Hume's essay 'Of Miracles' to prove the impossibility of his ever believing any report of the supernatural: 'no testimony is sufficient to establish a miracle, unless the testimony be of such a kind that its falsehood would be more miraculous than the fact which it endeavours to establish.' His reluctant commitment to Hume's scepticism comes through in his fine, late poem, 'Drinking Song':

> Then rose one Hume, who could not see,
>   If earth were such,
>   Required were much
> To prove no miracles could be:
>   'Better believe
>   The eyes deceive
> Than that God's clockwork jolts,' said he.

Unlike the sun on Gibeon, the laws of nature never stand still.

Hardy's wish to *see* an indubitable ghost is characteristic of his discontented scepticism, and as I shall argue in the following chapters his imagination operates under what Coleridge terms the 'despotism of the eye'. The dilemma is obviously familiar: as Tennyson puts it, 'We have but faith: we cannot know; / For knowledge is of things we see.' But Hardy does not follow Tennyson, who bases a sense of the supernatural upon the split between faith and sense-data, and nor does he take the way that Grigson suggests in his note and in many of his shorter poems. He does not seek to discover objects which may 'elicit and exert benediction'.

This mysticism of objects, often obsessive and usually unsatisfactory, is the predominant characteristic of Grigson's poetry. A poem called 'Objects' in *A Skull in Salop* has an epigraph from Wyndham Lewis: 'Moments of vision are blurred rapidly, and the poet sinks into the rhetoric of the will.' Inevitably, the phrase 'moments of vision' associates with Hardy, though Lewis was probably thinking of Schopenhauer and the Imagist movement rather than Hardy's poetry. Grigson's poem reads:

On a sill:
Black and white stripes,
A pink scarf, amethyst edge of a
Flannel, ballet shoes red,
Blue stockinged blunt
Feet of a bear, head
To a vaguely wood-
Coloured brick: I am surprised
Noticing suddenly
These, waiting there.

A starling nicks with its bill,
Sky is quite grey. Inside
I notice no fumble or blunder
Or fuss of the will.
No connection. I notice only
Extravagant wonder
Of items laid out on a long
White painted sill.

As so often with Grigson there is that marvellously managed sense of a voice speaking, a savoured fidelity to the rhythms of speech, with sharp, clear diction. But the poem fails to persuade me that he is doing anything more than accurately observe and describe a series of *things*. They don't 'exert benediction' because he simply tells us that he notices 'only / Extravagant wonder'. He is noticing a series of things and writing a poem of observation, not a perceptional or a visionary poem (i.e. one which redeems or transforms objects).

And Grigson's difficulty is that, committed to Hardy's poetry (though he has recently reneged on this commitment – or grown beyond it*), he leaves out one of its most important qualities – its humanism. Take 'Scullion':

> Blue eyes, red red nose, and bright
> ginger hair: on the pavement
> opposite goes one of our Breugel world
> without much to be glad of, I fear.

Grigson observes 'this kitchen hand ashore from a liner' and imagines him back in 1400 'cold in old ill-fitting hose'. He concludes:

> Our Breugel race has its jokes,
> I can only say it's not fair
> to combine such blue, red and white and sharp
> feet and such hair. I say, it's not fair.

And it's not fair to make a jokey composition out of the boy's clashing colours. He does it again in 'Lovers in a Train':

> Her eyebrows black, her fair falling hair
> from her sloped head on his
> green cardigan.

He is 'blue-chinned, a hairy man' who would have been a 'short-browed hard black-thatched' Roman charioteer. Though being in love, Grigson comments, they don't care about politics or the fact that the train is passing through an ancient landscape. He finishes by noticing the man's 'most startlingly red-tinted ear'.

Grigson is really more interested in colours and their combinations than in the two people, and so he arranges them, like the kitchen porter, into a composition, making a kind of cubist picture of them. He distances them historically (they are even remoter than Breugel) and transforms them into objects. In doing so he behaves like a patronising aesthete, and this is something – or someone – we don't associate with Grigson as critic, editor and anthologist. The difficulty

* See his essay, 'The Poet Who Did Not Care for Life', in *The Contrary View*.

is that to do other than turn them into things is to run the risk of being sentimental. In a very fine poem, 'Dead Poets: Recalling them in November', it is by facing up to this problem, by taking the risk, that Grigson is able to write so powerfully. He begins:

> Friends, my friends of so much
> Time gone, of languages
> Brighter than mackerel,
> It is beyond bearing that you are dead.

Then, as in 'Twins, More or Less, Still Necessary', he undercuts this tone of sentiment with a curt frankness:

> No, I bear it most days too easily.
> But there are moments when a drop falls
> And sends tremors over my bason, at 8 a.m.
> When light comes up behind
>
> Our hill and reveals flaws in the
> Window-glass shaped like comets or
> Skulls: to think of you warm, of you gone
> Is a cold air all round me then.

The voice drops and because we hear its tone and credit its authenticity, the objection is overcome. And in the final stanza, where he convicts himself of a selfish sentimentality and so purges the poem of precisely that emotion and of his self-conscious criticism of it, he is sternly and magnificently direct:

> So many. And in so many ways
> Of course myself I mourn, my
> Own ash throw on to that
> Frosty grey lawn.

Hardy is one of the poets behind the superb, spoken texture of Grigson's poetry and it's therefore a pity that Donald Davie didn't mention him, let alone give him a chapter, in *Thomas Hardy and British Poetry*. Possibly the history behind Grigson's squib, 'To Professor Donald Davie', in *Sad Grave of an Imperial Mongoose*, one of his most recent volumes, accounts for the omission. Unfortunate, too, was the timid punch Davie pulled at Douglas Dunn, for many of his poems work in ways that anyone who values Hardy's poetry ought to appreciate. 'The Hunched', for example, is a really fine poem:

They will not leave me, the lives of other people.
I wear them near my eyes like spectacles.
Sullen magnates, hunched into chins and overcoats
In the back seats of their large cars;
Scholars, so conscientious, as if to escape
The things too real, the names too easily read,
Preferring language stuffed with difficulties;
And the children, furtive with their own parts;
The lonely glutton in the sunlit corner
Of an empty Chinese restaurant;
The coughing woman, leaning on a wall,
Her wedding-ring finger in her son's cold hand,
In her back the invisible arch of death.
What makes them laugh, who lives with them?

I stooped to lace a shoe, and they all came back,
Mysterious people without names or faces,
Whose lives I guess about, whose dangers tease.
And not one of them has anything at all to do with me.

This tough vision of other lives carries its own refutation of the charge of 'inert observation' that Davie makes against some of Dunn's work.

What I detect in Davie's book is a dissatisfaction with a confused entity composed of Hardy's poetry, English suburban sprawl, and certain British poets. Somehow, poetry has been sold short. Hardy's poems 'instead of transforming and displacing quantifiable reality or the reality of commonsense, are on the contrary just so many glosses on that reality, which is conceived of as unchallengeably "given" and final.' To demonstrate the wrongness of this Davie quotes a poem by Mairi MacInnes called 'Hardly Anything Bears Watching' (the unintentional, subdued pun seeps into his argument). The poem ends:

When I was young,
The pavement kerbs were made of stone,
A substance like my finger-nails.

It is not like that any more.
I do not see
The essential life of inorganic things.
Humanity has covered all.

The attitude here, Davie says, is that 'to buy sympathy with the human, at the price of alienation from the nonhuman, is a hard bargain at best.' Davie clearly sympathises with this poetry of rocks and stones (bones and stones in Grigson's similar formulation). What we need, he suggests, is a poetry of hard objects. He is not asking us, as Colin Falck said in an essay called 'The Poetry of Ordinariness' which was prompted by Davie's book, 'to abandon the frying-pan of myth for the fire of old-fashioned positivism: we are to trade in the "superior" world of myth for a wholesale commitment to the actualities of what happens to happen.' In fact, Davie is very close to the position Falck himself elaborates in the last sentence of his essay when he says that the result of jettisoning a symbolist escape from ordinary life 'could be a true poetry of ordinariness (or to borrow Keats's phrase we could perhaps call it "poetry of earth"): a step towards setting our other-wordly longings to work within the only world we can hope to possess.' This is well said, but it in no way contradicts the recommendation contained in Davie's statement:

> Neither in Hardy nor in Auden is there any sign of that determination to render the particular scene, experience, or topic in all its particularized quiddity which we find in Ruskin, in Hopkins's poems (and his theories of 'inscape' and 'instress'), and, in the present day, in characteristic poems by Charles Tomlinson.

This is a rejection of the kind of valuation Hardy, Auden, and Larkin put on 'things' which 'Humanity has covered'. It's a rejection of all that Hardy meant when he noted:

> An object or mark raised or made by man on a scene is worth ten times any such formed by unconscious Nature. Hence clouds, mists, and mountains are unimportant beside the wear on a threshold, or the print of a hand.

Davie's rejection of a humanism which is central to Hardy's work finds an over-obvious and unfortunate echo in Calvin Bedient's essay, 'On the Poetry of Charles Tomlinson', where he says:

> Let others – Dylan Thomas, D. H. Lawrence, E.E. Cummings – mount nature in ecstatic egoism. They will not really see her, except distortedly, through the heat waves of their own desire for union; they will not be companioned. Let still others – Thomas Hardy, Robert Frost, Philip Larkin – suspect the worst of her, dread her, hint at wrinkled flesh beneath the flowered dress.

They, too, will be left with only themselves. Tomlinson, putting himself by, will gain the world.

Tomlinson's sharply perceiving eye and the mysterious clarities it seizes demand respect, but not in such sycophantic quantities. Hardy, Frost and Larkin are better poets, and one of the reasons why they are better is because their work engages with the lives of other people. And though Tomlinson's most recent volume, *The Way In*, moves towards this engagement, its faintness shows in his eagerness to push beyond it into a metaphysical dimension. An earlier and characteristic poem, 'Winter Encounters', does this:

House and hollow; village and valley-side:
  The ceaseless pairings, the interchange
In which the properties are constant
  Resumes its winter starkness. The hedges' barbs
Are bared. Lengthened shadows
  Intersecting, the fields seem parcelled smaller
As if by hedgerow within hedgerow. Meshed
  Into neighbourhood by such shifting ties,
The house reposes, squarely upon its acre
  Yet with softened angles, the responsive stone
Changeful beneath the changing light:
  There is a riding-forth, a voyage impending
In this ruffled air, where all moves
  Towards encounter. Inanimate or human,
The distinction fails in these brisk exchanges –
  Say, merely, that the roof greets the cloud,
Or by the wall, sheltering its knot of talkers,
  Encounter enacts itself in the conversation
On customary subjects, where the mind
  May lean at ease, weighing the prospect
Of another's presence. Rain
  And the probability of rain, tares
And their progress through a field of wheat –
  These, though of moment in themselves,
Serve rather to articulate the sense
  That having met, one meets with more
Than the words can witness. One feels behind
  Into the intensity that bodies through them
Calmness within the wind, the warmth in cold.

The graceful sense of mystery is attractive, but the bland statement: 'Inanimate or human / The distinction fails in these brisk exchanges –' worries me in the way that Grigson's reduction of people to objects does. And Grigson, though much less confidently, entertains similar metaphysical ambitions. He, too, wants to discover a still clarity of objects.

Though Tomlinson means that there is an energising quality, a sense of true communion and encounter, behind both the people's casual conversation and the 'changing light' and 'responsive stone', the effect is one of detachment and distance – the 'intensity' seems located beyond the human, not within the people who are talking to each other. The quiddity is reached too easily, partly because the scene and the people are not sufficiently particularised, though if they were then their names and the substance of their conversations – necessary details from my point of view – would probably make the essential quiddity much more difficult. Admittedly, this is an early poem which seeks, very ambitiously, to discover a sense of relatedness between light, landscape and a human group, but for me it doesn't prove its discovery with sufficient power.

There is a short poem by Yeats called 'Paudeen' which manages this most difficult of combinations – a connection between human, social reality and metaphysical certainty:

> Indignant at the fumbling wits, the obscure spite
> Of our old Paudeen in his shop, I stumbled blind
> Among the stones and thorn-trees, under morning light;
> Until a curlew cried and in the luminous wind
> A curlew answered; and suddenly thereupon I thought
> That on the lonely height where all are in God's eye,
> There cannot be, confusion of our sound forgot,
> A single soul that lacks a sweet crystalline cry.

This begins as a rejection of the tawdry sogginess of modern Ireland, its tourist trade and political mediocrities, and it's similar to Lawrence's fatuous rejection of industrialised England at the end of *The Rainbow* (an attitude with which Davie appears to sympathise as he associates an approval of the humanised landscapes of Hardy and Larkin with apathy about conservation). But Yeats does not propose a romantic isolation from society and a mystic's attachment to the curlew's cry and the 'luminous wind' as an alternative. Instead, he relates them back to the people he has rejected through the realisation that beyond the social and political babble – 'confusion of our sound forgot' – there is a reality where each and every one of the people he thinks of as utterly sordid has a pure integrity, a soul with a 'sweet, crystalline cry' like the curlew's. The recognition is won both in spite of and because of his heroic egoism.

My point is that a poetry of clearly observed scenes – a poetry characteristic of Grigson and Tomlinson – doesn't make this kind of connection and can, as a result, be terribly deadening. When Davie criticizes Hardy and Larkin for infrequently breaking into, 'without meaning to and without noticing', imaginative levels that Tomlinson continually inhabits, we ought to be aware of just how thin the air up there can be. Yeats, who is Hardy's opposite, knew this.

The terms of this discussion are clearly comparable with those Victorian debates about faith and doubt which Hardy followed, though nowadays the argument centres around questions of whether poetry should be entirely about social and political quotidian reality, or whether it should move more in the direction that Davie is recommending – towards the 'particularized quiddity'. Colin Falck suggests a compromise between the two, a setting of the possibilities for quiddity within a 'poetry of ordinariness' – in other words a joining of the ordinary with the extraordinary. Is this feasible? Or must we choose between Bentham and Coleridge? Between behaviourism and mysticism? Or between humanism and religion?

The difficulties are apparent in Hopkins's 'Harry Ploughman':

> Hard as hurdle arms, with a broth of goldish flue
> Breathed round; the rack of ribs; the scooped flank; lank
> Rope-over thigh; knee-nave; and barrelled shank –
> Head and foot, shoulder and shank –

Though he gives us a religious quiddity, Hopkins makes a grotesque piece of creaking wickerwork out of the man in whom he discovers it. And when he hears of Felix Randal's death, he shrugs his shoulders, says 'God rest him', and tells us that

> My tongue had taught thee comfrot, touch had quenched thy tears,
> Thy tears that touched my heart, child, Felix, poor Felix Randal.

He can't quite allow this to touch our hearts because, after all, his subject may be *felix* in a better place. Hardy would have wrung our hearts here and set the unique human being against the injustice of circumstances and the absence of God.

Can poetry, then, have both quiddity and humanity? In the last chapter, which is based on Hardy's *Moments of Vision*, I argue that there are moments in his work when he writes in ways that are both human, like a Dutch painting, and visionary. The poems I'm thinking of – 'Old Furniture' and 'During Wind and Rain' in particular – make use of objects, and they do so not by perceiving them in such a way that each becomes a transcendental *ding an sich*, or an inscape, but by revealing and releasing human qualities that seem to be present in them. Just at times Hardy makes this enormously difficult connection.

I
Perception

Hardy's account of his life is severely reticent. He wrote his autobiography in the third person and directed his second wife, Florence Hardy, to publish it under her name after his death. It is a piece of sustained ventriloquism from beyond the grave. From there he tells us that 'Thomas Hardy was born, about eight o'clock on Tuesday morning the 2nd of June 1840', in a thatched house that stood 'in a lonely and silent spot between woodland and heathland.' His family, he says, had all the characteristics 'of an old family of spent social energies' and he hints that because his father's happy-go-lucky disposition made him neglect his building business for his violin and walks on the heath, his mother's energies and ambitions were transferred from her husband to her son. Hardy left school at sixteen and went to work in an architect's office in Dorchester where he 'often gave more time to books than to drawing'. In the summer he would get up at four in the morning to study Greek and Latin before going to work and in the evenings he often played the fiddle at country dances, weddings and christenings. One morning as he sat down to breakfast he remembered that a man was to be hanged at eight o'clock that morning and he ran out on to the heath with his father's telescope. Just as he put it to his eye 'the white figure dropped downwards, and the faint note of the town-clock struck eight'. He went home terrified and wished 'he had not been so curious', but his intense curiosity never left him. Right to the end of his life he was a watcher.

Though there are hints of a period of depression during his youth, there is no mention of a religious crisis. He read Newman's *Apologia* when he was twenty-five and had a 'great desire to be convinced by him' but could find 'no first link to his excellent chain of reasoning'. He admits that when the poems he was writing during his early twenties were being rejected by magazines he considered reading theology at Cambridge because he felt that poetry would go better with the church than with his work as an architect. This plan, he says, fell through less from any practical difficulties than from 'a conscientious feeling, after some theological study, that he could hardly take the step with honour while holding the views which on examination he found himself to hold'. However, he continued to go to church, 'to practise orthodoxy' he calls it, and this was partly because he liked hymns, bible readings, church buildings and the graveyards so many of his poems are about. Some of his architectural work involved restoring old churches and it was during a business visit to Cornwall in 1870 that he met his first wife, Emma Lavinia Gifford, the niece of the rector whose church he had been commissioned to restore. By the time of their marriage in 1874 Hardy was earning a living wholly by his writing. He had published three novels – *Desperate Remedies, Under the Greenwood Tree* and *A Pair of Blue Eyes* – and the serial of *Far from the Madding Crowd* was being favourably received. He and Emma were happy for a few years and then, he hints, their marriage became unhappy, though they lived together for almost forty years until Emma's death in 1912.

That radical unhappiness which so permeates all his work was not the result of his first marriage, though it was clearly deepened and confirmed by their transition from an intense love to a corrosive misery. There is, as I've said, no suggestion of a crisis of faith or identity – nothing remotely comparable with Mill's or Carlyle's plunge into deadness and negation – but there are hints in his very guarded account of his life which point to a crisis that occurred when he was twenty-seven. Deliberately, he presents what sounds like a deep crisis of confidence as a simple spell of bad health: possibly, he suggests, the hot summer of 1867 and the stinking Thames mudflats outside his office conspired to weaken his constitution, possibly – again this is partly an evasive, physical explanation – he became ill because every evening after work he continued his rigorous system of self-education by shutting himself up in his rooms and 'reading incessantly, instead of getting out for air after the day's confinement'. Whatever the cause or causes of his illness he had to go back to Dorset to recuperate and he admits that he was beginning 'to feel that he would rather go into the country altogether'. But a permanent return to his native heath at that period would have meant recognising the failure of his literary ambitions. He had been studying, reading and writing with enormous diligence but to little practical purpose, and in 1867 he obviously felt he was getting nowhere. Though his intense hard work eventually had results when *Desperate Remedies* was published four years later, that characteristic note of sadness begins to gather round many of the notes he made in his journal from 1866 onwards. A description of a visit he paid to Hatfield a few days after his twenty-sixth birthday marks the beginning of that eternally returning journey:

> Went to Hatfield. Changed since my early visit. A youth thought the altered highway had always run as it did. Pied rabbits in the Park, descendants of those I knew. The once children are quite old inhabitants. I regretted that the beautiful sunset did not occur in a place of no reminiscences, that I might have enjoyed it without their tinge.

But that melancholy tinge, a youthful insistence that 'Change dissolves the landscapes', is there in this note he made a year earlier: 'My 25th birthday. Not very cheerful. Feel as if I had lived a long time and done very little.' His lack of cheerfulness increased and two months later he reflected (surely with some reference to a deepening sense of failure) that the 'anguish of a defeat is most severely felt when we look upon weak ones who have believed us invincible and have made preparations for our victory.' He made this note in August 1865, and later that month he remarked:

> The poetry of a scene varies with the minds of the perceivers. Indeed, it does not lie in the scene at all.

This brief and unemphatic note, made at a time of increasing melancholy, states an attitude which is at the centre of all his work. It is the considered outcome of that strenuous course of reading and thinking which he had been following since his arrival in London three years before, and it rests upon the assumption that our knowledge is subjective and that nature is a dead waste like the heath which stretched beyond the back wall of the house Hardy was born in.

At the beginning of *The Return of the Native* he describes Egdon Heath as a darkling landscape which accords with the sombre intellectual mood of the times and he means that nature, like God, is dead. The heath is simultaneously a very old and a modern landscape, a barren place which philosophy and science have laid waste. And in this passage from one of his *Spectator* essays (Marjorie Nicolson quotes it in *Newton Demands the Muse*, a study of Newton's influence on eighteenth century poetry) Addison also uses a heath as a symbol of the reality posited by Newtonian science:

> ...but what a rough unsightly Sketch of Nature should we be entertained with, did all her Colouring disappear, and the several Distinctions of Light and Shade vanish? In short, our Souls are

> at present delightfully lost and bewildered in a pleasing Delusion, and we walk about like the Enchanted Hero of a Romance, who sees beautiful Castles, Woods and Meadows; and at the same time hears the warbling of Birds, and the purling of Streams; but upon the finishing of some secret Spell, the fantastick Scene breaks up, and the disconsolate Knight finds himself on a barren Heath, or in a solitary Desart. It is not improbable that something like this may be the State of the Soul after its first Separation, in respect of the Images it will receive from Matter; tho' indeed the Ideas of Colours are so pleasing and beautiful in the Imagination, that it is possible that the Soul will not be deprived of them, but perhaps find them excited by some other Occasional Cause, as they are at present by the different Impressions of the subtle Matter on the Organ of Sight.
>
> I have here supposed that my Reader is acquainted with that great Modern Discovery, which is at present universally acknowledged by all Enquirers into Natural Philosophy: Namely, that Light and Colours, as apprehended by the Imagination, are only Ideas in the Mind, and not Qualities that have any Existence in Matter.

As Marjorie Nicolson shows, Locke's philosophy grew out of Newton's discoveries, and Berkeley was later to use this idea that colours have no existence outside the mind as a proof for his argument that material objects only exist through being perceived. Berkeley did not deny the existence of matter as Samuel Johnson supposed when he refuted him by bruising his foot against a stone, but he restricted its reality to our perceptions of it and reduced perceived objects to bundles of 'sensible qualities'. If, like Johnson, we object that a tree, to use Bertrand Russell's example, 'would cease to exist if no one was looking at it', then Berkeley would reply that 'God always perceives everything; if there were no God, what we take to be material objects would have a jerky life, suddenly leaping into being when we look at them; but as it is, owing to God's perceptions, trees and rocks and stones have an existence as continuous as common sense supposes.'

In the philosophy of Berkeley's successor, Hume, both God and the perceiving self disappear. Hume reduces the self to a heap of different perceptions which lack a simple identity and so the human mind becomes a random assemblage of what it perceives, the sum of its memories and perceptions. We are the prisoners of our own minds and know nothing outside ourselves. As Russell says of Locke's theory of knowledge: 'Each one of us...must, so far as knowledge is concerned, be shut up in himself, and cut off from all contact with the outer world.' This, says Hume, is 'the universe of the imagination', and it is the universe which Hardy's imagination began to take possession of in 1865 when he made his note on the poetry of a scene.

At that time he probably had little direct knowledge of the philosophers who enabled him make his note. There are no references in the *Life* to long hours spent reading Hume's *A Treatise of Human Nature* during the 1860s, though later Hardy acquired a copy of Green and Grose's edition of the *Treatise* which was published in 1874, and as an old man he listed Hume along with Darwin, Huxley, Spencer and Mill as an influence on his work. If he didn't actually read Hume until the 1870s he did have access to his ideas much earlier because when he was twenty-one he read Bagehot's great essay on Shelley – an essay that gives the best account there is of Shelley's enthusiastic response to Hume's philosophy. And Shelley was the poet who most fascinated Hardy. He mentions in the *Life* that he was very impressed by Bagehot's *Estimates of Some Englishmen and Scotsmen* – the collection in which this essay appeared – and there he would have read, and probably reread, several of Shelley's references to Hume in which he repeatedly stresses his agreement with the idea that 'nothing exists but as it is perceived'. In his essay 'On Life', for example, Shelley states:

> The view of life presented by the most refined deductions of the intellectual philosophy is that of unity: Nothing exists but as it is perceived. The difference is merely nominal between those two classes of thought which are vulgarly distinguished by the names of ideas and of external objects.

And in *A Defence of Poetry* he quotes Milton, making the mind exist in a state of satanic isolation:

> All things exist as they are perceived; at least in relation to the percipient. 'The mind is its own place, and of itself can make a Heaven of Hell, a Hell of Heaven.'

Hardy, as I've mentioned, was fascinated by Shelley's poetry and personality – 'our most marvellous lyrist' he calls him in the *Life* – and his attachment to the Shelley-cult also involved an identification with the philosophical assumptions behind his poetry. In stating that the poetry of a scene varies with the minds of its perceivers Hardy was tacitly aligning himself with Shelley, and at the very centre of the Victorian period was identifying not simply with that period's characteristic theological earnestness – reading Newman into the small hours – but with an earlier tradition of radical freethinking. Hence, partly, his inability to be convinced by Newman. He had already mapped out the terrain before he read Huxley, Mill, Hume or Comte.

In 1862, a year after he read Bagehot's essay on Shelley, he mentions Ruskin's *Modern Painters* in a letter to his sister, and Ruskin's famous chapter on the pathetic fallacy must have also influenced his 1865 note. There, Ruskin is arguing against Hume's scepticism when he attacks those philosophers who define the word 'blue' as 'the sensation of colour which the human eye receives in looking at the open sky, or at a bell gentian.' As this sensation, they argue, 'can only be felt when the eye is turned to the object, and as, therefore, no such sensation is produced by the object when nobody looks at it, therefore the thing, when it is not looked at, is not blue.' The consequence of this, Ruskin states, is the idea that 'it does not much matter what things are in themselves, but only what they are to us,' and the logical conclusion of this is the philosopher's belief that 'everything in the world depends upon his seeing or thinking of it, and that nothing, therefore, exists, but what he sees or thinks of.' Ruskin is arguing for the external existence of hard objects and against the ways in which cloudy, emotional language blurs and dissolves their reality. For him this blurred language is a characteristic of second-rate poetry, and he quotes these lines from 'The Sands of Dee' to prove it:

> They rowed her in across the rolling foam –
> The cruel, crawling foam.

He then states:

> The foam is not cruel, neither does it crawl. The state of mind which attributes to it these characters of a living creature is one in which the reason is unhinged by grief. All violent feelings have the same effect. They produce in us a falseness in all our impressions of external things, which I would generally categorize as the 'pathetic fallacy.'

Hardy's note obviously resembles Ruskin's definition of the pathetic fallacy but it differs from it in that he is not concerned with the truth or falseness of the received impression: for him the emotional impact of a scene varies with, and therefore depends upon, its perceiver's state of mind. He is not interested in qualities that belong to the scene itself, and when Ruskin asserts that the 'particles' which always have the power of producing a sensation of blueness, even when no one is looking at a gentian, have been 'everlastingly so arranged by its Maker', Hardy is not with him. His imagination occupies that sealed world of sense impressions Ruskin is trying to argue us out of. In this Humean universe we are the prisoners of a constant series of pathetic fallacies.

Originally, 'The Pathetic Fallacy', was Hardy's title for 'The Seasons of her Year':

I

White is white on turf and tree,
  And birds are fled;
But summer songsters pipe to me,
  And petals spread,
For what I dreamt of secretly
  His lips have said!

II

O 'tis a fine May morn, they say,
  And blooms have blown;
But wild and wintry is my day,
  My song-birds moan;
For he who vowed leaves me to pay
  Alone – alone!

This is a dull, drab poem which simply illustrates Ruskin's term and Hardy's own note. Its companion-piece, 'The King's Experiment', which again shows how our perceptions of a landscape vary with our emotions, suggests that Hardy had also absorbed Crabbe's influence – a poet he admired and was reading during the 1860s. In 'The King's Experiment' he shows how Hodge's reactions to landscape, like Orlando's in Crabbe's 'The Lover's Journey', are conditioned by his feelings. The result is another mediocre poem which versifies Crabbe's statement:

It is the Soul that sees: the outward eyes
Present the object, but the Mind descries;
And thence delight, disgust, or cool indiff'rence rise:
When minds are joyful, then we look around,
And what is seen is all on fairy ground;
Again they sicken, and on every view
Cast their own dull and melancholy hue;

Or, if absorb'd by their peculiar cares,
The vacant eye on viewless matter glares,
Our feelings still upon our views attend,
And their own natures to the objects lend.

Crabbe then demonstrates how, since love 'clothes each object with the change he takes,' Orlando's love for Laura makes a barren heath seem beautiful and a rich pastoral scene appear ugly when he believes she no longer loves him. Interestingly, Crabbe, like Addison, uses a heath as an emblem of a reality which is void of the light, colour and emotive content man invests it with, and this is the idea Hardy explores at the beginning of *The Return of the Native* when he says that Egdon Heath appeals to 'a more recently learnt emotion, than that which responds to the sort of beauty called charming and fair.' Anticipating *Letters from Iceland* and Auden's injunction in 'Missing' to 'leave for Cape Wrath tonight', he predicts that tourists will soon be visiting Iceland rather than conventionally 'charming' beauty spots like Baden-Baden. For Hardy, this modern landscape harmonises with the lonely nature of man's experience in a barren material world: it is 'absolutely in keeping with the moods of the more thinking among mankind'. This lets the pathetic fallacy in through the back door and allows him to make his darkling heath both inert and strangely animate, both indifferent to human feelings and yet in keeping with some of them. The product of Newtonian science and empirical philosophy, it is 'like man, slighted and enduring; and withal singularly colossal and mysterious in its swarthy monotony.' Solitude seems to 'look out of its countenance'.

A. N. Whitehead gives a fuller and more contemporary account of this barren universe in a passage which Marjorie Nicolson quotes from *Science and the Modern World* where he shows that for Locke:

> ...the mind in apprehending also experiences sensations which, properly speaking, are qualities of the mind alone. These sensations are projected by the mind so as to clothe appropriate bodies in external nature. Thus the bodies are perceived as with qualities which in reality do not belong to them, qualities which in fact are purely the offspring of the mind. Thus nature gets credit which should in truth be reserved for ourselves; the rose for its scent: the nightingale for its song: and the sun for his radiance. The poets are entirely mistaken. They should address their lyrics

> to themselves, and should turn them into odes of self-congratulation on the excellency of the human mind. Nature is a dull affair, soundless, scentless, colourless; merely the hurrying of material, endlessly, meaninglessly.

Egdon Heath represents, largely, this meaningless hurrying of material, though by describing it as 'full of a watchful intentness' Hardy gives it a contradictory personality of its own. But his response is substantially the same as Whitehead's: the only values left now are human ones; the perceiving mind counts, not the scene itself. And in a crucial passage in the *Life* he relates his preference for wasteland scenery to a humanist aesthetic which gives value to a sterile outer world:

> The method of Boldini, the painter of 'The Morning Walk' in the French Gallery two or three years ago (a young lady beside an ugly blank wall on an ugly highway) – of Hobbema, in his view of a road with formal lopped trees and flat tame scenery – is that of infusing emotion into the baldest external objects either by the presence of a human figure among them, or by mark of some human connection with them.
>
> This accords with my feeling about, say, Heidelberg and Baden *versus* Scheveningen – as I wrote at the beginning of *The Return of the Native* – that the beauty of association is entirely superior to the beauty of aspect, and a beloved relative's old battered tankard to the finest Greek vase. Paradoxically put, it is to see the beauty in ugliness.

And he discovers this beauty in 'Beyond the Last Lamp', which is set in a damp grimness near Tooting Common:

> While rain, with eve in partnership,
> Descended darkly, drip, drip, drip,
> Beyond the last lone lamp I passed
> Walking slowly, whispering sadly,
> Two linked loiterers, wan, downcast:
> Some heavy thought constrained each face,
> And blinded them to time and place.

This civic heath is the deadest, the direst, of landscapes, and it throws into relief the human misery it contains. Hardy says:

Without those comrades there at tryst
 Creeping slowly, creeping sadly,
 That lone lane does not exist.
There they seem brooding on their pain,
And will, while such a lane remain.

The ugly lane, like Hobbema's dull road and scenery, would be meaningless without the human figures that occupy it. They give a sad significance to dead matter.

Hardy's rejection of conventional scenic beauty as a value in itself was also the result of his reading of *The Origin of Species* which was first published in 1859 when he was nineteen. In the *Life* he tells us that he was among its 'earliest acclaimers' and he probably read it in London during the early 1860s. Darwin shows that our appreciation of beauty is just a matter of fashion and cultural conditioning:

> With respect to the view that organic beings have been created beautiful for the delight of man, – a view which it has lately been pronounced may safely be accepted as true, and as subversive of my whole theory, – I may first remark that the idea of the beauty of any particular object obviously depends on the mind of man, irrespective of any real quality in the object; and that the idea is not an innate and unalterable element in the mind. We see this in men of different races admiring an entirely different standard of beauty in their women; neither the Negro nor the Chinese admires the Caucasian beau-ideal. The idea also of beauty in natural scenery has arisen only within modern times. On the view of beautiful objects having been created for man's gratification, it ought to be shown that there was less beauty on the face of the earth before man appeared than since he came on the stage. Were the beautiful volute and cone shells of the Eocene epoch, and the gracefully sculptured ammonites of the Secondary period, created that man might ages afterwards admire them in his cabinet?

And in 'Let Me Enjoy' Hardy echoes Darwin's rejection of Paleyan deism:

Let me enjoy the earth no less
Because the all-enacting Might
That fashioned forth its loveliness
Had other aims than my delight.

About my path there flits a Fair,
Who throws me not a word or sign;
I'll charm me with her ignoring air,
And laud the lips not meant for mine.

Both the beauty of the natural scene and of his 'beau-ideal' exist in his mind and there his idea of them is not 'an innate and unalterable element'. The beauty he finds in nature is merely an accidental quality his mind brings to, say, a flower whose colour and scent – despite what Ruskin says – have a function which is totally unrelated to his appreciation of them. Human consciousness has no relevance to nature which, in Hardy's phrase, is a 'world of defect' where 'the emotions have no place'. There is a terrifying feeling of isolation in this idea. It's there in Shelley's echo of Satan ('The mind is its own place, and of itself can make a Heaven of Hell, a Hell of Heaven') and it's also present in Mill's *Autobiography*, not just in his account of the spiritual deadness his Benthamite education left him with, but in this brief mention of how he argued against the Benthamite, Roebuck, that:

> The intensest feeling of the beauty of a cloud lighted up by the setting sun, is no hindrance to my knowing that the cloud is vapour of water, subject to all the laws of vapours in a state of suspension.

Like Hardy, Mill has to resolve to enjoy a beauty which he knows is the accidental product of certain physical laws. The extreme loneliness implicit in this resolution is the loneliness of someone trapped in Hume's sceptical universe and having to make the best of its constraints.

We can catch something of the isolation involved in this sense of the irrelevance of feeling to fact in the curious illustration below which Hardy drew for 'In a Eweleaze near Weatherbury' (*Wessex Poems*, 1898). The poem begins:

The years have gathered grayly
  Since I danced upon this leaze
With one who kindled gaily
  Love's fitful ecstasies!
But despite the term as teacher,
  I remain what I was then
In each essential feature
  Of the fantasies of men.

His rather tame wish to throw over conventional morality and 'go the world with Beauty' is futile because now she would not 'balm the breeze'

> By murmuring 'Thine for ever!'
> As she did upon this leaze.

By superimposing a pair of wire-framed spectacles on a sketch of the eweleaze, Hardy represents himself in the illustration as an elderly man peering at a meadow where he once danced with a girl he loved.

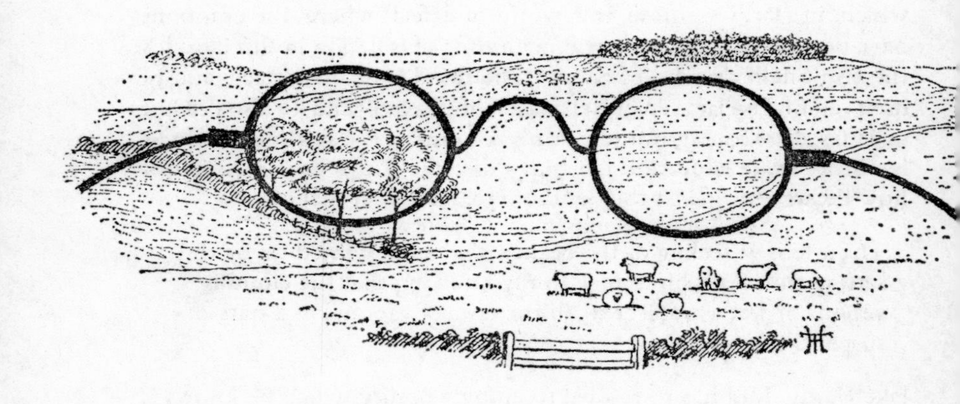

Metaphorically, he is also looking back at his past and realising that the moment has gone and only exists in his mind now. If the landscape exists in the past through the personal value it has for him, it also exists in the present where it holds absolutely no trace of the human figures who once danced on it. Except for a few inattentive sheep it's empty and commonplace. We look at the illustration and bring our knowledge of the poem to it just as Hardy brings his experience to the scene, but what we see are two physical objects – a landscape and a pair of spectacles – which have no apparent or necessary connection with each other and whose relationship is random and gratuitous, like objects in a surrealist picture. His looking at the scene, like his and our general experience of the outer world, has no relation to what he sees and is purely accidental.

This eerie sense that no objects – even the most domestic and familiar – have any relation to each other or to us is one of the qualities of these lines from 'During Wind and Rain':

> They change to a high new house,
> He, she, all of them – aye,
> Clocks and carpets and chairs
> On the lawn all day,
> And brightest things that are theirs....
> Ah, no; the years, the years;
> Down their carved names the rain-drop ploughs.

There is only what Hume would call a 'constant conjunction' between these objects which, indoors, gives them the appearance of being connected with each other. But they're really related only by familiarity or 'custom' which, for Hume, is just 'the effect of repeated perceptions'. Place some furniture on a lawn or a pair of spectacles on a field and the effect is disconcerting because their relationship appears unfamiliar and anomalous. Just as in ' "I Travel as a Phantom Now" ' man's consciousness is God's 'mistake', so his perception of the world is a casual anomaly that leaves no trace on the objects it registers. The values he brings to those objects don't belong to them. In Hume's terms all we know are the 'impressions' that things make on our senses, and so the 'poetry', the significance, of Hardy's eweleaze lies in his mind, not in the scene itself. The grey, cold, dispassionate illustration adds to the poem's theme – the impossibility of retrieving love – the indifference of the external world to both human emotions and the fact of its perception. It extends the poem's sense of the split in personal experience between past and present to include the anomalous relationship of man to the outer world which is the object of his knowledge. And the fact that their relationship is over and can never be renewed is mirrored in the total lack of relation between object and perceiver which the illustration expresses. There is no sense, as there is in Wordsworth and Coleridge, of a creative relationship between mind and fact.

Nowadays the word 'impression' which philosophers use to describe the way in which we know the external world has a less exact sense than it had for a Victorian writer like Hardy who was interested in philosophy. Hume defines an impression as

> all our more lively perceptions, when we hear, or see, or feel, or love, or hate, or desire, or will. And impressions are distinguished from ideas, which are the less lively perceptions, of which

we are conscious, when we reflect on any of those sensations or movements above mentioned.

Hardy uses this term many times to describe his own writing. In the *Life* he notes that 'the mission of poetry is to record impressions, not convictions', and in a preface to *Poems of the Past and the Present* he defends his poems against the possible charge that they 'possess little cohesion of thought or harmony of colouring' by saying:

> Unadjusted impressions have their value, and the road to a true philosophy of life seems to lie in humbly recording diverse readings of its phenomena as they are forced upon us by chance and change.

Again defending his poems, he says that they represent less a view of life than a 'series of fugitive impressions which I have never tried to co-ordinate'. His views are always tentative, '*seemings*, provisional impressions only'. They are 'mere impressions of the moment'. What he means is that each poem expresses a passing mood which is entirely personal and which shouldn't be evaluated in terms of its consistency or inconsistency with a systematic philosophy. He is insisting that he is a poet, not a rigid thinker, and that all the diffident, sceptical, passive qualities of his poetry are true to the patchy nature of our experience. His poems humbly record the impressions he receives.

In repeatedly describing his poems as impressions Hardy was deliberately aligning himself with both Hume and Shelley and so was following through and consolidating the identification with them which is implicit in his 1865 note. He knew the epistemological value of the word, for he noted that:

> We don't always remember as we should that in getting at the truth, we get only at the true nature of the impression that an object, etc., produces on us, the true thing in itself being still, as Kant shows, beyond our knowledge.

This is a later version of his note on the poetry of a scene and it shows his understanding of the way the term 'impression' limits and curtails our knowledge, restricting it totally to our sensations. We cannot know or relate to things in themselves; we are boxed in by our own feelings which completely condition our perceptions of things.

Hardy also knew that 'impression' has another and related significance when applied to painting. He was keenly interested in the visual arts and at one time considered becoming an art critic as an alternative to architecture, though like his plan of going into the church this came to nothing. He was, says Alastair Smart, 'one of the few people of his generation who fully appreciated Turner's last pictures', and on his return from an art exhibition during 1886 he carefully noted down his own definition of Impressionism:

> The impressionist school is strong. It is even more suggestive in the direction of literature than in that of art. As usual it is pushed to absurdity by some. But their principle is, as I understand it, that what you carry away with you from a scene is the true feature to grasp; or in other words, *what appeals to your own individual eye and heart in particular* amid much that does not so appeal, and which you therefore omit to record.

Again, what matters to him is not the scene itself but the personal value it has for the individual perceiver. So, when Mr Percomb sees Marty South:

> In her present beholder's mind the scene formed by the girlish spar-maker composed itself into an impression-picture of extremest type, wherein the girl's hair alone, as the focus of observation, was depicted with intensity and distinctness, while her face, shoulders, hands, and figure in general were a blurred mass of unimportant detail lost in haze and obscurity.

Being a barber and intent on making some money from the sale of her hair Percomb notices only her chestnut tresses.

Like Romantic poetry, Impressionism developed out of empirical philosophy. According to Arnold Hauser it reproduces 'the subjective act instead of the objective substratum of seeing' and by detaching 'the optical elements of experience from the conceptual' reduces artistic representation to 'the mood of the moment'. Hardy is very close to this definition when he refers to his poems as 'mere impressions of the moment', and Hauser's statement that Impressionism is 'the expression of a fundamentally passive outlook on life' is similarly close to Hardy's insistence on the humble, passive nature of his recordings. For him, as for Locke, the mind is passive in perception. Objects and events force themselves upon us as sensations.

Hardy stresses memory in his definition of Impressionism: the mind selects and records certain things, and the way he connected sight and memory through this significant word 'impression' shows in this semi-autobiographical passage from *A Pair of Blue Eyes*:

> Every woman who makes a permanent impression on a man is usually recalled to his mind's eye as she appeared in one particular scene, which seems ordained to be her special form of manifestation throughout the pages of his memory. As the patron Saint has her attitude and accessories in medieval illumination, so the sweetheart may be said to have hers upon the table of her true love's fancy, without which she is rarely introduced there except by effort; and this though she may, on further acquaintance, have been observed in many other phases which one would imagine to be far more appropriate to Love's young dream.
>
> Miss Elfride's image chose the form in which she was beheld during these minutes of singing, for her permanent attitude of visitation to Stephen's eyes during his sleeping and waking hours in after days. The profile is seen of a young woman in a pale gray silk dress with trimmings of swan's-down, and opening up from a point in front, like a waistcoat without a shirt; the cool colour contrasting admirably with the warm bloom of her neck and face. The furthermost candle on the piano comes immediately in a line with her head, and half invisible itself, forms the accidentally frizzled hair into a nebulous haze of light, surrounding her crown like an aureola. Her hands are in their place on the keys, her lips parted, and trilling forth, in a tender *diminuendo,* the closing words of the sad apostrophe:
>
> 'O Love, who bewailest
> The frailty of all things here,
> Why choose you the frailest
> For your cradle, your home, and your bier!'

Hardy based this realisation of Stephen Smith's ideal fantasy on a memory of Emma during one of his visits to Cornwall in the early 1870s and in a most curious way it resurfaced over forty years later in this stanza from 'In Front of the Landscape':

> Then there would breast me shining sights, sweet seasons
> Further in date;
> Instruments of strings with the tenderest passion
> Vibrant, beside
> Lamps long extinguished, robes, cheeks, eyes with the earth's crust
> Now corporate.

Elfride, who is surrounded by a glowing aureole like the other idealised, 'halo-bedecked' women in the poem, is singing part of Shelley's 'When the Lamp is Shattered' which is a dirge on the death of love, and the line 'Lamps long extinguished' echoes this, while the candle by Elfride's head is the physical equivalent of Shelley's symbolic lamp of the soul. In the novel she is about to become what Hardy calls in 'The Occultation' a 'late-irradiate soul' – an extinguished lamp whose 'light', Shelley says, 'in the dust lies dead'. The poem's vibrant, stringed instruments refer to Shelley's poetry and character, which Hardy also idealised, and to the now-dead women Hardy loved and fell out of love with and whose quivering, passionate natures he's comparing to Shelley's Aeolian lyres. And the line also refers to his memory of Emma playing a stringed instrument and singing a song (the ironic coincidence is of his making, I doubt if she actually sang Shelley's lyric). A whole series of memories – including a memory of one of his own novels which he based partly on his personal experience – have merged here, and the stanza moves from intense romantic love ('shining sights' like Elfride) to disillusion and death, unfurling a series of compressed images or impressions in a rhythm which envelops and frees, frees and envelops.

Desperate Remedies also contains a description of a 'permanent impression', this time a traumatically memorable one. Cytherea sees her father fall to his death, collapses in a faint and is carried home:

> Recollection of what had passed evolved itself an instant later, and just as they entered the door – through which another and sadder burden had been carried but a few instants before – her eyes caught sight of the south-western sky, and, without heeding, saw white sunlight shining in shaft-like lines from a rift in a slaty cloud. Emotions will attach themselves to scenes that are simultaneous – however foreign in essence these scenes may be – as chemical waters will crystallize on twigs and wires. Ever after that time any mental agony brought less vividly to Cytherea's mind the scene from the Town Hall windows than sunlight streaming in shaft-like lines.

De Quincey would call this fixed, eternally memorable impression of streaming sunlight an 'involute', a term he coins in an essay called 'The Affliction of Childhood'* where he describes how, as a boy, he

* See Hugh Sykes Davies' fascinating application of De Quincey's term to Wordsworth's poetry in his essay, 'Wordsworth and the Empirical Philosophers', in *The*

crept up to his dead sister's bedroom in the early afternoon. He expected to see her face, but instead:

> Nothing met my eyes but one large window, wide open, through which the sun of midsummer at mid-day was showering down torrents of splendour. The weather was dry, the sky was cloudless, the blue depths seemed the express types of infinity; and it was not possible for eye to behold, or for heart to conceive, any symbols more pathetic of life and the glory of life.

His sight of the sky, like Cytherea's, became charged with thoughts of death and, like Hardy, he comments on the recollection:

> I am struck with the truth that far more of our deepest thoughts and feelings pass to us through perplexed combinations of *concrete* objects, pass to us as *involutes* (if I may coin that word) in compound experiences incapable of being disentangled, than ever reach us directly, and in their own abstract shapes.

What both De Quincey and Hardy are saying in their very similar ways is that certain images – not necessarily the most appropriate ones – can become fixed in the memory and hold intense experiences connected with them. Each image *becomes* the experience and this means that the mind has the power to select and retain images and therefore cannot be passive. 'In their determination to show', Hugh Sykes Davies states, 'that all ideas, all thought, all the works of the mind were derived from sensory experience and from nothing else, the empirical philosophers from Locke onwards were led to present the mind as essentially passive and inactive.' Their tacit assumption is 'that experience tends to be continuous and homogenous: that it flows in through the senses upon the mind with an unremitting and undifferentiated force, no one piece of it being of greater importance than another'. But this cannot be the case, for we remember certain experiences intensely and forget others. Hardy's definition of Impressionism as what you select and remember of a scene, as well as being an inadequate definition itself, doesn't face up to this problem. Why is it that we remember some experiences while thousands of others just disappear the moment they've occurred? Is there some active power in the mind which enables it to retain certain moments? Much of Charles Tomlinson's poetry answers that there is, and part of Sykes

English Mind (ed. Hugh Sykes Davies and George Watson). I owe a great debt both to this essay and to R. L. Brett's essay on Hobbes in the same volume.

Davies' answer is a great passage from *The Prelude* where Wordsworth describes a particular scene – a wall, a single sheep, a hawthorn – which he saw a few days before his father's death. Like De Quincey, like Cytherea Marston in *Desperate Remedies*, he remembers that scene later and describes it again:

> And afterwards, the wind and sleety rain
> And all the business of the elements,
> The single sheep, and the one blasted tree,
> And the bleak music of that old stone wall,
> The noise of wood and water, and the mist
> Which on the line of each of those two roads
> Advanced in such indisputable shapes,
> All these were spectacles and sounds to which
> I often would repair and thence would drink,
> As at a fountain.

Notice how Wordsworth is repeating his description of the wall, sheep and hawthorn, and so charging them powerfully with the significance of what he is saying. This is just what Hardy does in 'Neutral Tones', one of his earliest and finest poems:

> We stood by a pond that winter day,
> And the sun was white, as though chidden of God,
> And a few leaves lay on the starving sod;
> – They had fallen from an ash, and were gray.

Unlike death and a blue sky this scene is appropriate to the emotion, as Wordsworth's bleak moorland also is. And in the last stanza Hardy presents this ashen scene as a total picture, an 'involute' or charged combination of emotion and concrete objects, which during his subsequent painful experience has become a permanently meaningful impression:

> Since then, keen lessons that love deceives,
> And wrings with wrong, have shaped to me
> Your face, and the God-curst sun, and a tree,
> And a pond edged with grayish leaves.

It has to be stressed that this isn't simply a generalisation slapped down on the description of a particular experience, an idea reached, in Hume's terms, by reflecting upon a sense impression. It is a stark image. The lesson that time and experience have taught him is presented visually, not conceptually, and like Wordsworth Hardy repeats his description of the scene. Because both their scenes are so starkly delineated and so sternly expressed it would be wrong to dismiss them as pathetic fallacies. It's as though the scene and the perceiver have become fused, instead of remaining separate like a landscape and a pair of spectacles. This is the kind of effect which the Imagist poets sought early in the next century and, just sometimes, achieved. Joyce's term for it is 'epiphany' and the endings of 'Two Gallants' and 'The Dead' in *Dubliners* are two of the best examples of his use of this visionary clarity. Larkin's 'The Whitsun Weddings', 'Money' and 'High Windows' also close in this way, each with a single, marvellous image:

> And immediately
> Rather than words comes the thought of high windows:
> The sun-comprehending glass,
> And beyond it, the deep blue air, that shows
> Nothing, and is nowhere, and is endless.

For Wordsworth such special moments and sights are, as Sykes Davies says, 'not part of the more usual texture of experience, for which the account given by the empirical philosophers will serve pretty well'. They are visionary images which transcend our ordinary experience. It would be stretching the point much too far to say that Hardy is with Wordsworth and against empiricism, and that he regarded the mind as being more than the passive receptacle of sense impressions, or the imagination as being not just another term for the memory. Hobbes puts it this way:

> This *decaying sense,* when we would express the thing itself, I mean *fancy* itself, we call *imagination,* as I said before: but when we would express the decay, and signify that the sense is fading, old, and past, it is called *memory*. So that imagination and memory are but one thing, which for divers considerations hath divers names.

This reduces the imagination to a sort of compost heap of sense impressions which the poet, Hobbes suggests, rakes over for the best phrases when he writes. Hardy's 'robes, cheeks, eyes with the earth's crust/Now corporate' makes his memory resemble a graveyard and a rubbish dump, a mound of 'decaying sense'. However, his term 'permanent impression' represents a compromise between this kind of dissolving passivity and an active account of the mind.

That the mind is merely passive seems to be the implication of an odd episode in *A Laodicean* where Captain De Stancy gazes at Paula through a chink in the wall of her gymnasium and sees what Hardy calls 'a sort of optical poem'. De Stancy's son, who is a photographer, is inducing his father to look at Paula and so fall in love with her, and the analogy that Hardy is covertly drawing is with a camera: Paula's image is being exposed on the sensitive plate of De Stancy's mind which his son hopes will retain it as a permanent impression. This could almost be a behaviourist's account of the growth of love as a programming of the mind to respond to a physical stimulus. And the photographic analogy between the mind and a camera is also apparent in 'Alike and Unlike':

> We watched the selfsame scene on that long drive,
> Saw the magnificent purples, as one eye,
> Of those near mountains; saw the storm arrive;
> Laid up the sight in memory, you and I,
> As if for joint recallings by and by.
>
> But our eye-records, like in hue and line,
> Had superimposed on them, that very day,
> Gravings on your side deep, but slight on mine! –
> Tending to sever us thenceforth alway;
> Mine commonplace; yours tragic, gruesome, gray.

The treatment of memory here is very similar to Locke's comparison of the mind to a sheet of 'white paper, void of all characters', that passively receives the simple ideas experience prints on it. And the empiricism of 'In a Former Resort after Many Years' is remarkably close to Locke:

> Do they know me, whose former mind
> Was like an open plain where no foot falls,
> But now is as a gallery portrait-lined,
> And scored with necrologic scrawls,
> Where feeble voices rise, once full-defined,
> From underground in curious calls?

His mind was once a blank sheet or 'open plain' without a footprint, and it now resembles the dark closet which Locke also compared the mind to. Locke argues that if 'the pictures coming into such a dark room but stay there, and lie so orderly as to be found upon occasion, it would very much resemble the understanding of man, in reference to all objects of sight, and the ideas of them'. His analogy is with a *camera obscura* where images could also be ordered and fixed like pictures in a gallery. And Hardy similarly compares his mind to a portrait gallery lined with a series of speaking pictures or 'optical poems'. He could scarcely be closer to Locke and to Hobbes's account of the poetic imagination. When he called his poems 'impressions' he meant it.

'The High-School Lawn' is an impressionist poem in several ways:

> Gray prinked with rose,
> White tipped with blue,
> Shoes with gay hose,
> Sleeves of chrome hue;
> Fluffed frills of white,
> Dark bordered light;
> Such shimmerings through
> Trees of emerald green are eyed
> This afternoon, from the road outside.
>
> They whirl around:
> Many laughters run
> With a cascade's sound;
> Then a mere one.
>
> A bell: they flee:
> Silence then: –
> So it will be
> Some day again
> With them, – with me.

The word 'eyed' stresses the 'direct optical perception' characteristic of Impressionist paintings, and the poem's isolated, floating colours are also characteristic. They're detached, as in such a painting, from the objects where they supposedly inhere and which they're normally associated with, though 'emerald green' is just the sort of stereotyped colour an Impressionist would avoid. Hardy either ignores the objects: 'Gray prinked with rose,' or specifies parts here and there: sleeves, shoes, frills. By concentrating on immediate visual appearances, the shimmering, ephemeral qualities of surfaces, he gives a sense of great freshness and immediacy. And this spontaneity is also there in the sound of the poem, particularly in the last stanza where he uses dashes, colons and a comma to catch the voice's tones and pauses. This careful fidelity to the speaking voice is Impressionistic, and so is the fact that the poem expresses a passing mood – the school bell rings like a bell of quittance and all the light and lively moving colours vanish, prompting an analogy between the animated variety and swiftness of life and the silent blankness of death. But this analogy is most definitely not an intrusive wisdom: it's on a par with his description of the colours, for, like them, it's a fugitive perception, a mere impression of the moment.

* * *

Hardy concludes 'The Profitable Reading of Fiction', one of the very few literary essays he wrote, with a most revealing remark about prudish readers who misinterpret the purport of an honest story:

> Truly it has been observed that 'the eye sees that which it brings with it the means of seeing.'

In his edition of Hardy's personal writings Harold Orel shows that this is a reminiscence of a passage from *The French Revolution*:

> For indeed it is well said, 'in every object there is inexhaustible meaning; the eye sees in it what the eye brings means of seeing.' To Newton and to Newton's Dog Diamond, what a different pair of Universes; while the painting on the optical retina of both was, most likely, the same!

Underlying Carlyle's remark is the central assumption of idealist philosophy that, as Basil Willey phrases it, the mind 'works actively in the mere act of perception; it knows not by passive reception, but by its own energy and under its own necessary forms.' As I've already suggested, Hardy appears to have sometimes held to a compromise between idealism and empiricism. In the *Life* he says that although he disagrees with Bergson's philosophy he is not 'a hard-hearted rationalist':

> Half my time (particularly when I write verse) I believe – in the modern use of the word – not only in things that Bergson does, but in spectres, mysterious voices, intuitions, omens, dreams, haunted places, etc., etc.

And in *The Woodlanders* he describes Edred Fitzpiers, who is a student of idealist philosophy, as having eyes that

> were dark and impressive, and beamed with the light either of energy or susceptivity – it was difficult to say which; it might have been chiefly the latter. That quick, glittering, empirical eye,

> sharp for the surface of things if for nothing beneath, he had not. But whether his apparent depth of vision were real, or only an artistic accident of his corporeal moulding, nothing but his deeds could reveal.

This 'empirical eye' belongs not to the idealist, but to the scientist and positivist who believes with Comte that the only real knowledge is based on 'observed facts'.

Hardy read Comte, and the tension between positivism and idealism apparent in his description of Fitzpiers is also there in 'Heiress and Architect', a cruelly humorous poem in which the architect represents pessimistic empiricism and the heiress idealistic imagination and romantic optimism. The description of the architect as 'the man of measuring eye' is a reminiscence of Thomson's 'To the Memory of Isaac Newton':

> Nor could the darting beam of speed immense
> Escape his swift pursuit and measuring eye.

The architect is also a man of science and his 'cold, clear view' belongs with much of Hardy to a habit of thought which is sceptical, empirical and agnostic. The undeviating rigidity of the architect's limited point of view and the sadistic relish with which he states it are meant to disturb. His dialogue with the heiress and the crushing movement of the poem down to his final refusal to design even a winding turret for her are reminiscent of 'The Convergence of the Twain'. He says:

> 'I must even fashion as the rule declares,
> To wit: Give space (since life ends unawares)
> To hale a coffined corpse adown the stairs;
> For you will die.'

The presentation of the architect's 'facile foresight', his Benthamite lack of imagination, criticises those qualities, while the heiress is shown to be both unrealistic and pretentious. The poem isn't so much a compromise as a presentation of two unsatisfactory extremes. Like Mill in his two great essays on Bentham and Coleridge, Hardy seems to be somewhere between a utilitarian empiricism and a romantic idealism. If his imagination, operating under what Coleridge terms the 'despotism of the eye', is imprisoned in a Humean universe of sense-data, he would prefer it to have a transcending freedom, though he knows this is impossible. Coleridge believes that it is possible, for as Mill shows in his essay he rejects an empirical epistemology which says that all our knowledge consists of generalisations from experience and that we know nothing but the facts which are present to our senses. For Coleridge, our understanding judges things in the phenomenal world while our reason knows things-in-themselves directly by intuition. The idealist philosopher discovers these things-in-themselves, this transcendental reality, through his analysis of perceptual processes in terms of certain organising principles or categories, such as time and space, which the mind does not acquire through experience, as the empiricist argues, but which it possesses *a priori*. And in the Dejection Ode Coleridge powerfully describes the empiricist's imaginative universe and his own unwilling, despairing experience of it:

> A grief without a pang, void, dark, and drear,
> A stifled, drowsy, unimpassioned grief,
> Which finds no natural outlet, no relief,
> In word, or sigh, or tear –
> O Lady! in this wan and heartless mood,
> To other thoughts by yonder throstle wooed,
> All this long eve, so balmy and serene,
> Have I been gazing on the western sky,
> And its peculiar tint of yellow green:
> And still I gaze – and with how blank an eye!
> And those thin clouds above, in flakes and bars,
> That give away their motion to the stars;
> Those stars, that glide behind them or between,
> Now sparkling, now bedimmed, but always seen:
> Yon crescent Moon, as fixed as if it grew
> In its own cloudless, starless lake of blue;
> I see them all so excellently fair,
> I see, not feel, how beautiful they are!

Like Crabbe in 'The Lover's Journey' Coleridge views the external world as dead. It is an 'inanimate cold world' from whose visible phenomena we can never hope to win the 'passion and the life'. And yet one's reaction in reading this stanza is to think that the line about the western sky's 'peculiar tint of yellow green' is very beautiful – Coleridge's point is that, yes, it may very well be so, but it's none the less an observed fact, and an observed fact is a dead fact. He has lost his vision of the world and can now only see, not feel. He is merely interested, a detached and sterile observer. The sky-tint which he sees is interesting in the same way that the plants which Crabbe observes in 'The Lover's Journey' are:

> Here on its wiry stem, in rigid bloom,
> Grows the salt lavender that lacks perfume;
> Here the dwarf sallows creep, the septfoil harsh,
> And the soft slimy mallow of the marsh.

Below these lines Hardy would have found a lengthy footnote in which Crabbe describes the different marsh flowers in even greater detail. This kind of accuracy was something Hardy admired.

For example, Crabbe describes a church tower in this way:

> The stony tower as grey with age appears;
> With coats of vegetation thinly spread,
> Coat above coat, the living on the dead;
> These then dissolve to dust and make a way
> For bolder foliage, nursed in their decay:
> The long-enduring ferns in time will all
> Die and depose their dust upon the wall.

Hardy read these lines and noted in his journal: 'A novel, good, microscopic touch in Crabbe (which would strike one trained in architecture). He gives surface without outline, describing his church by telling *the colour of the lichens*.' Hardy's parenthesis reminds us how well he understood the 'cold, clear view' in 'Heiress and Architect'. So did Coleridge, and when he says:

> O Lady! we receive but what we give,
> And in our life alone does Nature live:
> Ours is her wedding garment, ours her shroud!

he suggests, like Crabbe and Hardy, that we discover value in a dead world by projecting our emotions into it. However, there is a crucial difference: Coleridge does not mean that what we discover is therefore illusory, that we know only a subjective impression and that our experience of nature is just a constant series of pathetic fallacies. If we want to know something beyond the knowledge the inanimate world allows – i.e. beyond our sense impressions – then:

Ah! from the soul itself must issue forth
A light, a glory, a fair luminous cloud
Enveloping the Earth –
And from the soul itself must there be sent
A sweet and potent voice, of its own birth,
Of all sweet sounds the life and element!

This spirit of joy is something that 'the sensual and the proud' are ignorant of, and by them Coleridge means those who try to think under the 'strong sensuous influence' of empirical philosophy. T. S. Eliot makes a similar identification between sensuality and empiricism in 'Whispers of Immortality', and in 'The Dry Salvages' casually dismisses the tradition of Victorian thought which Hardy grew up in as 'superficial notions of evolution'.

For many Victorians Darwin's notions of evolution appeared to discredit not just God's existence but the sort of idealism which Coleridge so marvellously advocates. Here, the discussion became centred not on the structure of the human mind – whether it knows actively and intuitively or passively and mechanically – but on the structure of the eye. In *The Origin of Species* Darwin admits that the assumption that a highly sophisticated organ like the eye could have been formed by natural selection appears absurd, and in order to prove that it's not he draws an analogy between the gradual development of a primitive optic nerve and man's gradual perfecting of the telescope. But, having proved his point, he then goes back on it by asking whether we have any right 'to assume that the Creator works by intellectual powers like those of man?' Darwin is anxious not to offend the religious sensibilities of his readers and both his analogy and his rhetorical question must have been partly intended to reassure them, for they would have known that Paley employs exactly this analogy in *Natural Theology* as one of a series of proofs for the existence of God.

Mill refers to Darwin's discussion of the development of the eye in his essay, 'Theism', which Hardy also read. He uses it to explore the value of Paleyan arguments from design, and his position is again a compromise, though a narrower one, for he cautiously concludes that natural adaptations 'afford a large balance of probability in favour of creation by intelligence'. However, this was not the conclusion of Hardy's acknowledged mentor, Leslie Stephen, who uses Darwinian science in 'Darwinism and Divinity' to refute the arguments of natural theology:

> The eye and ear are no longer to be regarded as illustrating the cunning workmanship of the Divine artificer, but as particular results of the uniform operation of what are called the laws of nature. Instead of saying, He that made the eye, shall he not see? we confine ourselves to remarking that the development of eyes is part of the great process of the adaptation of the organism to its medium. In attacking this theory, with its inevitable anthropomorphism, Darwinism, it may be said, merely destroys the conceptions which have been abandoned by the most philosophical theists.

Stephen is an agnostic and empiricist, and in another essay called 'Newman's Theory of Belief' he attacks the intuitionist epistemology which is the basis of Newman's theology. Hardy read *A Grammar of Assent* and so would have been familiar with Newman's argument that animals organise their visual impressions instinctively: 'This perception of individual things amid the maze of shapes and colours which meets their sight, is given to brutes in large measures, and that, apparently, from the moment of their birth.' It is no mere physical instinct, Newman says, which enables the new-born lamb to recognise 'each of his fellow lambkins as a whole, consisting of many parts bound up in one'. This apprehension of individual things in the midst of a confused world of multiple phenomena is due to 'the dictate of conscience' which is the voice 'of a Master, living, personal, and sovereign.' Rejecting an empirical account of perception and its counter-arguments, Newman says:

> There are those who can see and hear for all the common purposes of life, yet have no eye for colours or their shades, or no ear for music; moreover there are degrees of sensibility to colours and to sounds, in the comparison of man with man, while some men are stone-blind or stone-deaf.... Accordingly, if there be those who deny that the dictate of conscience is ever more than a taste, or an association, it is a less difficulty for me to believe that they are deficient either in the religious sense or in their memory of early years, than that they never had at all what those around them without hesitation profess, in their own case, to have received from nature.

Leslie Stephen is referring to this when he explains:

> This exclusion of the witnesses on one side is generally justified

> by the analogy of the blind and seeing. It would be useless, it is said, to argue with a blind man about colours, or with a dull conscience about sin. The analogy breaks down in one important point. No seeing man ever had a difficulty in convincing a blind man of his blindness. The blind man cannot know what sight is, but he cannot help knowing that others possess some faculty of which he is deprived. No such process is applicable to the infidel. He is bold enough to maintain that he, too, has a conscience – that is, that he is as sensitive as the believer to the emotions described by that name. He only denies the interpretation put upon it by the theologian. He cannot be confuted, like the blind man, by any summary appeal to facts; for the facts to which the theologian appeals are beyond all verification by experience. Thus we see at once that from the outset all hopes of an objective test of religious truth must be abandoned. You can prove to a blind man that you see things at a distance. You cannot prove to the infidel that you see a transcendental world.

Hardy's attitude to this debate again seems slightly equivocal. There is a passage in *Far from the Madding Crowd* which resembles Newman's example of a new-born lamb's instinct. Gabriel Oak notices a calf

> about a day old, looking idiotically at the two women, which showed that it had not long been accustomed to the phenomenon of eyesight, and often turning to the lantern, which it apparently mistook for the moon, inherited instinct having as yet had little time for correction by experience.

This appears to be a compromise between all that Stephen means by 'verification by experience' and Newman by 'dictate of conscience'. The calf, Hardy suggests, has a dim, innate knowledge of the world.

Besides Newman, Mill and Stephen, Hardy also read Schopenhauer, and this passage from *The World as Will and Idea* caught his imagination:

> As the magic-lantern shows many different pictures, which are all made visible by one and the same light, so in all the multifarious phenomena which fill the world together or throng after each other as events, only *one will* manifests itself, of which everything is the visibility, the objectivity, and which remains unmoved in the midst of this change; it alone is thing-in-itself; all objects are manifestations, or, to speak the language of Kant, phenomena.

Hardy uses a similar analogy in 'A Plaint to Man':

> When you slowly emerged from the den of Time,
> And gained percipience as you grew,
> And fleshed you fair out of shapeless slime,
>
> Wherefore, O Man, did there come to you
> The unhappy need of creating me –
> A form like your own – for praying to?
>
> My virtue, power, utility,
> Within my maker must all abide,
> Since none in myself can ever be,
>
> One thin as a phasm on a lantern-slide
> Shown forth in the dark upon some dim sheet,
> And by none but its showman vivified.

Naturally, what is significant here is the fact that he has reversed Schopenhauer's application of the analogy. It is man, not the unconscious will, who endows his subjective, religious fancies (God is a 'phasm') with what he believes is an independent, objective existence. Quite clearly Hardy's sympathies are with Humean scepticism, though only he could make God say so. And only he could write an agnostic poem, 'The Impercipient', in the form of a hymn:

> That with this bright believing band
> I have no claim to be,
> That faiths by which my comrades stand
> Seem fantasies to me,
> And mirage-mists their Shining Land,
> Is a strange destiny.
>
> Why thus my soul should be consigned
> To infelicity,
> Why always I must feel as blind
> To sights my brethren see,
> Why joys they've found I cannot find,
> Abides a mystery.

Like Newman he compares agnosticism to blindness, but, as he well knew, this proves nothing. As Leslie Stephen says, you can prove to a blind man that you see things in the distance, but it's quite impossible to prove to an unbeliever that you can see a transcendental world.

Of course, such a transcendental world cannot be strictly 'seen' and to demand that it should be is, for Coleridge, to become a mechanistic philosopher who is 'restless because invisible things are not the objects of vision'. This is the kind of optical proof Hardy's persona is looking for in 'A Sign-Seeker':

> I mark the months in liveries dank and dry,
> The noontides many-shaped and hued;
> I see the nightfall shades subtrude,
> And hear the monotonous hours clang negligently by.
>
> I view the evening bonfires of the sun
> On hills where morning rains have hissed;
> The eyeless countenance of the mist
> Pallidly rising when the summer droughts are done.

This scientific interest in the phenomena of the visible world, which enables him to 'mete the dust the sky absorbs', makes him place great stress on sight. Each of the first five stanzas begins with a specific and deliberate act of perception.

The 'eyeless countenance' of the pallidly rising mist suggests both a blank face and a ghost. The blank face could be an objectification of the futility of the speaker's search, his empirical sight but visionary blindness, though the suggestion of a ghost carries with it a perfectly natural explanation. This is not the 'authentic, indubitable spectre' Hardy told William Archer he would trade ten years of his life for. And while the form and content of this poem are clearly Tennysonian, the effort being, inevitably, to discover some proof of immortality, Hardy's presentation of some of the evidence which the speaker would be prepared to accept is partly satiric. If a 'dead Love' were to kiss him in a dream and then leave 'some print to prove her spirit-kisses real', or if a recording angel, winging its way over a battlefield, were to 'drop one plume as pledge that Heaven inscrolls the wrong', then he would be convinced. Though he is presenting such wishes as glumly comic, the result of 'limitings', narrow attitudes that demand visible 'signs' and 'tokens', this does not mean that he is doing anything more than leave the question rather negatively open, a sceptical twist he uses in the ironic last stanza of 'He Abjures Love'. For one of the qualities of his scepticism is that the moment we read lines like:

> – I speak as one who plumbs
> Life's dim profound,
> One who at length can sound
> Clear views and certain,

we know that Hardy has moved away and another voice has taken over completely. This is what he meant when he called his poems 'unadjusted impressions' and said that many of them were 'dramatic or impersonative even where not explicitly so'. The very certainty of the conclusion in these lines raises doubts, and so the apparently solid ground reached in the last stanza is cut away exactly at the moment it's discovered and the position formulated:

> But – after love what comes?
> A scene that lours,
> A few sad vacant hours,
> And then, the Curtain.

If the sign-seeker's melancholy positivism is being gently guyed, like the romantic disillusion of 'He Abjures Love', this doesn't mean we're being offered an alternative. Hardy is suggesting that the speaker, in Coleridge's terms, is seeing but not feeling, just as Wordsworth in the Immortality Ode registers a sterile series of rainbows, roses, moons and stars, and knows that he's merely observing them because he has lost his visionary powers. Empiricism measures the world, makes time 'clang' mechanically past, is able to 'weigh the sun, and fix the hour each planet dips', but it can never make an observed fact of religious truth. Hardy is not saying that there is such a truth. In 'Heiress and Architect' he shows the antipathy between the scientific temperament which divides and measures, and the synthesising imagination which cherishes impossible visions, but all he does is *demonstrate* this in a rather experimental fashion. He doesn't come to rest on the idea that there are more things in heaven and earth than empirical philosophy can account for – an attitude that anyway can easily harden into a facile complacency and become a mere excuse for laziness. What he does is to sit on the fence and lean towards the positivists' camp while preferring to defect in the other direction.

2

Influences

Upon a poet's page I wrote
Of old two letters of her name;
Part seemed she of the effulgent thought
Whence that high singer's rapture came.
–When now I turn the leaf the same
Immortal light illumes the lay,
But from the letters of her name
The radiance has waned away!

The 'high singer' is Shelley. Hardy admired him more than any other poet and when he was working in London in the 1860s ('Her Initials' is dated 1869) he read him closely and carefully, pencilling hundreds of marks in the margins of the volume of Shelley he owned. Though there can scarcely be two more dissimilar poets, Shelley's influence on Hardy's work was vast – a fact which may seem surprising as Shelley's Romanticism has been largely discredited nowadays. No one now thinks 'O world, O life, O time' a great poem, though Hardy did. He revered Shelley and tracked him like a ghost. So, describing a childhood visit to London when he and his mother stayed at an inn where Shelley used to meet Mary Godwin 'not two-score years before', he conjectures that their room 'may have been the same as that occupied by our most marvellous lyrist'. And in his short story, 'An Imaginative Woman', he dramatises something of his fascination with 'the poet he loved' when he describes Emma Marchmill's reactions to the rough drafts of Trewe's poems which are 'like Shelley's scraps, and the least of them so intense, so sweet, so palpitating, that it seemed as if his very breath, warm and loving, fanned her cheeks from those walls'. Curiously, he lifted the extensive comparison of Trewe's drafts to Shelley's scraps from the introduction to Buxton Forman's 1882 edition of Shelley, and the confusion between love and Shelley's poetry in the story, with the subsequent disillusion described in 'Her Initials', is a movement entirely characteristic of the novels and poems.

What the poem also points to is a habit Hardy had of giving his reading a personal, private significance by marking his books – pages like walls became infused with memories and associations. For example, he pencilled seven dates and place-names in the margin of his bible next to one of his favourite verses: 'And after the earthquake a fire; but the Lord was not in the fire: and after the fire a still small voice' (1 Kings 19, 12). This chapter used to be read as a lesson on the ninth Sunday after Trinity and as Hardy heard it read out in church year after year – when he was an old man he made a special point of going to church simply to hear it – the verse must have gathered numerous personal associations and meanings which had nothing to do with what it actually means.

These associations are the subject of 'Quid Hic Agis':

When I weekly knew
An ancient pew,
And murmured there
The forms of prayer
And thanks and praise
In the ancient ways,
And heard read out
During August drought
That chapter from Kings
Harvest-time brings;
–How the prophet, broken
By griefs unspoken,
Went heavily away
To fast and to pray,
And, while waiting to die,
The Lord passed by,
And a whirlwind and fire
Drew nigher and nigher,
And a small voice anon
Bade him up and be gone,
I did not apprehend
As I sat to the end
And watched for her smile
Across the sunned aisle,
That this tale of a seer
Which came once a year
Might, when sands were heaping,
Be like a sweat creeping,

Or in any degree
Bear on her or on me!

The text served as a kind of mnemonic, enabling him to spring a whole series of memories simply by reading it or hearing it read. When this happened the circumstances surrounding many of the previous occasions on which he heard it must have become luminously present to him, together with his age, emotions and ambitions on each occasion, as well as a series of particular places and the people he knew or loved who were identified with them. Hot afternoons and the beloved dead came crowding back. The chapter was read on one Sunday each year as 'the lesson decreed' and it must have represented something fixed and predictable which was part of a predetermined and immutable pattern, like an anniversary, an annual holiday, or like Halley's comet in 'The Comet at Yell'ham' which will only 'return' – always an important word for Hardy – long after the woman he addresses has disappeared.

The hurrying Skeltonics of 'Quid Hic Agis' drip down like time ticking and scurrying through the static eternity of those drowsy afternoons:

So, like them then,
I did not see
What drought might be
With me, with her,
As the Kalendar
Moved on, and Time
Devoured our prime.

The musing gentleness of his voice comes over so perfectly in these lines. Like the 'still small voice' – a phrase which is an old cliché for conscience – we catch it 'clear'. And like Tennyson in 'The Two Voices' Hardy must have been attracted to the phrase because it describes a divine communication which is rather subtler than any spectacular wind, earthquake, fire or emissary angel. The phrase holds so many memories, while its whispered question: 'What doest thou here?' represents his sense of his own irrelevance not just to the fire and thunder on the battlefields in France at the time but to life generally now that he has outlived her love and his success.

Though he was an agnostic Hardy described himself as 'churchy'. He wanted to retain a church culture but to leave God out of it. So when a voice quotes another of his favourite biblical verses in ' "There Seemed a Strangeness" ', the Pauline revelation is not what is meant:

> 'Men have not heard, men have not seen
> Since the beginning of the world
> What earth and heaven mean:
> But now their curtains shall be furled,
>
> 'And they shall see what is, ere long,
> Not through a glass, but face to face;
> And Right shall disestablish Wrong:
> The Great Adjustment is taking place.'

By seeing 'what is' he does not mean that we shall see God but that we will soon discover a fuller and more scientific understanding of nature which will involve the final discarding of outmoded religious beliefs. This is what Hardy meant by the 'evolutionary meliorism' he claimed to profess, and in this poem the process of development is understood in terms of a gradual improvement in our powers of sight. Darwin's account of the development of the human eye is being given the broadest of applications. And the immediate source for this is a passage from W. K. Clifford's *Lectures and Essays* which Hardy copied into one of his commonplace books:

> Clifford's Theory of the Intellectual growth of mankind: 'as the physical senses (e.g. the eyes of the first animals with eyes) have been gradually developed out of confused & uncertain impressions, so a set of intellectual senses or *insights* are still in course of development, the operation of which may ultimately be expected to be as certain and immed^te. as ordinary sense-perceptions.'

Clifford was a bright young Victorian philosopher, mathematician and intellectual who was a friend of Leslie Stephen and who died young. He was interested in perception and wrote an essay which tries to refute Hume – this puts him in the special corner of hell Bertrand Russell designed for those who've made this doomed attempt. His work is rather ambiguous and this may have been what attracted Hardy to it. Like many men of his time Clifford concludes that the physical world is made up of 'atoms and ether... there is no room in it for ghosts'. However, he then wonders whether the universe may not be 'a vast brain' and the stars 'just atoms in some vast organism'. This is his version of Edward von Hartmann's *Philosophy of the Unconscious* and Clifford, with von Hartmann and Schopenhauer, has his effects on Hardy's conception of the Immanent Will in *The Dynasts.* When Clifford suggests that if human consciousness 'is the great mistake of the universe, it will not unsuitably fall to the devil', his reference to von Hartmann is echoed in ' "I Travel as a Phantom Now" ' where Hardy wonders: 'if Man's consciousness/Was a mistake of God's.' Hardy found the material world of atoms and ether stultifying and he wanted to believe in ghosts: this is one side of the fence he sat on. On the other he could quote St Paul in a context that entirely contradicts the meaning of the biblical verse.

In 'I Travel' his mind becomes a kind of ghost moving invisibly through a world of unsympathetic and gloomy people, and it's perhaps this wandering, travelling quality which is a feature of so much of his work that explains why the *Aeneid* was one of his favourite books. His mother gave him a copy of Dryden's translation when he was eight and like Shelley's poetry or 'that chapter in Kings' or verses like 'the whole creation groaneth and travaileth in pain together until now' it stayed in his mind, becoming a permanent impression. Aeneas's journey to the underworld in book six is one of the inspirations behind the 'Poems of 1912–13' and on a mythic level it embodies one of the deepest patterns of his imagination: the pattern of a native always trying to return to a lost past and then having, like Aeneas, to get on with the journey. There is an interesting echo of the *Aeneid* in 'The Souls of the Slain' where the ghosts of soldiers killed in the Boer War return to their native land, gathering like great moths or seagulls near the lighthouse on Portland Bill. The soldiers have come back to enjoy their fame, but a ghostly general, a 'senior soul-flame', appears and gently tells them that their families are not thinking of their glory and heroism but of 'dearer things':

> 'Some mothers muse sadly, and murmur
> Your doings as boys –
> Recall the quaint ways
> Of your babyhood's innocent days.
> Some pray that, ere dying, your faith had grown firmer,
> And higher your joys.

The poem has an extraordinary tenderness and wit: many of their sweethearts think it is 'not unattractive to prink/Them in sable for heroes,' while their wives don't think of their brave deeds, but of:

> –'Deeds of home; that live yet
> Fresh as new – deeds of fondness or fret;
> Ancient words that were kindly expressed or unkindly,
> These, these have their heeds.'

Most of the soldiers react stoically to the news that their glory counts for less than their 'old homely acts' and 'long-ago commonplace facts,' and they head for home, while 'those of bitter traditions' plunge into 'the fathomless regions/Of myriads forgot.'

Of course, we don't need to look outside Hardy's own work for this sort of moving commitment to ordinary, unheroic, human values, but this poem seems to me to be very close to these lines which Venulus quotes from Diomede – the 'royal hand that razed unhappy Troy' – in an anti-war speech in book eleven of the *Aeneid*:

> 'The Gods have envy'd me the sweets of Life,
> My much lov'd Country, and my more lov'd Wife:
> Banish'd from both, I mourn; while in the Sky
> Transform'd to Birds, my lost Companions fly:
> Hov'ring about the Coasts they make their Moan;
> And cuff the Cliffs with Pinions not their own.
> What squalid Spectres, in the dead of Night,
> Break my short Sleep, and skim before my Sight!'

Both Virgil and Hardy share a profoundly traditional wish to commemorate the soldiers who were killed in a foreign land and they both try to bind them to their country by imagining them returning to their native coasts as ghostly birds. Besides the attraction this theme of exile and return held, another reason why Hardy was so fond of the *Aeneid* must have been the imaginative identity he felt with Aeneas (Donald Davie has likened him to Virgil and this amounts to much the same idea.) 'Pious' Aeneas's efforts to fix his 'wand'ring gods' in a new place has a parallel in 'churchy' Hardy's wish for a compromise between a traditional Christian culture and the new rationalism; and Hardy, like Aeneas, had great filial piety. He probably also came to identify with what Venus's favouring and Juno's hatred of Aeneas means. These parallels operate on an imaginative, mythic level and they help to identify something of the qualities and directions of his work. His imaginative underworld is traditional, but he formulates it in a modern idiom:

Relativity. That things and events always were, are, and will be (e.g. Emma, Mother and Father are living still in the past).

But however much he may have been attracted to the *Aeneid's* themes of second marriage, the return to a past that has been lost and broken with, and the search for a new culture that retains links with the old, the poet who most appealed to him after Shelley, and who most helped to shape his imagination, was Browning. J. I. M. Stewart says that of all Browning's poems 'The Statue and the Bust', 'with its subdued allegory of the springs of artistic creation', was the poem which 'haunted Hardy most', and it's a poem we need to know if we're to really appreciate the relationship between Jude and Sue. In *Jude* he quotes both it and Shelley's 'Epipsychidion' (which was another of his favourite poems) because for him Browning's tale of procrastination and frustration represented a profound criticism of the Shelleyan idealism to which he was also strongly drawn. There is a copy of a pocket edition of Browning in the Hardy library in Dorchester which is full of pencil markings, many of them against lines he quotes in *Jude*. The flyleaf is inscribed: 'Thomas Hardy from Florence Henniker July 29th 1894,' and these lines from 'By the Fire-Side' which Hardy marked may well have some relevance to his relationship with her:

> And find her soul as when friends confer,
> Friends – lovers that might have been.

In the stanza before this Browning says:

> Oh, the little more, and how much it is!
> And the little less, and what worlds away!
> How a sound shall quicken content to bliss,
> Or a breath suspend the blood's best play,
> And life be a proof of this!

Hardy echoes this in 'At the Word "Farewell" ':

> No prelude did I there perceive
> To a drama at all,
> Or foreshadow what fortune might weave
> From beginnings so small;
> But I rose as if quicked by a spur
> I was bound to obey,
> And stepped through the casement to her
> Still alone in the gray.

'I am leaving you.... Farewell!' I said
As I followed her on
By an alley bare boughs overspread;
'I soon must be gone!'
Even then the scale might have been turned
Against love by a feather,
–But crimson one cheek of hers burned
When we came in together.

His presentation of the moment when he and Emma first admitted their love openly to each other is subtly ambiguous: the fifth and sixth lines are a curious mixture of fatalism and freewill, biological determinism and romantic love. This ambiguity enables him to be simultaneously true to Browning's 'moment, one and infinite' and to an existential ethic of absolute commitment to the moment's truth, and also to impose a pattern from hindsight which suggests the future, unhappy results of their first, fragile recognition of love. It is this kind of rigid, retrospective pattern which he imposes in 'The Convergence of the Twain':

Alien they seemed to be:
No mortal eye could see
The intimate welding of their later history,

Or sign that they were bent
By paths coincident
On being anon twin halves of one august event,

Till the Spinner of the Years
Said 'Now!' And each one hears,
And consummation comes, and jars two hemispheres.

This extreme determinism is partly implicit in 'At the Word "Farewell"', and it's significant that there Hardy transposes Browning's 'quickening' celebration of a crucial moment of recognition within a married love into a lyrical recollection of courtship and so makes their love platonic and Shelleyan.

'One shape of many names', a phrase from Shelley's *The Revolt of Islam*, is the epigraph of *The Well-Beloved* which is a study of platonic love. Hardy underlined it in a copy of Shelley which he bought in his early twenties and so his interest in the phrase – and it's the only interesting feature in Shelley's tedious fantasy – dates from roughly the period when he read Bagehot's essay. The context in which Shelley uses this phrase is a significant formulation of just those Humean ideas Bagehot discusses:

> What is that Power? Some moon-struck sophist stood
> Watching the shade from his own soul upthrown
> Fill Heaven and darken Earth, and in such mood
> The Form he saw and worshipped was his own,
> His likeness in the world's vast mirror shown;
> And 'twere an innocent dream, but that a faith
> Nursed by fear's dew of poison, grows thereon,
> And that men say, that Power has chosen Death
> On all who scorn its laws, to wreak immortal wrath.

Cythna has just rebuked the mariners for giving a 'human heart' to 'some immortal power' and so creating an anthropomorphic God, a 'Power' which tyrants find useful in justifying their régimes. For Shelley, the divine right of kings is founded on 'the will of strength' which is really the strength only of our opinions: it's therefore only powerful for as long as public opinion believes in the political, religious and moral systems that enslave mankind. Opinion is weaker:

> Than yon dim cloud now fading on the moon
> Even while we gaze, though it awhile avail
> To hide the orb of truth – and every throne
> Of Earth or Heaven, though shadow, rests thereon,
> One shape of many names: – for this ye plough
> The barren waves of ocean, hence each one
> Is slave or tyrant; all betray and bow,
> Command, or kill, or fear, or wreak, or suffer woe.

Each of these names is a 'sign' which sanctifies all power and man can emancipate himself simply by willing its non-existence – by refusing to worship a deity he himself has invented. And Hardy echoes this in *The Mayor of Casterbridge* when he describes how Henchard stands like a dark ruin 'obscured by the "shade from his own soul upthrown."' As Hillis Miller shows, the point here is that just as for Shelley 'God is not an independently existing Power who governs heaven and earth, so Henchard is not, as he sometimes thinks, the victim of a malign power imposing suffering upon him.' Hardy echoes Shelley again in 'A Plaint to Man' where his puppet deity asks man why he has created 'a form like your own' and in 'God's Funeral' where God is a 'man-projected Figure'. Like Shelley he is saying that man projects an image of his own making outside himself – an image which assumes an autonomous existence that is apparently independent of his own mind. For Shelley, reality is a 'vast mirror' where man sees his own reflected image, and Hardy adopts this idea but expresses it in terms of a projection screen.

In his essay on Shelley, Bagehot states that Hume 'professed to hold that there was no substantial thing, either matter or mind; but only "sensations and impressions" flying about the universe, inhering in nothing and going nowhere. These, he said, were the only subjects of your consciousness; all you felt was your feeling, and all you thought was your thought; the rest was only hypothesis.' And Bagehot explains that Shelley adopted Hume's doctrine because it was 'a better description of his universe than most people's'. Hardy also followed Hume (and was therefore consciously following in Shelley's footsteps as well) when he justified his own lack of a rigidly schematic view of life in this way:

> I have no philosophy – merely what I have often explained to be only a confused heap of impressions, like those of a bewildered child at a conjuring show.

Here, he is deliberately echoing Hume who says:

> what we call a mind is nothing but a heap or collection of different perceptions, united together by certain relations, and suppos'd, tho' falsely, to be endow'd with a perfect simplicity and identity.

Like Shelley, Hardy was a monist – this is the philosophy of 'unity' which Shelley mentions in a passage Bagehot quotes from his essay 'On Life': 'The view of life presented by the most refined deductions of metaphysics is that of unity: Nothing exists but as it is perceived.' And like Crabbe in 'The Lover's Journey' both Shelley and Hardy apply this idea to sexual relationships as well as to man's relation to the universe. The persona of 'Epipsychidion' states:

> In many mortal forms I rashly sought
> The shadow of that idol of my thought.

Here, the concept of unity in multiplicity, the 'one shape of many names', refers to love and not evil power; but in a sense love and evil are identical for both poets: the man projects his own ideals on to a series of women he loves (the 'many mortal forms'), and so love, like evil, is a protean force emanating from man's subjectivity and successively embodying itself in a series of perishable incarnations. Edred Fitzpiers in *The Woodlanders* reads both Shelley and idealist philosophy, and he defines love as 'a subjective thing', as 'joy accompanied by an idea which we project against any suitable object in the line of our vision, just as the rainbow iris is projected against an oak, ash, or elm tree indifferently'. And in the *Life* Hardy shows that love's subjectivity is again his subject in *The Well-Beloved* when he says that both that novel and the poem of the same name exemplify 'the theory of the transmigration of the ideal beloved one, who only exists in the lover, from material woman to material woman'. This is what he meant by choosing the phrase 'one shape of many names' as the novel's epigraph.

He uses the same idea in 'Rome: The Vatican – Sala delle Muse' which is his dialogue with a 'composite Muse', the one shape of the many differently named Muses. As a writer he resembles Jocelyn Pierston, the sculptor and inconstant, idealistic lover in *The Well-Beloved*. And he resembles Shelley too, for in 'Epipsychidion' he also identifies love and the imagination:

> Love is like understanding, that grows bright,
> Gazing on many truths; 'tis like thy light,
> Imagination! which from earth and sky,
> And from the depths of human fantasy,
> As from a thousand prisms and mirrors, fills
> The Universe with glorious beams, and kills
> Error, the worm, with many a sun-like arrow
> Of its reverberated lightning. Narrow
> The heart that loves, the brain that contemplates.
> The life that wears, the spirit that creates
> One object, and one form, and builds thereby
> A sepulchre for its eternity.

This is an ingenious, philosophical attack on monogamy: love, the mind and the imagination all require 'many truths' and not one absolute truth as their object. In 'Rome: The Vatican' the combined shape of the nine Muses reassures Hardy by telling him that the many Muses he loves are really this one form. They are 'but phases of one':

> 'And that one is I; and I am projected from thee,
> One that out of thy brain and heart thou causest to be –

Extern to thee nothing. Grieve not, nor thyself becall,
Woo where thou wilt; and rejoice thou canst love at all!'

Here, Hardy uses the sun and moon as symbols of apparently irreconcileable opposites. He envisions the 'One' in a haze of sunshine and compares the different Muses to the phases of the moon: they are 'but phases of one'. Shelley also employs this symbolism in 'Epipsychidion' where his persona details the many women in whom he sought his ideal and then states that at last:

like a noonday dawn, there shone again
Deliverance. One stood on my path who seemed
As like the glorious shape which I had dreamed
As is the Moon, whose changes ever run
Into themselves, to the eternal Sun.

He justifies the apparent promiscuity of his affections by saying that the essential property of love, a property which distinguishes it from 'gold and clay', is that 'to divide is not to take away'. Hardy justifies a similar promiscuity by saying that the different Muses to whom he's attracted are just different aspects of the one, essential shape. Like the Power which Shelley's moon-struck sophist worships, this shape is a 'shade from his own soul upthrown', an emanation or projection of his own subjectivity.

'The Chosen', with its list of past mistresses, is clearly similar to 'Epipsychidion':

I thought of the first with her eating eyes,
And I thought of the second with hers, green-gray,
And I thought of the third, experienced, wise,
And I thought of the fourth who sang all day.

And I thought of the fifth, whom I'd called a jade
And I thought of them all, tear-fraught;
And that each had shown her a passable maid,
Yet not of the favour sought.

Eventually he discovers another 'composite form', an ideal whose 'face was all the five's'. For Hardy, the artistic imagination and this kind of promiscuous idealism are closely identified, and this is the allegory to which the poem's epigraph refers. The poem describes the results of an attitude which reduces women to mere objects, the mirrors of a man's ideals, and it ends with the man's icy misery and barren worship of his composite ideal. This, too, is close to the icy sea in 'Epipsychidion', and the total effect of Hardy's closeness to Shelley may seem to suggest that he followed him uncritically. This is not the case for he was by no means a slavish adherent of the Shelley-cult – the way he plays 'The Statue and the Bust' against 'Epipsychidion' in *Jude* shows this. And 'The Statue and the Bust' like 'My Last Duchess' (Browning's study of male egotism is also behind 'The Chosen') again makes a link between the artist's imagination and an egocentric idealism, a worship of women which transforms them into art objects. Many of Browning's poems are psychological studies of this area of human relationships and, as Hardy obviously knew, Browning took Shelley for the quintessential exponent of this kind of selfish Romanticism.

Tess of the D'Urbervilles is Hardy's most acute study of these sexist attitudes. He describes Angel Clare's nature as being 'less Byronic than Shelleyan', and says that Clare 'could love desperately, but with a love more especially inclined to the imaginative and ethereal; it was a fastidious emotion which could jealously guard the loved one against his very self.' The parallel with Shelley is explicit here but the name 'Angel Clare' is also meant to remind us of him. It's taken from Arnold's famous description of Shelley as a 'beautiful and ineffectual angel, beating in the void his luminous wings in vain', a statement which rightly annoyed Hardy, who besides being deeply aware of Shelley's limitations, also revered him. In *Tess* the reverse and complementary side of Angel's tyrannically idealistic nature is represented by the satanic Alec D'Urberville who at one point in the story casts himself as a devil with a pitchfork. Like the shape in 'Rome: The Vatican' and the composite woman in 'The Chosen' Tess seems to Angel: 'a visionary essence of woman – a whole sex condensed into one typical form'. The cold radiance of Clare's spiritual nature, his egotistic idealism, is a 'hard logical deposit, like a vein of metal in a soft loam, which turned the edge of everything that attempted to traverse it'. This profound understanding is behind a fine poem called 'Without, not Within Her':

> It was what you bore with you, Woman,
>   Not inly were,
> That throned you from all else human,
>   However fair!

It was that strange freshness you carried
  Into a soul
Whereon no thought of yours tarried
  Two moments at all.

And out from his spirit flew death,
  And bale, and ban,
Like the corn-chaff under the breath
  Of the winnowing-fan.

The terrible honesty of the last stanza is close to this description of Angel's nature which is based on the line in Shelley's 'Ode to the West Wind' about autumn leaves being like 'ghosts from an enchanter fleeing':

> Tess stole a glance at her husband. He was pale, even tremulous; but, as before, she was appalled by the determination revealed in the depths of this gentle being she had married – the will to subdue the grosser to the subtler emotion, the substance to the conception, the flesh to the spirit. Propensities, tendencies, habits, were as dead leaves upon the tyrannous wind of his imaginative ascendency.

This presentation of Angel's powerful egotism is given fuller expression in the threshing scene where Tess and the other women 'serve' a threshing-machine, a 'red tyrant' operated by men. 'Serve' is also used in a sexual sense here for Hardy is saying that these women are being exploited and treated as objects. They are the mere slaves or servants of male sexual power and are blown like dead leaves or chaff by a 'tyrannous wind'. Like the heiress they are swayed by a 'shade'.

In 'Without, not Within Her' this tyrannous wind is poisonous and destructive, a withering influence on the woman. But in 'The Shadow on the Stone' the significance of 'throwing a shade', which is behind this presentation of male personality, is much more complex. A tree casts a shadow on a white stone reminding him of the way his wife's shadow used to fall when she was gardening:

  Yet I wanted to look and see
 That nobody stood at the back of me;
But I thought once more: 'Nay, I'll not unvision
 A shape which, somehow, there may be.'

So I went on softly from the glade,
And left her behind me throwing her shade,
As she were indeed an apparition –
My head unturned lest my dream should fade.

He knows that there is a perfectly natural explanation for the ghostly shadow he sees, but only by not turning his head and discovering that 'there was nothing in my belief' can he 'keep down grief'. Now that she is dead his love for her is intense and – inevitably – platonic or Shelleyan. This necessarily means that it is subjective, that both the ghost and his love are just a shade thrown by his own soul. Less emphatically than in 'Rome: The Vatican' he points to its subjective nature because he's trying to give his personal vision an autonomous existence outside his own imagination. He first describes how the shadows 'shaped in my imagining' to Emma's familiar 'shade', and the word 'shade' has several significances which react with each other: it means Emma's shadow, her ghost which has been led from the underworld shades by his imagination and love, and the sophist's shade which is really the emanation of himself. Like Orpheus he wants to look back, but if he does so he will recognise fully that she isn't there, that the shadow is simply thrown by the branches of the tree and has combined with the shadow thrown by his own imagination or memory. The act of looking back will involve the recognition that he has been metaphorically 'looking back', i.e. just remembering. He wants to forget that he's doing so because ocular proof (the evidence demanded in 'The Sign-Seeker') involves the dreary recognition of normality, the unvisioning of a shape he desperately wants to believe in.

The poem's softly hesitant speech rhythms, its intimate, musing quality, suggest that he's conducting a conversation, and at one point he talks directly to her:

'I am sure you are standing behind me,
Though how do you get into this old track?'

The poem as a whole seems to be directed at her as much as at the reader. It's as though we overhear him talking very gently, perhaps to her, perhaps to himself. This is a quality that some of the 'Poems of 1912–13' have, particularly 'The Phantom Horsewoman' where the sense of a gentle conversation taking place plays against the acknowledgement that what he sees is just a 'phantom of his own figuring'. In both poems he has to hope that Emma exists independently of his vision: that she does not exist only as he perceives her. This is what he reduces their relationship to in 'Without, not Within Her' – he idealised her and gave her qualities she didn't really possess. And yet if he failed to love her for what she really was, there was still 'that strange freshness' which she brought into his soul – like a scent of flowers contrasting with his deadly nightshade. This seems to me to represent a recognition of her otherness, to be a true statement of love.

Hardy is partly saying in 'The Shadow on the Stone' that he knows he wants to believe in the external, independent existence of a shadow thrown by his own soul, and in 'Shelley's Skylark' there is a similar conflict between positivism and a wish to believe in immortality. Though it's not one of his strongest achievements, it does reveal the difference between his positivism and Shelley's, because Shelley's Ode, which has been obscured by too much familiarity, essentially enacts an effort to break through the imprisonment of sense impressions into an invisible world of Platonic Forms. Shelley therefore calls the lark a 'blithe Spirit', an 'unbodied joy', while Hardy writes:

> Somewhere afield here something lies
> In Earth's oblivious eyeless trust
> That moved a poet to prophecies –
> A pinch of unseen, unguarded dust:
>
> The dust of the lark that Shelley heard,
> And made immortal through times to be; –
> Though it only lived like another bird,
> And knew not its immortality.

While Shelley exclaims: 'Bird thou never wert', Hardy insists upon the lark's physical existence, the fact that it was once a 'bodied' joy. Shelley transforms the lark into a series of visions, while with glum but touching regret Hardy realises the fact that it must have died and become a 'little ball of feather and bone'. Shelley compares the lark to the 'unseen' morning star which fades until 'we hardly see – we feel that it is there', and to a glow-worm which scatters its light 'unbeholden' among the grass and flowers that 'screen it from the view'; but Hardy is concerned that the lark is now also 'unseen' where it lies in some unknown position in the earth's 'oblivious eyeless trust'. For him, the lark's continued existence, its immortality, depends upon its being perceived:

Maybe it rests in the loam I view,
Maybe it throbs in a myrtle's green,
Maybe it sleeps in the coming hue
Of a grape on the slopes of yon inland scene.

He neatly introduces the characteristically Shelleyan 'throbs' and attempts to naturalise the lark's immortality in physical, visible terms. However, as he can only credit an observed fact – the authentic and unique pinch of dust – he unfortunately invokes some 'faeries' who are to go and find it. Like his sign-seeker he wants hard facts.

Almost inevitably a strong responsiveness to fact makes for an inability to believe in anything beyond the visible. Unlike Hopkins, Hardy seldom transforms observation into vision, and the moment of vision in 'In a Whispering Gallery' is sparked by his very inability to see across a 'hazed lacune'

If opposite aught there be
Of fleshed humanity
Wherewith I may commune;
Or if the voice so near
Be a soul's voice floating here.

The answer is obvious and yet he still offers the possibility of faith in uncharacteristically soft and gnomic couplets. A strong element in this wish to believe is his nostalgia for the rural anglicanism of his childhood:

On afternoons of drowsy calm
We stood in the panelled pew,
Singing one-voiced a Tate-and-Brady psalm
To the tune of 'Cambridge New.'

Combined with this wonderfully particular evocation of the church services is a dissatisfaction with 'subtle thought on things,' the rationalism that has replaced religious faith:

Yet, I feel,
If someone said on Christmas Eve,
'Come; see the oxen kneel

'In the lonely barton by yonder coomb
Our childhood used to know,'
I should go with him in the gloom,
Hoping it might be so.

'The Oxen' is Hardy's most delicate rendering of this mingled hope and nostalgia. Though he wanted to believe in ghosts and spirits he couldn't, as he told William Archer, get past Hume's famous principle that no testimony can really prove a miracle. There is always a 'natural solution' to any ghost story – a tree's shadow or the fall of a leaf:

> I marked when the weather changed,
> And the panes began to quake,
> And the winds rose up and ranged,
> That night, lying half-awake.
>
> Dead leaves blew into my room,
> And alighted upon my bed,
> And a tree declared to the gloom
> Its sorrow that they were shed.
>
> One leaf of them touched my hand,
> And I thought that it was you
> There stood as you used to stand,
> And saying at last you knew!

Here, far from being a traditional symbol of the soul, the dead leaf is intended as a mere fact, but in the most muted way its traditional significance is allowed to reverberate with his wish; and though he doesn't insist on it, there is possibly also an echo of the significance that dead leaves hold in the passage I quoted earlier from *Tess*, which would mean that he is again convicting himself of responsibility for Emma's death. The poem – it is one of his finest – has a kind of gentle tact. It speaks and faces the facts directly and yet has a softly oblique subtlety that insinuates that she is still there.

Hardy is largely committed to a scientific view of natural processes as merely an endless, meaningless hurrying of material. This description of spring in *Tess* shows just how disenchanted he could be with nature:

> The season developed and matured. Another year's instalment of flowers, leaves, nightingales, thrushes, finches, and such ephemeral creatures, took up their positions where only a year ago others had stood in their place when these were nothing more than germs and inorganic particles. Rays from the sunrise drew forth the buds and stretched them into long stalks, lifted up sap in noiseless streams, opened petals, and sucked out scents in invisible jets and breathings.

Here, spring is just a mechanical process which is sending another routine instalment of finches and thrushes rolling off the conveyor belt. Last year they were just so many molecules, so much raw material. This view of nature as predictable and valueless and very dull is echoed in 'Proud Songsters', one of Hardy's last poems:

> The thrushes sing as the sun is going,
> And the finches whistle in ones and pairs,
> And as it gets dark loud nightingales
> In bushes
> Pipe, as they can when April wears,
> As if all Time were theirs.
>
> These are brand-new birds of twelve-months' growing,
> Which a year ago, or less than twain,
> No finches were, nor nightingales,
> Nor thrushes,
> But only particles of grain,
> And earth, and air, and rain.

This appears to insist on a totally reductive and disenchanted view of spring with none of Mill's resolution to admire what he knows is really proceeding according to immutable physical laws. The 'brand-new birds' are mere consumer durables mass-produced in a natural factory. But just as Hardy is pressing his disenchanted materialism home, just as he insists upon reducing the singing birds to their basic, dull constituents, something strange happens. The mystery of their being, which the chemical equation seems about to completely account for, becomes suddenly uppermost with all the force of a last-moment surprise. They're only particles of grain – already the idea of growth is starting to surface here – they're earth and they're air – the list is becoming just slightly too long to have the decisive force of a simple, negative reduction. And then the word 'rain' suddenly and so aptly completes the rhyme that the question of what their exact basic constituents are is left open at the very moment when it should have been neatly answered and summed up. The mechanism is suddenly refreshed and transformed.

The same last-minute admission is made in 'To an Unborn Pauper Child' where five stanzas are spent detailing the miseries that await the child:

Must come and bide. And such are we –
Unreasoning, sanguine, visionary –
That I can hope
Health, love, friends, scope
In full for thee; can dream thou'lt find
Joys seldom yet attained by humankind!

That he can still wish the child perfect happiness, despite all the evidence to the contrary, represents a fundamental reverence for the mysteries of life. The basic respect implicit in this sense that life somehow eludes all our efforts to understand it emerges in the puzzled wonder of 'The Year's Awakening':

How do you know, deep underground,
Hid in your bed from sight and sound,
Without a turn in temperature,
With weather life can scarce endure,
That light has won a fraction's strength,
And day put on some moments' length,
Whereof in merest rote will come,
Weeks hence, mild airs that do not numb;
O crocus root, how do you know,
How do you know?

The repeated question haunts and sets its lack of a neat answer against the dismissive 'merest rote' of the natural conveyor belt. This also happens in 'An August Midnight':

A shaded lamp and a waving blind,
And the beat of a clock from a distant floor:
On this scene enter – winged, horned, and spined –
A longlegs, a moth, and a dumbledore;
While 'mid my page there idly stands
A sleepy fly, that rubs its hands...

The strong, firm beat of the first line and more muted trisyllabic second line, which lulls but still retains the dramatic suspense and tension of the first, together create a sense of mystery which, perhaps, is dispelled by the entrance of a few insignificant insects. Indoors, they start to behave in a slightly comic fashion:

–My guests besmear my new-penned line,
Or bang at the lamp and fall supine.

It's as though they've gauchely blundered into his presence. He's mockingly superior, then tolerant:

> 'God's humblest, they!' I muse. Yet why?
> They know Earth-secrets that know not I.

Before his jokey anthropomorphism can completely patronise them he turns back on this attitude and suddenly respects them. Again, this is an example of Hardy's ability to deny part of his temperament and surprise us with an openness and sense of awe which is the result of his refusal to settle for an easy solution. There is more than the obvious irony in 'At the Railway Station, Upway':

> The man in the handcuffs smiled;
> The constable looked, and he smiled, too
> As the fiddle began to twang;
> And the man in the handcuffs suddenly sang
> With grimful glee:
> 'This life so free
> Is the thing for me!'
> And the constable smiled, and said no word,
> As if unconscious of what he heard;
> And so they went on till the train came in –
> The convict, and boy with the violin.

At a deeper level 'this life so free' is what Eliot means in *Four Quartets* by the 'inner freedom from the practical desire', and what Schopenhauer means by the 'pure perception' and sense of freedom which occur when we transcend our mechanical instincts; though 'grimful glee', unfortunately, is one of Hardy's facile alliterative coinages, a mechanical reflex.

This distinction between practical routine and a mysterious freedom is also covertly present in 'The Fallow Deer at the Lonely House':

> One without looks in to-night
> Through the curtain-chink
> From the sheet of glistening white;
> One without looks in to-night
> As we sit and think
> By the fender-brink.

We do not discern those eyes
Watching in the snow;
Lit by lamps of rosy dyes
We do not discern those eyes
Wondering, aglow,
Fourfooted, tiptoe.

The couple are silent and alone, but they're not entirely isolated because, even though they don't know it, the deer is watching over them like a perfectly natural angel and irradiating the domestic routine of their lives with its 'lamps of rosy dyes'. Its invisible presence, the hushed tone of the poem, create a gentle sense of awe and bring outside nature to their indoor fireside order. There is a feeling of co-operation here which relates outside to inside, the human pair to the watching creature. And this living, sympathetic relationship is obviously much more meaningful than the grey juxtaposition of a landscape and a pair of spectacles.

This co-operation also takes place in ' "I Sometimes Think" ' which begins as a complaint that no one has heeded all the decent things he has done in his life and then, through a characteristic scepticism about what he's just said, offers a contradictory affirmation:

Yet can this be full true, or no?
For one did care,
And, spiriting into my house, to, fro,
Like wind on the stair,
Cares still, heeds all, and will, even though
I may despair.

The third and fourth lines, with their marvellously sure movement, sweep in naturally; the speech rhythms tug gently against the metre, and there is something of the same musical extension that there is in:

Yea, to such freshness, fairness, fulness, fineness, freeness,
Love lures life on.

By contrast 'A Jog-Trot Pair' is extremely unromantic:

Trite usages in tamest style
Had tended to their plighting.
'It's just worth while,
Perhaps,' they had said. 'And saves much sad good-nighting.'

This Horatian comedy set in a trim suburban garden ends with an unremarkable question and an impulsive answer:

> Who could those common people be,
>   Of days the plainest, barest?
>   They were we;
> Yes; happier than the cleverest, smartest, rarest.

The sudden affirmation here springs directly and surprisingly out of a recognition of their unassuming ordinariness. And this also happens in 'The Something that Saved Him' which describes a state of acute spiritual despair:

>   In that day
> Unseeing the azure went I
>   On my way,
> And to white winter bent I,
>   Knowing no May.

Life gets duller and duller, more claustrophobic and impossible, then there is a 'feeble summons to rally', and then:

>   The clock rang;
> The hour brought a hand to deliver;
>   I upsprang,
> And looked back at den, ditch and river,
>   And sang.

Like the handcuffed convict he suddenly sings. There is the same 'spiriting' of a natural and joyful impulse, a pure freedom, into an apparently rigid and mechanical pattern that there is in 'Proud Songsters'. This is the song the darkling thrush sings, the unequivocal commitment to the moment that Browning celebrates; though unlike 'At the Word "Farewell"' these poems carry no allusions to the poet who, after Shelley, exerted the most considerable influence on both Hardy's prose and poetry. Stripped of the theological optimism they signify in Browning's poetry, these infinite moments are always won in despite of an ingrained, reductive pessimism.

3

Sounds and Voices

Because he used to play the fiddle at country dances and weddings when he was a boy, it's not surprising that some of Hardy's poems – 'Timing Her' for example – are written 'to an old folk-tune'. There is a tune behind 'Dead "Wessex" the Dog to the Household' which is sung by the ghost of his favourite dog:

> Do you think of me at all,
>   Wistful ones?
> Do you think of me at all
>   As if nigh?
> Do you think of me at all
> At the creep of evenfall,
> Or when the sky-birds call
>   As they fly?

Reading these lines I can hear the tune of 'She'll be Coming down the Mountain' and there must be many other poems which Hardy based on the songs and tunes he knew.

Sometimes a poem will catch the cadence of another poem, and reading Dryden's lines on Dido's death in his translation of the *Aeneid* I'm struck by a sense of familiarity which has nothing to do with the omnipresent eye:

> Thrice op'd her heavy Eyes, and sought the Light,
> But having found it, sicken'd at the Sight;
> And clos'd her Lids at last, in endless Night.

The great chorus on the eve of Waterloo in *The Dynasts* begins:

> The eyelids of eve fall together at last,
> And the forms so foreign to field and tree
> Lie down as though native, and slumber fast!

The cadence of 'lids at last' is caught up in Hardy's lines which anticipate the endless darkness that is soon to fall on the massed thousands of soldiers. As he was writing the chorus a memory of Dryden's lines must have drifted into his mind and helped him shape what he wanted to say. Though the connection between these lines is remote, there is nothing very unusual in the fact that Hardy is echoing Dryden. We don't, for example, have to look very far to know who is behind this stanza:

> For winning love we win the risk of losing,
> And losing love is as one's life were riven;
> It cuts like contumely and keen ill-using
> To cede what was superfluously given.

This is from an early sonnet and the Shakespearean influence hasn't been subdued, supposing it ever could be, into a style that is authentically Hardy's own.

'Friends Beyond' has a sound which is both uniquely its own and yet reminiscent of another poem:

> William Dewy, Tranter Reuben, Farmer Ledlow late at plough,
> Robert's kin, and John's, and Ned's,
> And the Squire, and Lady Susan, lie in Mellstock churchyard now!
>
> 'Gone,' I call them, gone for good, that group of local hearts and heads;
> Yet at mothy curfew-tide,
> And at midnight when the noon-heat breathes it back from walls and leads,
>
> They've a way of whispering to me – fellow-wight who yet abide –
> In the muted, measured note
> Of a ripple under archways, or a lone cave's stillicide.

Bailey states that the long lines 'suggest the measure of "Locksley Hall" ', and then adds the rider: 'but the short lines, in Hardy's terza-rima pattern, slow down the rush of Tennyson's poem.' Tennyson writes:

> 'Tis the place, and all around it, as of old, the curlews call,
> Dreary gleams about the moorland flying over Locksley Hall.

Surely the whispering softness of Hardy's lines is a long way from this? Their texture and sound seem much closer to:

> Oh Galuppi, Baldassaro, this is very sad to find!
> I can hardly misconceive you; it would prove me deaf and blind;
> But although I take your meaning, 'tis with such a heavy mind!

Here you come with your old music, and here's all the good it
brings.
What, they lived once thus at Venice where the merchants were
the kings,
Where Saint Mark's is, where the Doges used to wed the sea with
rings?

The sounds of the third and fourth syllables in the first line of each poem are identical, almost like a key-note starting the tune, and Hardy's:

'Gone,' I call them, gone for good, that group of local hearts and
heads,

is close to Browning's:

'Dust and ashes, dead and done with, Venice spent what Venice
earned.'

The friends' assertion that by dying they have transformed 'unsuccess' into 'success' picks up a characteristic theme of Browning's which emerges in these lines from the 'Toccata':

Some with lives that came to nothing, some with deeds as well
undone,
Death stepped tacitly and took them where they never see the
sun.

This theme of failure and success is also there in Browning's 'Rabbi Ben Ezra' which Hardy had read out to him on his deathbed along with the 'Rubaiyat of Omar Khayyam', the poem Browning is attacking:

For thence, – a paradox
Which comforts while it mocks, –
Shall life succeed in that it seems to fail:
What I aspired to be,
And was not, comforts me:
A brute I might have been, but would not sink i' the scale.

As Hardy formulates it in his poem, the idea of success is tenderly comic, a sympathetic sophistry Browning would have appreciated.

The great quality of 'Friends Beyond' and the 'Toccata' is the effect they achieve of intimate, musing, musical speech. In the last four syllables of 'Robert's kin, and John's, and Ned's' the trochaic beat shifts over into iambic speech. We can hear the voice pausing, then adding

'and John's, and Ned's',

just as in 'Neutral Tones', where a various mixture of iambs and anapaests builds a powerfully dulled monotone, Hardy patiently adds that the leaves 'had fallen from an ash, and were gray'. That little comma, like the comma in the conclusive: 'And then, the Curtain', is vital. Hardy's deployment of commas is always deftly significant. So is Browning's:

> 'Dust and ashes!' So you creak it, and I want the heart to scold.
> Dear dead women, with such hair, too – what's become of all the gold
> Used to hang and brush their bosoms? I feel chilly and grown old.

This – the second line especially – has all the spontaneity of natural speech. Browning's character says that Galuppi is 'like a ghostly cricket creaking where a house was burned' (a line Hardy quotes in the preface to his selection of Barnes's poetry), and this strange, ghostly quality – a soft, intermittent chirring – is there in Hardy's poems too. It's 'a way of whispering', a 'muted, measured note' which we can also hear in Browning's 'By the Fire-Side', one of Hardy's favourite poems:

> With me, youth led... I will speak now,
> No longer watch you as you sit
> Reading by fire-light, that great brow
> And the spirit-small hand propping it,
> Mutely, my heart knows how –
>
> When, if I think but deep enough,
> You are wont to answer, prompt as rhyme;
> And you, too, find without rebuff
> Response your soul seeks many a time
> Piercing its fine flesh-stuff.

Browning is describing how they communicate in a kind of perfect telepathy, like Sue and Jude who 'when they talked on an indifferent subject... there was ever a second silent conversation passing between their emotions, so perfect was the reciprocity between them'. This silent musing is a kind of spirit-talk, the music of intimate speech.

Hardy quotes these lines from the 'Toccata' in the *Life*:

> Did young people take their pleasure when the sea was warm in May?

Balls and masks begun at midnight, burning ever to mid-day,
When they made up fresh adventures for the morrow, do you say?

That last 'do you say?' has such a wonderfully soft, questioning tone, is so authentically the sound of someone talking very gently in his own mind. There is a very fine distinction in these poems between speaking out loud to someone and communicating in the 'silent conversation' of people who know each other very well. This whispering, thinking speech is there in Hardy's 'The Shadow on the Stone' and in 'After a Journey' where he talks ever so gently to Emma:

Summer gave us sweets, but autumn wrought division?
Things were not lastly as firstly well
With us twain, you tell?

As in the 'Toccata' the final 'you tell?' both characterises his voice and gives a sense of reciprocity, as though she's actually there to hear and reply.

Browning, then, is much closer to 'Friends Beyond' than Tennyson, though they both are among the brash, breezy 'stout upstanders' who optimistically shout that 'things are all as they best may be, save a few to be right ere long' ('In Tenebris' II). Hardy is parodying them both here and attacking a complacent optimism which asserts that 'nothing is much the matter; there are many smiles to a tear'. Against this kind of faith and clanging rhetoric – the rhetoric of Tennyson's 'Let the great world spin forever down the ringing grooves of change' – Hardy pits his own bitter despair:

Wintertime nighs;
But my bereavement-pain
It cannot bring again:
Twice no one dies.

Flower-petals flee;
But, since it once hath been,
No more that severing scene
Can harrow me.

These are minimal stanzas. The poem's short, sharp, first lines: 'Birds faint in dread,' 'Leaves freeze to dun,' 'Tempests may scath,' 'Black is night's cope,' are direct statements of reality, terse and totally unrhetorical.

Tennyson and Browning also impinge on 'Beeny Cliff':

A little cloud then cloaked us, and there flew an irised rain,
And the Atlantic dyed its levels with a dull misfeatured stain,
And then the sun burst out again, and purples prinked the main.

As Donald Davie says, the poem has an 'elaborately cunning metre'. It is 'in septenaries, but they are very artfully masked, especially near the start'. This stanza begins with an iambic beat:

A litt|e cloud | then cloaked | us,

and then becomes trochaic after the pause marked by the comma (the third foot is effectively 'then cloaked us'):

and there | flew an | irised | rain

And the | Atlantic | dyed its | levels | with a | dull mis|featured | stain,

and then restores tranquillity by changing back into more relaxed iambs:

And then | the sun | burst out | again, | and purp|les prinked | the main.

The irised rain is an echo of Browning's 'own soul's iris-bow' in the prologue to *Asolando* (it's his positive, idealist version of the sophist's shadow), while the purples, as Donald Davie has so brilliantly shown, are Virgilian. They are 'the spiritual light of sexual love', and the intense love they communicate is salted with a slight sadness in 'A little cloud then cloaked us'. This sadness becomes briefly disconcerting towards the end of the second line where the rhythm and sound of 'a dull misfeatured stain' seems to thicken into the metallic trochaics of 'Locksley Hall'. The hard sound disturbs as though the future has crowded in with its staining ugliness and imperfections and introduced another, much deeper kind of sadness. But it blows over like a brief depression and then the light glares out intensely as it does after rain – though as Davie shows this is more than a merely natural, physical effect. By 'purple' Hardy means *purpureus*, a spiritual brilliance.

The end of the second line is a musical moment, a dark tone like the demanding gravity of the 'dominant's persistence' which overshadows the softer, plaintive notes in the 'Toccata':

What? Those lesser thirds so plaintive, sixths diminished, sigh on sigh,
Told them something? Those suspensions, those solutions – 'Must we die?'
Those commiserating sevenths – 'Life might last! we can but try!'

'Were you happy?' – 'Yes.' – 'And are you still as happy!' – 'Yes. And you?'
– 'Then, more kisses!' – 'Did *I* stop them, when a million seemed so few?'
Hark, the dominant's persistence till it must be answered to!'

This is an extraordinary evocation of shifting emotions, a musical impressionism. And the trochaics in 'Beeny Cliff' often shed a similar delicacy and softness for an inexorable rhythm which has all the momentum of Tennyson's great world spinning forever down 'the ringing grooves of change' like the steam train he meant. Hardy uses these hurtling trochaics in 'A Death-Day Recalled', the poem immediately before 'Beeny Cliff', to represent the rattling swiftness of indifferent natural processes:

Beeny did not quiver,
Juliot grew not gray,
Thin Vallency's river
Held its wonted way.
Bos seemed not to utter
Dimmest note of dirge,
Targan mouth a mutter
To its creamy surge.

This rushing mechanism, as much as a feeling of ecstatic happiness, is there in the strong rhythm of 'Beeny Cliff'. And now and then a softer, wistful tone that is like the tone of the 'Toccata' comes through:

And the sweet things said in that March say anew there by and by?

But in the last stanza, when a darker mood threatens to disturb the total mood of the poem, the trochaic rhythm smooths over the disturbance like a steamroller and lets the mood of intensity carry on. The first line is romantic and trochaic:

What if | still in | chasmal | beauty | looms that | wild weird | western | shore,

the next begins as an iambic line:

The wom|an now | is –

and then there is a hiatus which might be a catch in the voice, like a sob, but instead the euphemism 'elsewhere' covers it over so that if the voice drops it comes conveniently to rest, and this allows the metre to reassert itself after the pause – again Hardy seems to be including an amphibrach:

| is – élsewhere |.

This forms a transition to the full trochaic beat:

whóm the | ámbling | póny | bóre,

Ánd nor | knóws nor | cáres for | Béeny, | ánd wìll | láugh there | névermóre.

Because it's set so solidly in the mould the last line doesn't express despair. Only in the middle of the previous line is there a threat to smash the mould, but it's quickly suppressed; while the last word 'nevermore' is muted by the rhythm so that it can't resound in the cavernous isolation of Poe's 'The Raven'.

Another technique which Hardy uses to create a mechanical beat is the double-rhyme found in many ballads and bawdy songs. He uses it in the fourth line of each stanza of 'Midnight on the Great Western' to underline the fact that the boy's fate is being determined for him. Determinism and a steam engine are again combined, though the thumping rhythm is iambic rather than trochaic: 'Bewrapt past knowing to what he was going'; 'That twinkled gleams of the lamp's sad beams'. And he also uses these propelling double-rhymes in the refrain of 'The Wind's Prophecy' where the wind contradicts his retrospectively naive expressions of fidelity to the girl he's about to abandon: 'Like bursting bonds the wind responds'; 'Low laughs the wind as if it grinned'. Nature is a deterministic mechanism whose processes are running on to their inevitable conclusion – his meeting with Emma. This situation is re-told from her point of view in 'A Man was Drawing Near to Me' which is also modelled on a ballad stanza – i.e. an essentially narrative form – and this gives a feeling of growing suspense, as though the man is getting closer, like a demon lover, like a murderer:

> There was no light at all inland,
> Only the seaward pharos-fire,
> Nothing to let me understand
>   That hard at hand
>   By Hennet Byre
> The man was getting nigh and nigher.

She has been idly thinking of 'legends, ghosts' and not about other people or her approaching fate. She didn't know that in the quiet spread of evening:

> Where Otterham lay,
> A man was riding up my way.

There is something beautifully natural and quietly inevitable in the tone, movement and rhyme of these lines. Then:

> There was a rumble at the door,
> A draught disturbed the drapery,
> And but a minute passed before,
> With gaze that bore
> My destiny,
> The man revealed himself to me.

The rhythms of destiny, of the lovers' convergence, are eerily caught in this poem. It moves with a terrible determination. There is a hint of the sense of sexual cruelty which is overtly present in 'Heiress and Architect' and 'The Convergence of the Twain', and her thoughts of ghosts and the poem's setting – a 'grey night of mournful drone' – make it clear that it's designed to inspire the same fascinated terror that a ghost story does. The line, 'The man had passed Tresparret Posts', is really frightening, partly because they're not identified: they sound like a gallows.

Each stanza of 'A Broken Appointment,' a poem about a failed meeting, is elaborately designed:

> You did not come,
> And marching Time drew on, and wore me numb. –
> Yet less for loss of your dear presence there
> Than that I thus found lacking in your make
> That high compassion which can overbear
> Reluctance for pure lovingkindness' sake
> Grieved I, when, as the hope-hour stroked its sum,
> You did not come.

Effectively, this is one long, expertly contrived stanza, a cunning and intricate escapement mechanism which strokes out the finality of 'You did not come' and, in the second stanza, 'You love not me.' Each is the last stroke of the 'hope-hour' and is appropriately final and absolute. This is one of the few instances of Hardy's use of the grand style, a style whose plangent sonorities are oddly combined with a Donne-like intricacy where an essentially spoken sentence twists over the stanzaic pattern. It's unusual for Hardy to write in the style of Tennyson's 'Ulysses' and employ a rhetoric which demands an elocutionary voice, but this poem unfortunately solicits just the reading that Dylan Thomas gives it on a record of one of his poetry readings. It asks to be read loudly and emptily, with all the fatuous sonorities of Gielgud reciting Shakespeare. The poem dramatises an emotion which is unashamedly passive and self-pitying, its argument is a piece of emotional blackmail in which the man pleads for the woman's pity because he knows he can't have her love. And yet one can't help being impressed by its sheer power and brilliance.

'Standing by the Mantlepiece', a curious monologue spoken as if by Hardy's friend Horace Moule who committed suicide in 1873, illustrates what I mean by these plangent sonorities. It begins well:

> This candle-wax is shaping to a shroud
> To-night. (They call it that, as you may know) –
> By touching it the claimant is avowed,
> And hence I press it with my finger – so.

He is addressing a mysterious woman and the parentheses and pauses marked by dashes flavour the stanza with the authenticity of real speech. We can hear him talking gently to her, but then the tone shifts:

> To-night. To me twice night, that should have been
> The radiance of the midmost tick of noon,
> And close around me wintertime is seen
> That might have shone the veriest day of June!

This is the elocutionary voice hamming the resonant lines and ending on the loudly facile rhyme 'June–noon'. And it's only in the last stanza that the tones of the speaking voice reassert themselves:

> And let the candle-wax thus mould a shape
> Whose meaning now, if hid before, you know,
> And how by touch one present claims its drape,
> And that it's I who press my finger – so.

This is actual speech with an actual gesture in the last line and a pause which roughens the line's regularity. It has the ghostly chirring that

Hardy admired in Browning. Indeed, Hardy found his own style, his own voice, by rejecting a mellifluous monotony:

> It surely is far sweeter and more wise
> To water love, than toil to leave anon
> A name whose glory-gleam will but advise
> Invidious minds to eclipse it with their own.

This is from an early and unremarkable sonnet called 'Her Reproach', and had Hardy continued to write in its Shakespearian style he would never have achieved the fame he's talking about. But, in the final couplet which follows this quatrain, he's already shedding its ponderous style:

> And over which the kindliest will but stay
> A moment; musing, 'He, too, had his day!'

The last line sets commas and a semi-colon in among the iambs and this draws it away from a facile regularity. Like 'Friends Beyond' its speech is 'musing', a soft whisper instead of a loud, cold resonance. This makes it the only good line in the poem.

'In Death Divided', like 'A Broken Appointment', is addressed to Florence Henniker and has also been read and recorded by Dylan Thomas. Inevitably, it's highly sonorous:

> I shall rot here, with those whom in their day
> You never knew,
> And alien ones who, ere they chilled to clay,
> Met not my view,
> Will in your distant grave-place ever neighbour you.

Behind this poem is the situation of 'The Statue and the Bust', which so fascinated Hardy, and another poem called 'Bifurcation' which he marked in the copy of Browning which Florence Henniker gave him (he appears to have had a platonic affection for her and his letters to her have been published under the title *One Rare Fair Woman*). Although he probably understood Browning's poetry better than anyone – he once said he could have written a book about him – he sometimes omits Browning's fundamental criticism of those dreary platonic relationships where the lovers indulge an intense, but fastidious passion for each other and selfishly refuse their opportunity, content to waste into a pair of 'frustrate ghosts'. Lines like 'No linking symbol show thereon for our tale's sake' are so remote from Browning's terse

same hard 'd' and 't' sounds that Hardy uses in 'dull misfeatured stain'.

He justifies his use of rhythm in a fascinating, though tetchy passage in the *Life*:

> Years earlier he had decided that too regular a beat was bad art. He had fortified himself in his opinion by thinking of the analogy of architecture, between which art and that of poetry he had discovered, to use his own words, that there existed a close and curious parallel, both arts, unlike some others, having to carry a rational content inside their artistic form. He knew that in architecture cunning irregularity is of enormous worth, and it is obvious that he carried on into his verse, perhaps in part unconsciously, the Gothic art-principle in which he had been trained – the principle of spontaneity, found in mouldings, tracery, and such like – resulting in the 'unforeseen' (as it has been called) character of his metres and stanzas, that of stress rather than of syllable, poetic texture rather than poetic veneer; the latter kind of thing, under the name of 'constructed ornament', being what he, in common with every Gothic student, had been taught to avoid as the plague. He shaped his poetry accordingly introducing metrical pauses, and reversed beats; and found for his trouble that some particular line of a poem exemplifying this principle was greeted with a would-be jocular remark that such a line 'did not make for immortality.'

The effort is to humanise and redeem the tyranny of technical facility and introduce into a regular sequence and mechanical pattern just those surprising spontaneities I discussed at the end of the last chapter. In ' "Why Do I?" ' Hardy apparently designs another clockwork poem:

> Why do I go on doing these things?
> Why not cease?
> Is it that you are yet in this world of welterings
> And unease,
> And that, while so, mechanic repetitions please?
>
> When shall I leave off doing these things? –
> When I hear
> You have dropped your dusty cloak and taken you wondrous wings
> To another sphere,
> Where no pain is: Then shall I hush this dinning gear.

But this is not the stale, routinely competent piece he suggest it is. The line:

> And that, while so, mechanic repetitions please?

is marvellous. The voice suddenly drops with 'while so' and becomes intimate, as though he's speaking to Emma softly, gently. And it's entirely characteristic of our voices not to keep an even level. When we talk our tones and inflections are constantly shifting and are usually not frozen into one posture. Only demagogues – the Byron of *Childe Harold*, not *Don Juan* – shout all the time. And by drawing a different tone, another shading, against the beat of what is otherwise a perfectly regular iambic line Hardy refuses to orate. In 'Beeny Cliff' the euphemism 'elsewhere' introduces a different vocal shading, but it opens the way to a reality he doesn't want to face. Here, the drop in the voice which must accompany any parenthetical remark tugs against the line and humanises it. It's spontaneous and 'unforeseen', and it releases the rest of the line so that 'mechanic repetitions' moves nimbly forward, its bunched syllables varying upon and echoing each other in a quick flurry, then pausing very slightly again before coming to rest on 'please?' This drop in the voice and fidelity to the way in which we actually do speak (a kind of acoustic impressionism) is a quality that characterises Hardy's best poems.

Perhaps its value and significance can best be demonstrated if we suppose that Ben Jonson had begun 'To Penshurst' with this line:

> Penshurst, thou art not built to envious show,

instead of:

> Thou art not, Penshurst, built to envious show.

As I hear it, he would have immediately contradicted all that he goes on to say about the building's deeply human qualities. The distinction Jonson draws in his poem between other mansions' 'proud ambitious heaps' of polished marble and Penshurst's local stone and unpretentious architecture is obviously one that Hardy would have appreciated, for it's essentially his distinction between the beauty of human association and the beauty of aspect, between a beloved ancestor's battered tankard and the finest Greek vase. Jonson doesn't begin with a clarion call, a declamatory blast of wind through cold metal: he begins almost by stepping backwards, by addressing the building and then introducing its name in a parenthesis which involves a change in vocal tone. The poem is in couplets but because Jonson often draws the sense out through several lines and will often happily complete it in the middle of a line, they are seldom closed and never polished. Sense and rhyme never chime glibly. And this studied roughness, which is what Hardy means by 'poetic texture rather than poetic veneer', represents a rejection of rhetoric and polished smoothness. Local stone and wood are chosen as the true materials, not marble or metal.

Take the end of 'Logs on the Hearth':

> My fellow-climber rises dim
> From her chilly grave –
> Just as she was, her foot near mine on the bending limb,
> Laughing, her young brown hand awave.

The lithe springiness of the last line is magnificent. There is a similar moment in *The Woodlanders* when Grace Melbury sees Giles Winterbourne:

> He looked and smelt like Autumn's very brother, his face being sunburnt to wheat-colour, his eyes blue as corn-flowers, his sleeves and leggings dyed with fruit-stains, his hands clammy with the sweet juice of apples, his hat sprinkled with pips, and everywhere about him that atmosphere of cider which at its first return each season has such an indescribable fascination for those who have been born and bred among the orchards. Her heart rose from its late sadness like a released bough; her senses revelled in the sudden lapse back to Nature unadorned. The consciousness of having to be genteel because of her husband's profession, the veneer of artificiality which she had acquired at the fashionable schools, were thrown off, and she became the crude country girl of her latent early instincts.

The taut 'give' of a living branch, the heart moving impulsively 'like a released bough', is the effect of the poem's last line. Because the material is springy wood this entails a rejection of any glossy 'veneer of artificiality'. The natural speech-pause at the comma and the shades of stress on

/ \ / /
'young brown hand awave',

with the unique human gesture this describes, make the line authentic and natural, with a naturalness that is the result of a deliberate and difficult rejection of poetic veneer in favour of poetic texture.

The first stanza of '"My Spirit will not Haunt the Mound"' shows the way those parenthetical qualifications we all use in our everyday speech to amplify and define what we're saying can give an otherwise standard poem a unique quality of its own:

> My spirit will not haunt the mound
> Above my breast,
> But travel, memory-possessed,
> To where my tremulous being found
> Life largest, best.

The phrase 'memory-possessed', which is held between commas, and the use of the single, pausing comma in 'largest, best' are the two features which freshen this verse. The last verse establishes the obvious with an almost Jamesian scrupulosity:

> And there you'll find me, if a jot
> You still should care
> For me, and for my curious air;
> If otherwise, then I shall not,
> For you, be there.

The voice arrives at a definition and what matters is not the definition itself but the sense Hardy creates through it of Emma actually talking to him. The third foot of the first line is broken by a comma and so the line is immediately rescued from an easy regularity. This pause is in addition to the equivocal pauses and hoverings at the line-endings and the pauses in the third, fourth and fifth lines. These pauses give the sense of an exact definition being arrived at and their tone introduces a subtle, strange beauty, for this is again a ghostly poem in both its content and sound. There is a more even tone in the second verse, though I like the nimble alliteration in the first line and the pit-patting of 'hither and thither':

> My phantom-footed shape will go
> When nightfall grays
> Hither and thither along the ways
> I and another used to know
> In backward days.

The quality of this poem is best described by Frost's phrase 'sentence-sound'. Frost's sense of this sound, his delighted relishing of it, makes him offer this provocative definition: 'A sentence is a sound in itself on which other sounds called words may be strung.' The writer doesn't invent these sounds, he 'only catches them fresh from talk, where they grow spontaneously.' For Frost, the 'possibilities for tune from the dramatic tones of meaning struck across the rigidity of a limited meter are endless', and like Hardy he is resolutely on the side of the unique and quirky, valuing 'the straight crookedness of a good walking stick' rather than a 'mechanically straight' line. Again, springy wood is the chosen material. Both it and that special tone of voice or 'sentence-sound' are there in the last line of Frost's 'Birches':

> One could do worse than be a swinger of birches.

And this spoken quality is also marvellously present in the poetry of Edward Thomas, who was both a friend of Frost's and an admirer of Hardy's work. He justified Frost's way of writing by calling attention to his insistence upon 'absolute fidelity to the postures which the voice assumes in the most expressive intimate speech'. The vocal shifts and pauses in ' "My Spirit will not Haunt the Mound" ' show the absolute fidelity Hardy had to the ways in which intimate speech moves. His friend, William Barnes, formulates a similar idea in his famous statement:

> Speech was shapen of the breath-sounds of speakers, for the ears of hearers, and not from speech-tokens (letters) in books...and therefore I have shapen my teaching as that of a speech of breath-sounded words, and not of lettered ones.

And these beautiful lines from Barnes's 'My Orcha'd in Linden Lea' have this kind of spoken authenticity:

> I be free to goo abrode,
> Or teäke ageän my homeward road
> To where, vor me, the apple tree
> Do leän down low in Linden Lea.

It seems appropriate that, again, a lovely natural line like the last should be about a bending bough. The third line's 'vor me' is close to Hardy's 'for you' in ' "My Spirit will not Haunt the Mound" ', less in the obvious similarity than in the sense of an intimate speech-tone shading across the line. It also sets up an internal rhyme within the couplet – a couplet that is used with slight variations as a refrain in the poem – and this tautens the lines. As Grigson shows in his edition of Barnes, the last, lithely perfect line uses a *cynghanedd* which is 'the Welsh repetition of consonantal sounds in the two parts of a line, divided by a caesura'. The figure reads: DLNDNL/NLNDNL. Hardy greatly admired Barnes's 'ingenious internal rhymes, his subtle juxtapositions of kindred lippings and vowel-sounds'; and, as Samuel Hynes notes, the line 'Yellowly the sun sloped low down to westward' in Hardy's great elegy for Barnes, 'The Last Signal', uses the *cynghanedd*. The consonantal pattern is: LLSNSLLNS. This pattern and a series of internal rhymes are part of his tribute to Barnes.

Though he preferred his own use of these metrical techniques, Hopkins also had a great admiration for Barnes's fidelity to speech-sounds, his 'Westcountry instress' as he termed it. The opening of 'Felix Randal' shows Hopkins's attentiveness to speech-tones and to the way we arrange words when we speak:

> Felix Randal the farrier, O is he dead then? my duty all ended

Hardy's fidelity to speech which Barnes and Browning must have helped him to perfect and encouraged him to achieve comes over in these rather similar lines which begin 'Exeunt Omnes':

> Everybody else, then, going,
> And I still left where the fair was?...

This sounds completely authentic. We catch a tone that is puzzled and resigned, as though he's suddenly breaking out of a momentary fit of absent-mindedness and realising what's happening. Hopkins, Hardy and Browning (whom Hopkins disliked but must have learnt from) all value the uniqueness of speech-tones – their instress – and with this valuation goes a total respect for the absolute uniqueness and integrity of people and things: 'All things counter, original, spare, strange.' Each in his own way is a Gothic artist, an enemy of veneer and 'constructed ornament'.

A characteristic feature of Hardy's poetry is the frequency with which he introduces direct speech, and this is partly due to Browning's influence. Their poems are often a collocation of different voices:

> And will any say when my bell of quittance is heard in the gloom,
>   And a crossing breeze cuts a pause in its outrollings,
> Till they rise again, as they were a new bell's boom,
>   'He hears it not now, but used to notice such things'?

The last line is both Hardy's voice and his rendering of someone else's, and though its sense reveals itself quite logically the whole stanza sounds as though it's being spoken by someone thinking the idea out:

the third line seems an amplification, an additional amplification that isn't strictly necessary, though, logically, it is. In the *Life* Hardy suggests that his poetry has some resemblance to Donne's, and this ability to base a stanza upon rhythms that are both logical and natural is a characteristic they share:

> Twice or thrice had I loved thee,
> Before I knew thy face or name;
> So in a voice, so in a shapeless flame,
> Angels affect us oft, and worshipped be;
> Still when, to where thou wert, I came,
> Some lovely glorious nothing I did see,
> But since my soul, whose child love is,
> Takes limbs of flesh, and else could nothing do,
> More subtle than the parent is
> Love must not be, but take a body too,
> And therefore what thou wert, and who
> I bid Love ask, and now
> That it assume thy body, I allow,
> And fix itself in thy lip, eye, and brow.

'So in a voice, so in a shapeless flame' is a natural figure, a speech cadence which carries and powerfully organises the developing argument. These lines of Hardy's are twisted and yet natural:

> – Yea, as the rhyme
> Sung by the sea-swell, so in their pleading dumbness
> Captured me these.

The back-to-front organisation of these lines is appropriate to the poem's theme of 'lost revisiting manifestations' and to its Miltonic sense of difficulty. The line 'Sweet, sad, sublime' in the next stanza of 'In Front of the Landscape' has a cadence that appealed to Hardy for he uses it again in 'To the Moon':

> 'What have you looked at, Moon,
> In your time,
> Now long past your prime?'
> 'O, I have looked at, often looked at
> Sweet, sublime,
> Sore things, shudderful, night and noon
> In my time.'

The alliteration, bunched stresses and the varying line-lengths produce that fricative terseness which is what Hardy means by 'poetic texture'. 'Then, welcome each rebuff/That turns earth's smoothness rough', as Browning says in 'Rabbi Ben Ezra'. But for Browning this is a theodicy as well as a poetic because the difficulty involved in pronouncing his rough, scraping sounds becomes, curiously, an argument for God's existence through a justification of pain along the very puritanical lines that it's good for us. It makes us strive; we are 'baffled to fight better'. In 'To the Moon', as almost always in Hardy, pain is accidental and unjust. And in the refrains in 'During Wind and Rain' the injustice of life's conditions is partly represented by buffeting stresses:

> /   \   /   \   /   /
> How the sick leaves reel down in throngs
> /   \   /   \   /   /
> See, the white storm-birds wing across
> /   /   /   /
> And the rotten rose is ript from the wall
> /   \   /   /   \   /
> Down their carved names the rain-drop ploughs.

The last line is particularly tough and scraping. It almost screeches, like chalk on a blackboard.

The greatness of 'At Castle Boterel' is partly owing to Hardy's marvellous skill in making us participate in a process that seems to be actually taking place as we read and listen:

> As I drive to the junction of lane and highway,
>   And the drizzle bedrenches the waggonette,
> I look behind at the fading byway,
>   And see on its slope, now glistening wet,
>   Distinctly yet
>
> Myself and a girlish form benighted
>   In dry March weather. We climb the road
> Beside a chaise. We had just alighted
>   To ease the sturdy pony's load
>   When he sighed and slowed.

The opening stanza contracts and then carries over into the next with the deftest of movements so that time shifts and expands backwards and the weather changes simply and unobtrusively. The patient simplicity and directness of the verses carry a feeling of awe with them and we never think that a statement of fact like: 'We climb the road/ Beside a chaise' is anything other than remarkable. It makes the ordinary marvellous. The tiny detail: 'When he sighed and slowed' is so natural and life-like, and because it alliterates and connects with 'road' through the rhyme, the emotion that is established becomes almost unbearable:

> It filled but a minute. But was there ever
> A time of such quality, since or before,
> In that hill's story? To one mind never,
> Though it has been climbed, foot-swift, foot-sore,
> By thousands more.

The strength and power of this verse stems from Hardy's way of building a stanza out of short terse units. There is a complete absence of rhetoric and a complete fidelity to a voice talking and apparently discovering what to say at that moment. Frost says that a poem 'can never lose its sense of a meaning that once unfolded by surprise as it went'; and 'At Castle Boterel', like so many of Hardy's poems, is faithful to this slowly unfolding principle of surprise and spontaneity.

'The Going', which is about their failure to communicate, works wholly in terms of a conversation which he desperately wishes were not one-sided:

> Why, then, latterly did we not speak,
> Did we not think of those days long dead,
> And ere your vanishing strive to seek
> That time's renewal? We might have said,
> 'In this bright spring weather
> We'll visit together
> Those places that once we visited.'

The last stanza moves from a resigned acceptance of the fact that nothing can now be done:

> Well, well! All's past amend,

to the stark, unbearable recognition:

> Unchangeable. It must go.

Then through a relapse upon his own inadequacy and weakness:

> I seem but a dead man held on end
> To sink down soon...

it moves into his final, impulsive declaration of grief:

> O you could not know
> That such swift fleeing
> No soul foreseeing –
> Not even I – would undo me so!

This spontaneous, surprising declaration sounds like a rebuke. It's almost as though she has died to spite him or test his love and has succeeded only too well. Here, he's demanding an answer from her and in 'The Voice' she begins to 'call' to him before their true dialogue is finally discovered in 'The Phantom Horsewoman'. So, at the very beginning of a sequence that contains some of his finest poems, the tones and inflections of his voice – a questioning voice that is searching for hers – texture each stanza and give 'The Going' that cunning, Gothic irregularity, that spoken authenticity, which frees all his best poems from the tyranny of a machine-made metrical regularity. As Auden says in 'The Horatians', this tone of voice is

> neither truckle nor thrasonical but softly
> certain (a sound wood-winds imitate better
> than strings).

4
Observations of Fact

Hardy's sensitivity to the cadences of actual speech is matched by his insistence throughout his work on what is authentically visible. Like Leslie Stephen and Frederic Harrison – both positivists and friends of his – he followed Comte in accepting that all real knowledge is based on observed facts, and this ruled out religious faith almost automatically: the 'quick, glittering, empirical eye' is 'sharp for the surfaces of things' but for nothing beneath them. It can never penetrate beyond surfaces and know things in themselves. For Ruskin this keen sight is essentially religious, and in a passage in *Modern Painters* which Hardy knew (he copied it into one of his commonplace books) he resembles any agnostic positivist when he insists that we must observe things closely:

> the greatest thing a human soul ever does in this world is to *see* something, and tell what it *saw* in a plain way.... To see clearly is poetry, prophecy, and religion, – all in one.

Hardy made this note in 1900, but he first read *Modern Painters* during the 1860s and throughout his life he acted on Ruskin's recommendation to observe closely. Like the architect in his early poem, 'Heiress and Architect', he developed a 'cold, clear view' of things, though for him this faculty of conscious, deliberate observation seldom, if ever, combined 'prophecy and religion' with poetry. He trained his eyes to seize the most distinctly visible feature in his field of vision and then he described it.

This is what happens in this description of Gladstone at the time of the Home Rule Bill:

> Saw Gladstone enter the Houses of Parliament. The crowd was very excited, not only waving their hats and shouting and running, but leaping in the air. His head was bare, and his now bald crown showed pale and distinct over the top of Mrs. Gladstone's bonnet.

Another note from this period shows the same insistence on the visibility of things:

> Cold weather brings out upon the faces of people the written marks of their habits, vices, passions, and memories, as warmth brings out on paper a writing in sympathetic ink. The drunkard looks still more a drunkard when the splotches have their margins made distinct by frost, the hectic blush becomes a stain now, the cadaverous complexion reveals the bone under, the quality of handsomeness is reduced to its lowest terms.

Here, he obeys Ruskin, observes closely and clearly and tells what he sees. Similarly, in his description of Gladstone he quaintly concentrates on one of the scene's most *distinct* features and touches it into life by using Gladstone's bald head as a focal point. For Hardy this type of accurate seeing is absolutely essential. The poet's task is 'to find beauty in ugliness' and this means that any and every object – no matter how prosaic – is worth noticing. In some ways this opens up a whole new poetic territory, in others, because it's a reflex action prompted by disillusion, it simply binds and restricts the eye to the dead surfaces of fact:

Brush not the bough for midnight scents
  That come forth lingeringly,
And wake the same sweet sentiments
  They breathed in you and me
When living seemed a laugh, and love
  All it was said to be.

Within the common lamp-lit room
  Prison my eyes and thought;
Let dingy details crudely loom,
  Mechanic speech be wrought:
Too fragrant was Life's early bloom,
  Too tart the fruit it brought!

'Shut out that Moon' brings the blinds firmly down on the pathetic fallacies of romantic moonlight and dark, Keatsian scents. The eye is imprisoned by drab contemporary fact, and behind this positivistic commitment to a prosaic ugliness lies Hardy's rejection of conventionally beautiful landscapes in favour of the greater – because more modern – reality of waste heaths and barren mountains. And yet it's not as simple as this. 'Afterwards', one of his finest poems, is about just this compulsive positivism (noticing *things*), but these perceived objects are not 'dingy details' or dead facts:

> When the Present has latched its postern behind my tremulous
> stay,
> And the May month flaps its glad green leaves like wings,
> Delicate-filmed as new-spun silk, will the neighbours say,
> 'He was a man who used to notice such things'?

It would be wrong to insist that the green leaves or the other 'things' in the poem – hawk, hedgehog, stars, passing-bell – exist simply as observed facts. The act of observation becomes a kind of vision here (this is the last poem in *Moments of Vision*) and deliberate scrutiny, the cold clear view of things, passes into a reverence for what is observed. The fresh green leaves are like butterflies hatching from their chrysalids, their texture is like fresh silk, and here, because of a hint of mulberry-feeding silkworms, there is a suggestion of a process that is both natural and man-made. In order to make such a comparison Hardy has obviously had to give spring leaves more than a casual glance, but his precise observation of them doesn't result in a coldly accurate description. The way he matches their sheens and also compares the fluttering leaves to one of the most wonder-inducing of natural processes – the hatching of a butterfly – means that his attitude to them is more than one of merely scientific interest. The butterfly is an ancient symbol of the soul and the poem is about survival after death, but it realises immortality in physical, visible terms. Resurrecting angels and winged souls are naturalised as fluttering leaves, as things. This also happens in 'Voices from Things Growing in a Churchyard':

> These flowers are I, poor Fanny Hurd,
> Sir or Madam,
> A little girl here sepultured.
> Once I flit-fluttered like a bird
> Above the grass, as now I wave
> In daisy shapes above my grave,
> All day cheerily,
> All night eerily!

Again, immortality is realised as an observed fact.

Hardy's matching of filmy leaves with fresh silk in 'Afterwards' is particularly curious in that he's joining a natural fact with a process that involves leaves, silkworms and spinning wheels and so suggests a co-operation between nature and human skills. He knew that Paleyan natural theology with its Great Designer is bunk, but there are moments when its basic idea seems feasible on an aesthetic level. What I mean by this is best shown by Arthur Koestler's descriptions in *The Act of Creation* of 'the new landscapes seen through an electron microscope':

> They show the ultra-structure of the world – electric discharges in a high voltage arc which look like the most elaborate Brussels lace, smoke molecules of magnesium oxide like a composition by Mondrian, nerve-synapses inside a muscle suspended like algae, phantom-figures of swirling heated air, ink molecules travelling through water, crystals like Persian carpets, and ghostly mountains inside the micro-structure of pure Hafnium, like an illustration to Dante's Purgatorio. What strikes one is that these landscapes, drawn as it were in invisible ink, possess great intrinsic beauty of form.

These shapes are not meant to be seen, and yet, once seen, they look like designs (Paley would interrupt here and say a design presupposes a Designer). The structure of matter, then, resembles certain man-made patterns, fresh leaves are like new-spun silk, electric discharges like Brussels lace. So hidden, natural forms appear to be echoed in human designs. This is what I mean by suggesting that Hardy's positivistic observation has passed into vision – the kind of vision found in Hopkins. (The common influence is Barnes, who delighted to match and contrast colours and shades: snow-white washing against a clear blue sky is one of the examples Grigson cites). For Hopkins 'inscape' is perceived or 'stressed' by looking at nature very closely. It's as though Crabbe, down on his knees examining a saltwort, changes into Coleridge and starts to see visions. By 'instress' Hopkins means the perception of a unique beauty, an individually distinctive pattern, and in a brief journal-entry he also compares an observed natural phenomenon to silk:

> Waterfalls not only skeined but silky too – one saw it fr. the inn across the meadows: at one quain of the rock the water glistened above and took shadow below, and the rock was reddened a little way each side with the wet, wh. sets off the silkiness.

Unusually for Hopkins, this sounds bogus. We can accept that certain natural colours and shades match, but to insist that the texture of the

26-11-2004 2:37PM
Item(s) checked out to Navaratnam, Subas

TITLE: Greek literature / edited by P.E.
BARCODE: 31888005699351
DUE DATE: 04-01-05

TITLE: Thomas Hardy : the poetry of perc
BARCODE: 31888007121560
DUE DATE: 04-01-05

water here is 'set off' by the wet rock is to suggest that nature is displaying a tasteful colour-sense. Hopkins is responding as an aesthete and transforming a waterfall into an ornamental prop in a private landscape garden. In this instance the metaphysical intentions behind his aestheticism are unpersuasive, and doubtless Hardy would have disclaimed having any such intention when he wrote the first stanza of 'Afterwards'. His aim is to objectify himself in the details he describes. This will be achieved through the association which he has with these objects in the minds of people who themselves used to observe his habit of noticing 'such things'. In this way his perception is reified and becomes as much a fact as its objects.

Hume's principle of 'custom', which he defines as 'the effect of repeated perceptions', illustrates what Hardy is doing in 'Afterwards': as a positivist who also wants to represent an idea of immortality he must make it convincing, and to be convincing it must be visible. Custom, for Hume, enables us to attribute a 'continued existence' to objects which otherwise have no obvious connection with each other; 'nor is it', he says, 'from any other principle but custom operating upon the imagination, that we can draw any inference from the appearance of one to the existence of another'. So each time Hardy's neighbours notice certain things they will immediately associate him with them, remembering that they were once a 'familiar sight' to him, and so will necessarily make him spring back into a kind of existence in their memories. His 'constant conjunction' with certain objects – the phrase is Hume's – will ensure that they will always associate him with them and so will always remember him. For Hume, we make sense of the world by seeing certain things again and again, and in this way we link a series of familiar impressions together and construct an apparently solid and durable world for ourselves. Hardy's stress on habitual sight echoes this: he will be the missing term which his neighbours will introduce into a familiar equation. In other words, his inseparable connection with certain objects will not be broken by his death and disappearance from his neighbours' sight. However, there are a series of short breaks in the poem's perceptual sequences:

> If it be in the dusk when, like an eyelid's soundless blink,
> The dewfall-hawk comes crossing the shades to alight
> Upon the wind-warped upland thorn, a gazer may think,
> 'To him this must have been a familiar sight.'

One of the functions of the comparison between the bird's flight and 'an eyelid's soundless blink' is to remind us of that act of perception which is taking place and which is part of the poem's subject. Like the filmy leaves and spun silk this curious simile is a fitting of man to nature, and it's also an enactment of the nightjar's swiftness, its almost instantaneous flight to the thorn. Hearing and sight are both momentarily closed off.

There are two other examples of occlusion in the poem. In the first line where the Present latches its postern behind his 'tremulous stay', Hardy identifies his being shut off from sight and life by death with the back door of a house closing behind him. But no sooner have we read this line than the next introduces spring, and because he is associated with the flapping leaves his memory is freshly revived. The last stanza contains another example of this idea of disappearance and reappearance:

> And will any say when my bell of quittance is heard in the gloom,
>   And a crossing breeze cuts a pause in its outrollings,
> Till they rise again, as they were a new bell's boom,
>   'He hears it not now, but used to notice such things'?

There is a hiatus, a break in a visible or audible sequence, a 'soundless blink'. And in the third stanza he says that even if it should be pitch dark when he dies there will still be a dimly visible object – a hedgehog – to recall him to mind, or:

> If, when hearing that I have been stilled at last, they stand at the
>   door,
>   Watching the full-starred heavens that winter sees,
> Will this thought rise on those who will meet my face no more,
>   'He was one who had an eye for such mysteries'?

Despite this reverence for the mysteries of nature the poem's notion of immortality is decidedly agnostic and humanist. There is a neat religious reference in: 'Till they rise again, as they were a new bell's boom.' The phrase 'rise again' is familiar – 'and the third day he shall rise again' – while the word 'new' also holds familiar biblical connotations: 'Therefore if any man be in Christ, he is a new creature; old things are passed away; behold, all things are become new.' The immortality which the agnostic poet anticipates is compared gently and with sad irony to the Christian's expectations of the resurrection of the dead and the life everlasting. We are back with the winged, new leaves.

'The Occultation', which is also in *Moments of Vision*, similarly describes a hiatus and then applies it to the possible survival of something which has disappeared. The verb 'to occult' is a term used in astronomy and it means 'to cut off from view by passing in front':

> When the cloud shut down on the morning shine,
> And darkened the sun,
> I said, 'So ended that joy of mine
> Years back begun.'
>
> But day continued its lustrous roll
> In upper air;
> And did my late irradiate soul
> Live on somewhere?

In 'Afterwards' he will survive after death as a kind of percept, a memory that will be activated when his neighbours look at certain objects associated with him. There, a sequence of observations is only apparently and temporarily interrupted by the death of the principal observer, while in this poem the observer wonders whether he may not infer the survival somewhere of his 'late irradiate soul', his vanished 'joy', just as he infers the continued existence of the sun when it's concealed by a cloud. Though the reference is probably as much to the end of a love affair as to the woman's death, the principle is the same as it is in 'Afterwards': an abrupt closing-off followed by a reminder that the perception of a thing, rather than the thing itself, has disappeared. The bell of quittance is still tolling in the gloom even though the occluding breeze makes it impossible to hear it for a moment.

In 'The Occultation' survival is presented as a metaphysical possibility but in 'Afterwards' it's rendered in human, secular terms: the poet will be remembered after his death. Both in this and the setting of 'Afterwards' are reminiscent of the moment in Gray's Elegy (another of Hardy's favourite poems) when the 'hoary-headed Swain' relates how he and the other villagers often used to see the poet out on one of his customary walks:

> 'One morn I miss'd him on the custom'd hill,
> Along the heath and near his fav'rite tree;
> Another came; nor yet beside the rill,
> Nor up the lawn, nor at the wood was he;

'The next with dirges due in sad array
Slow through the church-way path we saw him borne.

There are a number of minor verbal echoes of the Elegy in Hardy's poem but what matters is that he, like Gray, describes a series of totally familiar, 'custom'd' scenes which are so much associated with the poet that his personality has become part of them. The landscape is humanised through the memories and associations that inhere in it. Both Gray and Hardy point to the sacredness of habitual action and because they describe themselves in the third person, as they appear to others who observe them, they succeed in giving themselves an objective existence. Both conceive of immortality in secular, social terms, though Gray's melancholy epitaph, his talking headstone, is totally unsatisfactory compared with Hardy's casually voiced: 'He was a man who used to notice such things.'

There are more such observed things in 'Genoa and the Mediterranean':

Out from a deep-delved way my vision lit
On housebacks pink, green, ochreous – where a slit
Shoreward 'twixt row and row revealed the classic blue through it.

And thereacross waved fishwives' high-hung smocks,
Chrome kerchiefs, scarlet hose, darned underfrocks;
Often since when my dreams of thee, O Queen, that frippery mocks.

Bailey supplies more facts in his handbook to the poems: the 'deep-delved way' is a railway tunnel, nearly two miles long, just before Genoa's Station Piazza Principe. This information may be useful because if you apply it the poem seems to be deliberately organised around the first fleeting impressions of Genoa that flashed on Hardy's eyes as his train sped out into Mediterranean sunshine from a tunnel whose darkness would have made the colours all the more vivid and intense, like a vision after resurrection. Unusually, he describes numerous bright colours – pink, green, ochre, blue, scarlet, chrome – whose brightness might be due to this sudden transition from darkness to light. Bailey treats the poem as a photograph that 'presents the Hardy's first impression of Genoa', but doesn't appear to realise that the passage which he quotes from Emma's diary flatly contradicts this: 'dull weather, no blue sea'. I'm pointing to this because I think it's important that we take seriously Hardy's remark that 'the exact truth as to material fact...is a student's style'. This poem is organised very skilfully around various observed facts but Hardy naturally isn't tied to a literal transcription of the facts which happened to meet his eyes one day in 1887 when the train carrying him and his wife emerged from the last tunnel before Genoa's main station. He has carefully composed the visible scene by leading the eye, as in a painting, through the glaring, alkaline colours that clutter the foreground to the distant chink of cool 'classic blue'. This is the tourist's glimpse of that 'Epic-famed' sea whose classical beauty, he suggests, has been 'wronged' by Genoa's dowdy state of undress. Naturally he's being facetious here because he prefers the mundane, backstreet actuality of washing, housebacks and railway sidings to the city's epic fame and marbled beauty. He prefers, in other words, the dingy beauty of human association to a statuesque beauty of aspect.

This preference for scenes which have human associations is reflected in the ugly, banal setting of 'In a Waiting-Room':

> On a morning sick as the day of doom
>   With the drizzling gray
>   Of an English May,
> There were few in the railway waiting-room.
> About its walls were framed and varnished
> Pictures of liners, fly-blown, tarnished.
> The table bore a Testament
> For travellers' reading, if suchwise bent.

This is by no means an entirely successful poem: the lines are flaccid, the opening quatrain doesn't manage a combination of the portentous and the banal as 'Genoa' does, and the comparison later of the children's sudden appearance to the eastern flame of a 'high altar' overstates a deliberate incongruity. These faults are probably due to the way the poem's form vacillates uneasily between a fully fledged monologue spoken by a dramatic character, and one spoken by that surrogate persona present in many of Hardy's poems. Nevertheless it does have some of the strengths and virtues that characterise his best work. Its strength lies in its observation of a drab reality and in the way it extracts beauty from ugliness by infusing it with human associations. The poem has a different meaning for each person in it – it varies with its perceivers. For the bagman the waiting-room was just a place where he could absentmindedly scribble his accounts in the margins of a bible, for the soldier and his wife – they have a 'haggard look/Subdued to stone by strong endeavour' – it's the scene of their tragic parting, and for the children the room is beautiful because it contains pictures they see as being 'lovely'. And it's then that the room becomes beautiful for the speaker. The episode's 'smear of tragedy' is transformed by the children and their excited happiness spreads 'a glory' through the squalid, gloomy room. Though it's not insisted on, there is a pathetic irony in the different significances the pictures hold for the couple and the children: they are looking forward to seeing the ships and hearing the band play, while the soldier and his wife are not because he will be sailing on one of them, probably to the brassy strains of a military band. The poetry of this scene may vary with its perceivers, but the detached narrator feels that the children give it a value which is more permanent than the fluid relativism of its variable values. The drab room is given a human connection by the emotions of the people who wait in it.

The observing eye, sharp for the stories implicit in things, is at work in 'A Gentleman's Second-Hand Suit':

> Here it is hanging in the sun
>   By the pawn-shop door,
> A dress-suit – all its revels done
>   Of heretofore.
> Long drilled to the waltzers' swing and sway,
>   As its tokens show:
> What is has seen, what it could say
>   If it did but know!
>
> The sleeve bears still a print of powder
>   Rubbed from her arms
> When she warmed up as the notes swelled louder
>   And livened her charms –
> Or rather theirs, for beauties many
>   Leant there, no doubt,
> Leaving these tell-tale traces when he
>   Spun them about.

'On looking close', Hardy says, the suit seemed rather old-fashioned and he goes on, inevitably, to ask where the man and the women he danced with now are:

> Some of them may forget him quite
>   Who smudged his sleeve,
> Some think of a wild and whirling night
>   With him, and grieve.

The smudges are like clues to a mystery and he carefully scrutinises them, like a detective trying to piece together the events and experiences behind them. This clearly isn't one of his better poems but it does suggest something of the interested observation and human sympathy he brought to inanimate fact. It's a poem of observation, not vision. And my comparison of its cold scrutiny to a detective training his magnifying glass on a fingerprint is not an idle one for Hardy made it himself. He once sat for Sir William Rothenstein who recalled that he

> remarked on the expression of the eyes in the drawing that I made – he knew the look he said, for he was often taken for a detective. He had a small dark bilberry eye which he cocked at you unexpectedly.

Like a detective, the positivist needs a visible fact, a 'print', to work on. What matters is 'the wear on a threshold...the print of a hand'; indeed, any lump of dead fact that holds a trace of humanity – like the marks of fingers baked on old bricks. Experience can saturate bricks and plaster:

'Babes new-brought-forth
Obsess my rooms; straight-stretched
Lank corpses, ere outborne to earth;
Yea, throng they as when first from the Byss upfetched.

'Dancers and singers
Throb in me now as once;
Rich-noted throats and gossamered flingers
Of heels; the learned in love-lore and the dunce.

'Note here within
The bridegroom and the bride,
Who smile and greet their friends and kin,
And down my stairs depart for tracks untried.

So says the old house to the brash modern house beside it in 'The Two Houses'. These are the 'shades' which he tells the new house will 'print on thee their presences as on me'.

The poem's mixture of tender sympathy and eerie wit is characteristic; and so is its insistence that what's dead and gone can still be seen, is still somehow there. This happens again in 'Haunting Fingers' where the musical instruments in a museum mutter to each other like the dead in 'Friends Beyond', though sadly:

And they felt past handlers clutch them,
Though none was in the room,
Old players' dead fingers touch them,
Shrunk in the tomb.

The harpsichord laments how:

'My keys' white shine,
Now sallow, met a hand
Even whiter.... Tones of hers fell forth with mine
In sowings of sound so sweet no lover could withstand!'

And its clavier was filmed with fingers
Like tapering flames – wan, cold –
Or the nebulous light that lingers
In charnel mould.

The objects become phosphorescent – fact is spiritualised and the spiritual becomes a visible object. The dead fingers are like 'tapering flames'. Hardy is seeking to realise and objectify immortality in a series of observed facts, and it is this kind of immortality which he anticipates in 'Afterwards' and tries to discover in 'Shelley's Skylark'. He insists everywhere on things being visible, and one of the curious features of 'To my Father's Violin', 'The Two Houses' and 'Haunting Fingers' is the shape which the stanzas make on the page – though this is not so very unusual as all his poems are intended to have a distinctive shape. Like George Herbert he tries to ensure that each poem is a unique object with its own special identity.

Each stanza of 'To my Father's Violin' seems roughly to imitate the body of a violin, like an early concrete poem:

In the gallery west the nave,
But a few yards from his grave,
Did you, tucked beneath his chin, to his bowing
Guide the homely harmony
Of the quire
Who for long years strenuously –
Son and sire –
Caught the strains that at his fingering low or higher
From your four thin threads and eff-holes came outflowing.

There is a tune in these lines – a smart jolly tune which contrasts with its lugubrious second line and which carries over that line like the rhythm of 'Beeny Cliff' bridging the faltering pause at 'elsewhere'. It is still firmly there at the beginning of the last stanza:

> He must do without you now,
> Stir you no more anyhow
> To yearning concords taught you in your glory.

But as Hardy turns to describe the actual state of the violin the tune begins to falter and share in its disintegration:

> While, your strings a tangled wreck,
> Once smart drawn,
> Ten worm-wounds in your neck,
> Purflings wan
> With dust-hoar, here alone I sadly con
> Your present dumbness, shape your olden story.

Looking at the real object seems to destroy his compelling evocation of the sounds his father once drew from it. And when we read each stanza of the poem we both hear this tune and see the shape of a violin roughly before us on the page. He literally does 'shape' its story, so that again this is a positivist's poem, a visible and audible fact.

Heaven in these poems is part museum, part junk shop, while in 'Voices from Things Growing in a Churchyard' and 'Transformations' it's a sunny graveyard where the dead are busily and happily turning into green shoots on the yew tree or 'entering this rose'. Hardy starts with the familiar and uninspiring idea of pushing up daisies and makes it work. There is nothing of Dylan Thomas's windy, rhetorical assertion that 'Though they be mad and dead as nails/Heads of the characters hammer through daisies.' Instead he lets the characters speak for themselves and populates a heaven that is actual:

> – I am one Bachelor Bowring, 'Gent,'
> Sir or Madam;
> In shingled oak my bones were pent;
> Hence more than a hundred years I spent
> In my feat of change from a coffin-thrall
> To a dancer in green as leaves on a wall,
> All day cheerily,
> All night eerily!

It is this idea of naturalised immortality that Eliot is partly slighting in 'The Dry Salvages' when he says:

> We, content at the last
> If our temporal reversion nourish
> (Not too far from the yew-tree)
> The life of significant soil.

Eliot means that significance is not one of the properties of soil, but Hardy gives distinct human personalities to some of the plants and trees it nourishes and so suggests that it is meaningful. Bowring's gruff certainties and self-importance follow Fanny Hurd's twittering meekness, Thomas Voss has 'turned to clusters ruddy of view' and Lady Gertrude is splendid in laurel. Each speaker has a unique voice, a 'murmurous accent', as well as surviving naturally and visibly. Again, this positivistic concept of immortality is also social because people who move in society must be seen in order to be. But underneath the robust social comedy of the graveyard there is also a mysteriousness and an ecstatic energy. It's there in the 'radiant hum' and dancing freedom of 'Voices from Things' and at the end of 'Transformations' where

> they feel the sun and rain,
> And the energy again
> That made them what they were!

The physical basis of life gives Hardy no cause for despair in these poems and unlike Eliot he feels no need to reject a non-significant biological materialism, for it enables him both to create character and imply the forces underlying it. There is more than the obvious joke in the fact that Eve Greensleeves, 'the handsome mother of two or three illegitimate children', has now been changed into an 'innocent withwind', a climbing plant that is also called 'virgin's bower'. She has been kissed by many men:

> Beneath sun, stars, in blaze, in breeze,
> As now by glowworms and by bees.

This beautifully suggests a feeling of dazzling light, breezes and warmth which also become the expression of her free sexuality. As ever she is eternally virgin and promiscuous. Each of her names has uninsistent reverberations which also help to give a profound sense of female character. She is made to live more deeply than in her social personality as the subject of long-vanished village ribaldry.

Just as he must think of Shelley's lark living on in the 'coming hue' of a grape, Hardy tries throughout this poem to realise a number of unique human lives in a series of visible objects and though there is nothing narrow in his response to visibility here, this kind of positivism can be imaginatively limiting, even stultifying. In the end we really face the fact and it's simply and inanimately there, like the battered violin. When the deceptive, illusory and borrowed light of the moon has been shut out – when the pathetic fallacy has been exposed and rejected – then there only remains a 'common lamp-lit room' where the eyes and mind are 'prisoned'. The positivist's facts are just dingy surfaces. For Donald Davie, Hardy's poems never get beyond this 'quantifiable reality', a reality that is about as inspiring as a dual carriageway on a grey afternoon (Hardy's equivalent is a railway waiting-room). To speculate about, to try to get inside, the lives of the people who occupy that mundane reality is one way out of this imaginative dead end, but it leads only so far because sooner or later we come back to the worm-eaten violin, the second-hand suit, the meaningless soil. We come back to the realisation that the only afterlife is a secular one in which the dead are remembered, for a while, by the living. But in both 'Transformations' and 'Voices from Things' there is a quality somewhere around the edges of this eventually constraining positivistic humanism which is liberating and totally imaginative (and just in this instance I'm identifying humanism with social comedy). There is a kind of witty seriousness beyond the comedy of Bachelor Bowring and Lady Gertrude. It's there throughout the poem, though it can be sensed especially in Eve Greensleeves's voice – less so in Lady Gertrude's, for she is more simply social and superficial, and her shining laurels inevitably suggest a certain sterility in her character, a glinting or glistening light on a stagnant darkness. Eve Greensleeves, on the other hand, climbs in many flowers, lacks this artificial veneer and is constantly kissable, while Bachelor Bowring has been so solidly 'pent' in such good quality oak that it has taken him over a century to perform his 'feat of change' from rigid prisoner to leafy dancer. It seems appropriate that old Squire Audeley Gray, who grew weary of life and 'in scorn withdrew', should also be an evergreen like Lady Gertrude for there must always have been a deadness at the centre of his life too – there seems to be a natural morality as well as a natural concept of immortality in the poem.

At the end of 'On the Physical Basis of Life', the essay Bailey refers to in his account of this poem, Huxley says that 'the errors of systematic materialism may paralyse the energies and destroy the beauty of a life', and the materialism of Hardy's poem is not as systematic as it appears to be – in fact it's profoundly committed to a series of escapes from narrow sepulchres and coffins which, as in 'Heiress and Architect', represent the straight lines and rigidities of a limiting system. The 'dead humus of buried bodies lives again in plants', but the poem doesn't stop at this idea of the heads of characters bashing through daisies. Fanny Hurd is not just the 'daisy shapes' above her grave – she is the wavy movement of the daisies where she once 'flit-fluttered like a bird' and she is there in the eerie-cheery, swaying sound of the poem. She is still a meek virgin soul, and that essentially religious word is the right one because the poem's sense of awe at the forces of life and the forces in human character is not that of the 'sentimental materialist' one of Hardy's reviewers called him. An irreducible sense of mystery attaches to each character and voice.

5

Mnemonic Silhouettes

Ruskin's chapter on 'The Nature of Gothic' in *The Stones of Venice* is the best introduction I know to both Browning's and Hardy's work. Like Hardy in his justification of the Gothic art-principle behind his poetry, Ruskin sees irregularity and imperfection as essential constituents of Gothic art, and when he describes the Gothic builders' 'love of fact' he distinguishes a feature that is central to Hardy's art and to the way his imagination works. 'Genoa and the Mediterranean' and 'A Gentleman's Second-Hand Suit' are based upon certain observed facts: upon what Hardy in a delighted phrase calls 'the fresh originality of living fact', and what Browning terms 'pure crude fact', a sort of inspiring gold. Ruskin says that the Gothic builders were both men of facts and men of design, and that a co-operation took place between the shaping artist and the 'natural objects' that supplied his material. This co-operation between fact and imagination is the theme of one of Hardy's finest poems, 'The Abbey Mason', which is his great tribute to the unknown artist who invented the 'perpendicular' style of Gothic architecture.

Unable to solve a technical problem, the architect stares at his drawing-board which is drenched by 'freezing rain':

> He closelier looked; then looked again:
> The chalk-scratched draught-board faced the rain,
>
> Whose icicled drops deformed the lines
> Innumerous of his lame designs,
>
> So that they streamed in small white threads
> From the upper segments to the heads
>
> Of arcs below, uniting them
> Each by a stalactitic stem.

The 'weather's whim' supplies his inspiration and he solves his problem, creating a new style of architecture. But he has no reward as his abbot insists that the hand of God revealed the forms his 'invention chased in vain'. He 'copied, and did not create'. However, a later abbot shows more understanding and pays him a belated tribute:

> 'Nay; art can but transmute;
> Invention is not absolute;
>
> 'Things fail to spring from nought at call,
> And art-beginnings most of all.
>
> 'He did but what all artists do,
> Wait upon Nature for his cue.'

For Ruskin's 'fact' and 'design' Hardy substitutes 'Invention' and 'Nature'. Like his best novels the poem is both a narrative and a myth: a story about an unknown fourteenth-century mason which is also a myth of the imagination and its sources. For Hardy, a co-operation must take place between fact and imagination which joins them indissolubly together, and this is similar to the living relationship between the mind and its objects which Coleridge invokes as a lost power and ideal in the Dejection Ode. In 'The Abbey-Mason' Hardy's stress falls more on the factual and experiential side of this relationship – though he is of course insisting on the fatuity of a purely empirical account of the imagination. In this note from the *Life* he places greater emphasis on its transforming powers:

> The 'simply natural' is interesting no longer. The much decried, mad, late-Turner rendering is now necessary to create my interest. The exact truth as to material fact ceases to be of importance in art – it is a student's style – the style of a period when the mind is serene and unawakened to the tragical mysteries of life; when it does not bring anything to the object that coalesces with and translates the qualities that are already there, – half hidden, it may be – and the two united are depicted as the All.

There is a complex series of references behind Hardy's use of this idea in 'The House of Silence':

> '–Ah, that's because you do not bear
> The visioning powers of souls who dare
> To pierce the material screen.'

In saying that the poet's imaginative vision penetrates the visibility of fact, Hardy is echoing one of Browning's late poems which is a 'parley' with Christopher Smart:

Smart, solely of such songmen, pierced the screen
'Twixt thing and word, lit language straight from soul, –
Left no fine film-flake on the naked coal
Live from the censer.

Browning marvels at how Smart was suddenly possessed of visionary powers when all his life he had been a dull mediocrity, a 'drab-clothed decent proseman', and it's easy to see what he is really doing in this indifferent poem: he is examining his own character and indirectly discussing and justifying his twin, but uncomplementary identities of society diner-out and visionary poet. Henry James based his great story, 'The Private Life', on Browning's mystifying union of a wholly commonplace personality with poetic genius, and Hardy, who met Browning often in London society during the 1880s, was also puzzled and fascinated for he told Edmund Gosse:

> The longer I live the more does B[rowning]'s character seem *the* literary puzzle of the 19th Century. How could smug Christian optimism worthy of a dissenting grocer find a place inside a man who was so vast a seer and feeler when on neutral ground?

And in 'So Various' (the title is from Dryden's famous lines on Buckingham) Hardy describes himself in similar terms: at times he seems just a 'dunce', at others he is a 'learned seer'. He did exemplify characteristically Victorian values of ordinariness and respectability, and this was partly strategic as Charles Morgan observed:

> He was not simple; he had the formal subtlety peculiar to his own generation; there was something deliberately 'ordinary' in his demeanour which was a concealment of extraordinary fires – a method of self-protection common enough in my grandfather's generation, though rare now.

This helps to show some of the implications behind his allusion to Browning in 'The House of Silence' where he deliberately locates his 'poet's bower' somewhere in the stockbroker belt and ironically dignifies his red-brick suburban villa with an apparently inappropriate epithet. And when he says in 'To Shakespeare' that the Bard displayed a 'life of commonplace', he again stresses this connection between imagination and ordinariness. His imagination works upon commonplace facts – housebacks and washing, for example – and he makes no claims for its importance and uniqueness as a Romantic poet would.

If the 'material screen' is the substance which his imagination penetrates and transmutes into art, it's also a screen in the sense of being a respectable social front which he has erected in his capacity of prosperous, middle-class citizen in order to conceal and protect his exercise of 'visioning powers'. This represents a compromise between values whose essential incompatibility was one of the legacies of Romanticism. The cult of the lonely, heroic, anti-social genius which Byron vulgarises in *Manfred* is tucked away, fairly safely, behind a pair of bay windows. Partly, this is an adjustment to social and cultural change.

'Architectural Masks' makes a large cultural point very concisely:

I

There is a house with ivied walls,
And mullioned windows worn and old,
And the long dwellers in those halls
Have souls that know but sordid calls,
And daily dote on gold.

II

In blazing brick and plated show
Not far away a 'villa' gleams,
And here a family few may know,
With book and pencil, viol and bow,
Lead inner lives of dreams.

III

The philosophic passers say,
'See that old mansion mossed and fair,
Poetic souls therein are they:
And O that gaudy box! Away,
You vulgar people there.'

The artist, or the cultured member of the middle classes, guards his imaginative privacy, just as Wemmick in *Great Expectations*, like so many of Dickens's characters, is one man in the office and another at home. Hardy is saying that the material of art, as well as the social class of the artist and his readers, has changed: he works with brick and mortar now, hiding his imagination behind a red brick ordinariness, like the ghostly double in 'The Private Life'. A view of both the poet's relation to his society and of the poetic imagination and its materials is implicit in that concealed allusion to Browning in 'The House of Silence'. Hardy's point is that a reciprocity exists between prosaic ordinariness and imaginative vision. Yet, how does he transform the matter-of-fact reality he inhabits into art?

One way is by specialising observed facts into distinctive shapes or mnemonic images. His description of the pale distinctness of Gladstone's bald head is one example of a characteristic technique of selecting and describing an especially visible shape, of watching 'that pattern among general things which his idiosyncrasy moves him to observe' and then retaining such a pattern in what he termed the 'mindsight' or visual memory. In 'At Castle Boterel' he says:

> I look behind at the fading byway,
> And see on its slope, now glistening wet,
> Distinctly yet
>
> Myself and a girlish form benighted
> In dry March weather.

The phrase 'distinctly yet' has a significant cadence which emerges earlier in his work. In *The Woodlanders* Fitzpiers rides off into the sunset on a white horse: 'his plodding steed made him distinctly visible yet'. 'Distinctly visible now', 'distinctly visible', 'distinctly seen' – the phrase is varied and repeated in the novels and stories where it carries something of the powerful fascination sheer visibility held for him. In 'At Castle Boterel' he describes his memory of what he once saw so adroitly that he merges actual sight with 'mindsight', because by using 'look behind' and 'look back' both literally and figuratively he makes their meanings combine and so creates a tremendous sense of presence. The woman's form that appears to his mindsight on the sloping road is visualised so distinctly that it's as though she is actually still alive and simple receding into the distance like Fitzpiers. Her 'phantom figure' is 'shrinking, shrinking' as if it's being obscured by the rain and darkness as well as diminishing in the distance. Time 'has ruled from sight/ The substance now', and so the rain, darkness and distance become embodiments of time. They give it a spatial dimension and become physical metaphors like the action of looking back.

The authenticity and controlled intensity of this poem guarantee that its reality is, as Donald Davie asserts in his properly furious repudiation of Hillis Miller, 'metaphysical' rather than 'psychological merely'. Davie says that if the poem's 'time of such quality' persists 'indestructible in a metaphysical reality, then it is *truly* indestructible – because a man's mind survives the death of his body, or because quality exists as perceived by a Divine Mind, or...' The idea is left open, but the connection is clearly with Berkeley rather than Hume. If this poem begins with a mnemonic image and ends with that image weakening and disappearing, it also lifts it above a purely mnemonic, subjective, psychological existence. The poem's distinction between 'substance' and 'phantom' is familiar from *The Well-Beloved*, but it would be wrong to say that Hardy is insisting on the subjectivity of what he sees and loves, for the 'one phantom figure' that remains 'on the slope, as when that night/Saw us alight' sounds so completely, so patiently, *out there* that she becomes a vision rather than a memory. Again, it is the sound of this poem which guarantees such a certitude.

This difference of reality and quality becomes clearly audible if we compare 'At Castle Boterel' with 'Green Slates' which also describes a memory of a place he and Emma visited during their courtship:

> It happened once, before the duller
> Loomings of life defined them,
> I searched for slates of greenish colour
> A quarry where men mined them;
>
> And saw, the while I peered around there,
> In the quarry standing
> A form against the slate background there,
> Of fairness eye-commanding.

Fifty years later a sight of these slates reminds him of the scene in the quarry. The poem is trite and its triteness is reflected in the facile sound of the quatrains, but it does give a useful description of the way his memory operates: his eye isolates a form against a background so that the form becomes sharply defined and is then retained by his memory as a clearly visible image. We can see this way of remembering in a letter he wrote to *The Times* in 1906, on the 100th anniversary of Mill's birth. He describes Mill addressing an election meeting one afternoon in 1865:

> He stood bareheaded, and his vast pale brow, so thin-skinned as to show the blue veins, sloped back like a stretching upland, and conveyed to the observer a curious sense of perilous exposure. The picture of him as personified earnestness surrounded for the most part by careless curiosity derived an added piquancy – if it can be called such – from the fact that the cameo clearness of his face chanced to be in relief against the blue shadow of a

church which, on its transcendental side, his doctrines antagonized.

Hardy explains that this memory of his may be worth recording because writers like Carlyle and Leslie Stephen 'have held that anything, however imperfect, which affords an idea of a human personage in his actual form and flesh, is of value in respect of him.' And he clearly took this seriously for he quotes from Carlyle's letter on the subject in a preface he contributed to a book called *Wessex Worthies:*

> In all my poor historical investigations it has been and always is, one of the most primary wants to procure a bodily likeness of the personage enquired after – a good portrait if such exists; failing that, even an indifferent if sincere one. In short, any representation made by a faithful creature of that face and figure which he saw with his eyes, and which I can never see with mine, is now valuable to me, and much better than none at all.

Carlyle goes on to stress the importance of securing 'an authentic visible shadow' of the face of an historical figure so that he can conceive 'the actual likeness of the man'. Carlyle's positivism and, in this case, his humanism obviously appealed to Hardy, and in 'Green Slates', 'At Castle Boterel' and his letter to *The Times* he describes a mnemonic picture, a tiny portrait of an actual human figure in a scene, which may have lain dormant in his memory until it was 'defined' – in the sense both of 'interpreted' and 'given a clear outline' – by time and experience. However, in 'At Castle Boterel' the effort is to give the memory-trace an external existence and make it part of the place.

In 1879 Hardy watched the funeral of Napoleon's grand-nephew as it passed through Chislehurst, and as usual he noted down his careful observations:

> Was struck by the profile of Prince Napoleon as he walked by bareheaded, a son on each arm: complexion dark, sallow, even sinister: a round projecting chin: countenance altogether extraordinarily remindful of Boney.

And he tells us in the *Life* (as usual in the third person as though his wife is actually writing) that 'this sight of Napoleon's nephew... had been of enormous use to him, when writing *The Dynasts,* in imagining the Emperor's appearance.' So when we read one of the scene directions in *The Dynasts* – and these are among the great triumphs of his powers of visualisation – we can be sure that if there is an historical figure in it Hardy had his face vividly in his mind:

> A chilly but rainless noon three days later. At the back of the scene, northward, rise the Michaelsberg heights; below stretches the panorama of the city and the Danube. On a secondary eminence forming a spur of the upper hill, a fire of logs is burning, the foremost group beside it being Napoleon and his staff, the latter in gorgeous uniform, the former in his shabby greatcoat and plain turned-up hat, walking to and fro with his hands behind him, and occasionally stopping to warm himself. The French infantry are drawn up in a dense array at the back of these.

The scene is brilliantly present, a moving picture which seems to be an 'authentic visible shadow' not just of Napoleon but of his staff and the place where they are. What Hardy did when he saw Napoleon's nephew was to sight his profile almost as though he was taking a photograph of him. Presented with a scene, his eye appears to have actively sought its most distinctly visible feature – the sharp outline of a form or face against a background – and then to have grasped and remembered that unique, bounded shape.

This is how he describes Dick Dewy in *Under the Greenwood Tree*:

> Having come more into the open he could now be seen rising against the sky, his profile appearing on the light background like the portrait of a gentleman in black cardboard.

Dewy and the Mellstock choir who 'advanced against the sky in flat outlines, which suggested some processional design on Greek or Etruscan pottery' are based on childhood memories, and Hardy's mnemonic technique must have been partly instinctive, partly a matter of training. Sir William Rothenstein's remark about his habit of unexpectedly cocking his eye at someone is one testimony to his very deliberate method of looking. His architectural training must have helped him form it, and so must the method of studying paintings which he evolved while he was working as an architect and which shows just how deliberate his observation could be:

> His interest in painting led him to devote for many months, on every day that the National Gallery was open, twenty minutes after lunch to an inspection of the masters hung there, confining his attention to a single master on each visit, and forbidding his

> eyes to stray to any other. He went there from sheer liking, and not with any practical object; but he used to recommend the plan to young people, telling them that they would insensibly acquire a greater insight into schools and styles by this means than from any guide-books to the painters' works and manners.

He sounds almost like a behaviourist here. The aim is to school the mind to receive the imprint of a particular style through the disciplined observation of successive examples of that style, and though he disclaims any 'practical object' he clearly developed an intensely practical method of study and learning. The method was often the same when he was faced with a particular scene: his eye sought distinctive form and shape among the clutter of other impressions and retained it in his memory. The novels are full of his memories of paintings; and, as Alastair Smart has shown, both the illustrations which he drew for the first edition of *Wessex Poems* – they include a poor profile of Napoleon – and many of the descriptive passages in the novels where he concentrates on an illuminated face, reveal his 'unique sensitivity to shape and especially to outline'. As Smart also demonstrates, the effect of an illuminated face surrounded by darkness is an effect Hardy took over from the Rembrandts he so carefully studied in the National Gallery. Like thousands upon thousands of people he stood in front of those paintings and looked at them, but he trained himself to remember them with unusual clarity and then – which is something else – he made them part of his imagination.

In a scrap called 'The Figure in the Scene' he tells how he sketched Emma at Beeny Cliff:

> It pleased her to step in front and sit
> Where the cragged slope was green,
> While I stood back that I might pencil it
> With her amid the scene.

It began to rain and his sketch was smudged 'leaving for curious quizzings yet/The blots engrained.' He went on with his sketching as she sat there ominously 'hooded' with 'only her outline shown':

> –Soon passed our stay;
> Yet her rainy form is the Genius still of the spot,
> Immutable, yea,
> Though the place now knows her no more, and has known her not
> Ever since that day.

Hardy's copy of the sketch with the poem's opening lines is reproduced in Pinion's *Companion*. It's an unremarkable poem, but it has interesting links with 'At Castle Boterel', 'Beyond the Last Lamp' and 'The Abbey-Mason', three poems where rain also falls and blots form. In 'The Abbey-Mason' it falls on the mason's 'draught' (the same word is used in both poems) and it precipitates his imaginative solution to the problem that has been obsessing him. Hardy is saying that if time, or the rain which represents it, dissolves outline and blurs form, it also creates them as it's only by looking far back down the perspective of the years that memory can recover and visualise the distinct shapes of the past. These images must, as Abbot Horton says in 'The Abbey-Mason', 'wait upon Nature for their cue'. It's the lapse of time which crystallises them into their distinctive shapes. Here, I'm pointing to the passive side of Hardy's concept of imagination: what is brought to the mind, rather than what the mind brings to experience. Both 'The Abbey-Mason' and 'The Figure in the Scene' use a sketch stained by rain as a natural symbol of the work of sheer, random, unhappy experience in generating a work of art. This is the factual side of the imagination.

In 'The Whitewashed Wall' a woman's habit of turning and kissing to her blank chimney-corner is explained by the fact that a friend of her son's once drew his silhouette on the wall when the fire-light cast his shadow there. Later, the wall was accidentally given a fresh coat of whitewash which erased his profile:

But she knows he's there. And when she yearns
For him, deep in the labouring night,
She sees him as close at hand, and turns
To him under his sheet of white.

The last line is a surprise. Its mixture of strangeness and familiarity redeems what otherwise appears to be a fairly average poem. It doesn't state but deftly implies that her son is dead, sleeping under the counterpane of his white shroud, and that she's reconciled to this because, to her, he seems very present, not absent and separate. She has kept his lifelike profile in her memory and because his profile is also outside her, though hidden, she can turn to it and imagine he is near her. Hardy makes symbolic use of actual profiles in several other poems, warning against drawing them in 'Why did I Sketch?', which is the companion-piece of 'The Figure in the Scene', because not to draw them is to 'half forget', and in 'The Dame of Athelhall' describing a married woman fleeing with her lover in a coach which travels so quickly that

> the will to bind
> Her life with his made the moments there
> Efface the years behind.

As they near their port of departure, her bracelet slips from her 'fondled arm' and its 'cameo of the abjured one' starts her thinking:

> The gaud with his image once had been
> A gift from him:
> And so it was that its carving keen
> Refurbished memories wearing dim,
> Which set in her soul a twinge of teen,
> And a tear on her lashes' brim.

In his letter to *The Times* Hardy speaks of his memory of the 'cameo clearness' of Mill's face, and here he describes how her memory is suddenly revived by an actual cameo of her husband. (A memory is sparked by a profile on a coin in 'In the Old Theatre, Fiesole'.) The past catches up with the present as a sentimental loyalty, forcing her to return to a husband who is ironically delighted at her disloyalty. The symbol Hardy uses is entirely natural and the words 'efface' and 'bind' gain in significance when her bracelet slips its 'bond' and reveals her husband's face. She looks, remembers, and again puts herself in bondage to a deterministic process that destroys their fragile, present illusion of freedom and happiness.

'Heredity' also shows Hardy's keen sensitivity to the lines of the human face. In it the family face, which transcends oblivion, again represents a deterministic force that patterns life:

> The years-heired feature that can
> In curve and voice and eye
> Despise the human span
> Of durance – that is I;
> The eternal thing in man,
> That heeds no call to die.

The eerie sound carries something of Hardy's fascination with shape and pattern. In his great essay, 'Memories of Church Restoration', he says that although limestones or sandstones have passed into the 'form' of a Gothic church, it is 'an idea independent of them – an aesthetic phantom without solidarity, which might just as suitably have chosen millions of other stones from the quarry whereon to display its beauties'. This, he says, is 'the actual process of organic nature herself, which is one continuous substitution. She is always discarding the matter, while retaining the form.' He then goes on to set against this view the uniqueness of each particular example of Gothic architecture and the human associations that accrue to it and which he characteristically considers more valuable than its aesthetic qualities. But he's clearly fascinated by the other uniqueness of Shape, the independent idea or 'aesthetic phantom'. This shape must be platonic and impersonal. It is inhumanly perfect in 'Heredity' and 'At a Lunar Eclipse' where the serene profile of the earth bears no relation to its 'torn troubled form', its imperfect and human reality. However, the word 'form' in the last line of 'The Comet at Yell'ham' carries all the force of a tremendous recognition of loss – the loss of a loved human uniqueness that is defined against a determined, natural event:

> It will return long years hence, when
> As now its strange swift shine
> Will fall on Yell'ham; but not then
> On that sweet form of thine.

In 'Drummer Hodge' Hardy's effort is to rescue a sense of absolute human uniqueness from the casual burial of a young soldier whose name is the equivalent of 'yokel' and who was never anything more than cannon fodder:

> His landmark is a kopje-crest
> That breaks the veldt around;
> And foreign constellations west
> Each night above his mound.

A sense of place was a most important part of personal identity for Hardy and so he uses the Afrikaan equivalents of Wessex terms like 'coomb' and 'wold' to impose a sense of custom and locality on the blank, foreign landscape. He also uses the distinct shape of the kopje-crest outlined against the veldt's barren uniformity to assert that Hodge's memory survives. In doing so he erects a kind of natural tradition on this darkling 'unknown plain', a consoling and redeeming visibility. 'Portion of this yew/Is a man my grandsire knew', Hardy says in 'Transformations', and here Hodge will 'grow to some Southern tree' so that he might almost be back in Mellstock among the friends beyond.

Hardy's acute sensitivity to the memorably visible is again apparent in a beautiful poem called 'Lying Awake' which he published not long before his death:

> You, Morningtide Star, now are steady-eyed, over the east,
> I know it as if I saw you;
> You, Beeches, engrave on the sky your thin twigs, even the least;
> Had I paper and pencil I'd draw you.
>
> You, Meadow, are white with your counterpane cover of dew,
> I see it as if I were there;
> You, Churchyard, are lightening faint from the shade of the yew,
> The names creeping out everywhere.

This is a really fine poem which speaks simply and directly. The breath-pausing commas and semi-colons seem inked in with a loving scrupulousness. By comparing the dew on the meadow to a counterpane he implies that he is actually lying outside, as though already in the churchyard and under his sheet of white. Here, the 'steady-eyed' morning-star, like the 'strange-eyed constellations' which watch over Drummer Hodge, is the observer whose dawning vision guarantees the existence of the beeches, meadow and the carved names Hardy is unable to see. It's as though the star is deputising for God in an agnostic version of a Berkeleyan system.

Hardy noted in one of his commonplace books that:

> Berkeley established the subjective character of the world of phenomena; that this world I perceive *is* my perceptions, & nothing more. But besides these perceptions there is also a spirit, a *me* that perceives them. And to get rid of this imaginary soul or substance was the work of Hume.

And although his sympathies were with Hume, there is a Berkeleyan quality in 'Lying Awake', 'Drummer Hodge' and, as Donald Davie is suggesting, in 'At Castle Boterel'. The star's steady sight locks all the other objects into place. Hardy apostrophises all of them and so transforms them into active beings – the beeches are engraving their twigs on the sky, a use of the pathetic fallacy which seems entirely convincing. This is similar to his comparison of fresh leaves to silk, and the effect he's describing – the twigs' sharp, black, exact outlines –

seems both a natural and an artistic process. A co-operation between eye and object, fact and imagination, is taking place. The outline, like the profiles I've been discussing, is a visual memory, but a memory that appears to be working actively outside his mind. The last line is hushed and miraculous, a positivist's idea of the resurrection where the dead come 'creeping out' as the growing light, like a focusing eye, makes their names and memorials legible. This is the real resurrection.

6
Eidetic Images

Besides dark outlines and silhouettes there is another way in which Hardy embodies memory in his work. Many poems contain images which the memory appears to project onto the bare, external world, like colour slides on a screen. These images assume a virtually autonomous existence outside the poet or his persona, and are quasi-visionary or 'eidetic'* images. 'After a Romantic Day' describes how these visions are formed:

> The railway bore him through
> An earthen cutting out from a city:
> There was no scope for view,
> Though the frail light shed by a slim young moon
> Fell like a friendly tune.
> Fell like a liquid ditty,
> And the blank lack of any charm
> Of landscape did no harm.
> The bald steep cutting, rigid, rough,
> And moon-lit, was enough
> For poetry of place: its weathered face
> Formed a convenient sheet whereon
> The visions of his mind were drawn.

Hardy alludes to the crushing last line of *In Memoriam* VII – 'On the bald street breaks the blank day' – in order to underline the fact that the

* 'Eidetic' means 'of or relating to voluntarily producible visual images that have almost photographic accuracy'. Koestler describes how in an experiment on eidetic memory the subject is asked 'to inspect a picture for about thirty seconds without staring (to eliminate after-images), then to look at a grey screen. The average person sees nothing; the eidetic "projects" the image onto the screen and behaves as if the picture were actually there....It seems, therefore, that eidetic images "are seen in the literal sense of the word." ' Hardy was evidently interested in this kind of perception for he transcribed the following passage into one of his commonplace books: 'Mental representⁿ· so intense as to become mental presentation is a faculty of mind apt especially to be met with among certain artists.... "You have only to work up imagination to the state of vision & the thing is done" (Blake).'

youth has irradiated a drab and confined environment with his romantic visions and memories (the manuscript's biblical sub-title, 'Your young men shall see visions', again stresses this).

Unlike Tennyson, who is able to christianise his urban landscape through metaphor and covert biblical allusion, Hardy demonstrates how dead matter, like the landscapes in Crabbe's 'The Lover's Journey', merely serves as a screen for his travelling lover's fantasies. The two are entirely separate, like the architect and the heiress, like a prosaic utilitarianism and a fantasy – a fantasy that is an impoverished substitute for real vision and imagination. The lover is enclosed by his own solipsism – the railway cutting confines his sight – but he could see the slope's 'weathered face' were it not for the visions he has imposed on it. This face represents not just an ugly, drab actuality but all the wear and tear of ordinary, unromantic experience. Unaware of the threat to his visions this environment poses, the youth is an idealist like Fitzpiers and visualises only the dream. His visions and the deceptive light shed by the feminine moon are identified because both fall on the 'convenient sheet' of the cutting, just as the image on a lantern-slide is thrown on a projection screen. The falling moonlight symbolises the pathetic fallacy: it is a 'frail light' because the lover's emotion is subjective and liable, the implication is, to flit from girl to girl. He is another moon-struck sophist worshipping his own shadowy image, and so the poetry of this particular scene is entirely dependent on his state of mind. As the composite Muse tells the poet-lover in 'The Vatican: Sala delle Muse':

> I am projected from thee,
> One that out of thy brain and heart thou causest to be –
> Extern to thee nothing.

Hardy was indebted to Shelley for this type of subjective idealism – specifically to those Humean elements in Shelley's poetry which I discussed earlier. And though 'After a Romantic Day' is not an important poem in itself it significantly reveals the use he made of these ideas.

He uses projected visions again in 'In Front of the Landscape' where the external, 'customed' locality of coomb, upland and chalk-pit is glimpsed through a phantasmagoria of spectral visions which his memory has imposed on it. These memories of people whom he slighted when they were alive

now show hourly before the intenser
Stare of the mind
As they were ghosts avenging their slights by my bypast
Body-borne eyes,
Show, too, with fuller translation than rested upon them
As living kind.

Now that they're dead, the people whom his physical sight barely used to register have become intensely visible to his sighted mind. They cover the outer landscape like a thick mist.

The word 'translation' is a technical term which means: 'The expression or rendering of something in another medium or form, e.g. of a painting by an engraving or etching.' Hardy uses it as a metaphor for his sight of the past people he ignored and who appeared on his retina as casual, insignificant images. He means that, initially, his perception was merely a passive registering of a series of images which later activated themselves. There is an example of an impression becoming active in *A Pair of Blue Eyes* when Elfride reveals that she was once in love with another man: 'The word fell like a bolt, and the very land and sky seemed to suffer.... The scene was engraved for years on the retina of Knight's eye: the dead and brown stubble, the weeds among it, the distant belt of beeches shutting out the view of the house, the leaves of which were now red and sick to death.' Here, Knight sees what his mind brings means of seeing, and the scene's 'poetry' is the product of his emotions. This is another of those 'involutes' or 'permanent impressions' which I discussed in the first chapter, and it again reveals Hardy's compromise between an active and a passive account of the mind, for the outer scene and Knight's emotions become fused in the way that landscape and feeling weld together in 'Neutral Tones' and in that visionary passage from *The Prelude* which Sykes Davies quotes in his essay. Hardy's use of 'engraved' and 'translation' in the prose and poem suggests that he can favour an active account of mental processes, and this active relationship between eye and object is also there in his use of 'engrave' in 'Lying Awake'.

In the note on Turner's late paintings which I quoted in the last chapter Hardy distinguishes between amateurish transcripts of fact and this active encounter between mind and object where the mind again 'translates' qualities in the object. For Hardy, this unifying, visionary engagement of fact and imagination is characteristic of late-Turner, and these lines from 'In Front of the Landscape' possibly show Turner's influence:

> Ancient chalk-pit, milestone, rills in the grass-flat
> Stroked by the light,
> Seemed but a ghost-like gauze, and no substantial
> Meadow or mound.

This is an accurate and intense evocation of light. The use of 'stroked' has an authoritative precision, but as the poem contains no colours it can only resemble a black-and-white engraving of a Turner painting – a lesser rather than a 'fuller translation'.

Hardy is also using 'translation' in its biblical sense in this poem: 'By faith Enoch was translated that he should not see death.' The remembered people, though they're now dead, appear more visibly alive than when they were 'living kind'. They live on immortally in his memory. His mindsight projects images outside itself so intensely that they're hypostatised as physical obstacles, a 'tide of visions' which he has to wade through. This is close to a passage in *The Hand of Ethelberta* where Christopher Julian regularly passes a girl on a certain stretch of road and the more he passes her the less he notices her:

> He was a man who often, when walking abroad, and looking as it were at the scene before his eyes, discerned successes and failures, friends and relations, episodes of childhood, wedding feasts and funerals, the landscape suffering greatly by these visions, until it became no more than the patterned wall-tints about the paintings in a gallery; something necessary to the tone, yet not regarded. Nothing but a special concentration of himself on externals could interrupt this habit, and now that her appearance along the way had changed from a chance to a custom he began to lapse again into the old trick. He gazed once or twice at her form without seeing it: he did not notice that she trembled.

Notice the use of 'custom', 'visions' and 'landscape' as in the poem, and also the analogy between the actual landscape on which memories are imposed and the wall-tints in a picture gallery. In both the poem and this passage subjective vision assumes a substantive, autonomous existence. It becomes a self-subsistent thing, a physical object whose essential property is the capacity for being looked *at* which it shares with any object or painting.

In calling these objectified images 'eidetic' I'm suggesting that there is a link between Hardy's use of visual memories and the rare type of visual memory psychologists term 'eidetic'. This is not to say that Hardy possessed such a memory, merely to notice and explore the similarities some of the uses he makes of memory have with this type. The most accessible account of such a memory is a short and fascinating study called *The Mind of a Mnemonist* by the distinguished Russian neurophysiologist, A. R. Luria. It's the story of a man who possessed an extraordinary memory, a photographic memory which he could discipline to retain any series of details, no matter how long, random or complex. Luria refers to him throughout his book as S. and he describes how one of S.'s techniques was to isolate and visualise the things he wanted to remember against imaginary backgrounds – usually the doors and walls of the street where he grew up and which he could recall in exact detail. This is similar to Hardy's technique of isolating a profile against a dark background, but it must be stressed that S. possessed absolutely no literary gifts, despite the extraordinary synaesthesia and vivid realisation his memory gifted him with. He found reading, especially poetry, 'a struggle against images that kept rising to the surface in his mind'. These images tended to jam and force him away from the sense of the passage. He thought always in visual images, never in abstractions: 'something' and 'nothing' were both clouds to him. Often he lived in a haze of images, a solipsistic state where inner and outer reality became so mixed and confused that there was 'no real border-line between perceptions and emotions', and where 'images of the external world would blend and become part of diffuse experiences'. In other words, his memories appeared to be outside him, and even walking along a street could be like pushing his way through a dense thicket of images. This is remarkably close to the state of mind Hardy describes in both *The Hand of Ethelberta* and 'In Front of the Landscape' where he seems to be pushing his way through a thick mist of memories. Like Luria he is describing the dilemma of a man who can remember too much, and in presenting it as a dilemma, as a distressingly over-active power of memory, he raises all kinds of very important epistemological questions about personal identity and the nature of memory itself – questions which are the subject of those controversies about the structure of the mind which I touched on in the first chapter.

Discussing Luria's study and a subsequent work called *The Man with a Shattered World*, which is about a man whose memory had been almost totally destroyed, Oliver Sacks pointed to the dangers of mnemotechny if it is practised obsessively. S.'s memory, he said, ceased to be a 'living and personal memory' and became instead 'an enormous register of facts, of impersonal images, arbitrarily memorised, arbitrarily connected, and arbitrarily systematised in a convenient mechanical form'. Sacks then said:

> *The Mind of a Mnemonist* is a sort of Lockean allegory, a Lockean nightmare: a cautionary tale of a man whose being is sacrificed to a *tabula rasa.* If Locke were right about the nature of human nature, if Luria were right in supposing, as he once wrote, that the mechanical faculties of analysis and synthesis form 'the inalienable essence of man', the Mnemonist would be a superman, a genius. In reality we see that he is nothing of the sort: he is as pathetic, as pathological, as he is prodigious and phenomenal. His story is a paradigm of polytechnical modern man who is bursting with unalive, mechanical possessions and power.

Sacks's discussion of Luria's two books was published in *The Listener* in 1973 and it provoked a fascinating correspondence which, as Sacks pointed out in his great closing letter, was about the ancient controversy

> which divided Socrates and Plato from the Sophists – who saw all knowledge as teachable skills and saleable commodities; it is the controversy which divided Leibniz from Locke – Leibniz's *New Essays* from Locke's *Essay*; it is the controversy which divided Hume in himself, leading him along the path of disintegration and back, to the acknowledgement (in the closing sections of Book One of his *Treatise*) that human nature, enduring individuality, could never be comprehended as a mere sum of perceptions, sense-data or 'facts', but had to be approached, *from the start,* in terms of 'Personal Identity'; it is, finally, the inner controversy which at one time broke Wittgenstein in two, but which served to lead him from the dead-end of the *Tractatus* to the spaciousness and fertility of his later philosophy. We have Selves and we have Organs – and neither can be reduced to the terms of the other. In his last letter (to Wilhelm von Humboldt, 17 March 1832) Goethe wrote: 'The Ancients said that the animals are taught through their organs; let me add to this, so are

men, but they have the advantage of teaching their organs in return.'

One correspondent felt the controversy had a quaintly eighteenth-century air and was largely irrelevant because of modern scientific advances. Whether this was fair or not, it certainly sounded familiar, for, as I've already mentioned, it dealt with the kind of issues Newman, Leslie Stephen, Carlyle and Mill argued about in the nineteenth century: issues of whether the mind is merely the passive receptacle of sense impressions, of whether, as Sacks affirms, it has active powers, a 'constitutional knowledge, an innate and germinal Idea of the world.' For Sacks, there is 'always *something* – something to be *tended* – however damaged or ill-developed the brain may be.' Hardy was keenly interested in this kind of controversy and it's implicit even in a stray remark about Jude's kneeling to the moon being a 'curious superstition, innate or acquired'. Again, as in the passage I quoted from *Far from the Madding Crowd* where a new-born calf mistakes a lantern for the moon, Hardy proposes a non-committal compromise between the innate idea and empirically acquired knowledge.

Sacks's phrase 'a Lockean nightmare' fits the speaker's situation perfectly in 'Wessex Heights':

There are some heights in Wessex, shaped as if by a kindly hand
For thinking, dreaming, dying on, and at crises when I stand,
Say, on Ingpen Beacon eastward, or on Wylls-Neck westwardly,
I seem where I was before my birth, and after death may be.

In the lowlands I have no comrade, not even the lone man's friend –
Her who suffereth long and is kind; accepts what he is too weak to mend:
Down there they are dubious and askance; there nobody thinks as I,
But mind-chains do not clank where one's next neighbour is the sky.

In the towns I am tracked by phantoms having weird detective ways –
Shadows of beings who fellowed with myself of earlier days:
They hang about at places, and they say harsh heavy things –
Men with a wintry sneer, and women with tart disparagings.

Down there I seem to be false to myself, my simple self that was,
And is not now, and I see him watching, wondering what crass
cause
Can have merged him into such a strange continuator as this,
Who yet has something in common with himself, my chrysalis.

I cannot go to the great grey Plain; there's a figure against the
moon,
Nobody sees it but I, and it makes my breast beat out of tune;
I cannot go to the tall-spired town, being barred by the forms
now passed
For everybody but me, in whose long vision they stand there
fast.

There's a ghost at Yell'ham Bottom chiding loud at the fall of
the night,
There's a ghost in Froom-side Vale, thin-lipped and vague, in a
shroud of white,
There is one in the railway train whenever I do not want it near,
I see its profile against the pane, saying what I would not hear.

As for one rare fair woman, I am now but a thought of hers,
I enter her mind and another thought succeeds me that she
prefers;
Yet my love for her in its fulness she herself even did not know;
Well, time cures hearts of tenderness, and now I can let her go.

So I am found on Ingpen Beacon, or on Wylls-Neck to the west,
Or else on homely Bulbarrow, or little Pilsdon Crest,
Where men have never cared to haunt, nor women have walked
with me,
And ghosts then keep their distance; and I know some liberty.

The enormous iambic couplets create a terrifying monotony. This is the sort of 'monotonic delivery' Hardy recommends for the speeches in *The Dynasts*, which should be 'something in the manner traditionally maintained by the old Christmas mummers, the curiously hypnotizing impressiveness of whose automatic style' is that of 'persons who spoke by no will of their own.' The poem sounds what it is – a speech delivered by someone in a state of such acute depression that he has almost totally lost his own will. In the lowlands he is a 'strange continuator', the passive victim of a deterministic process.

Hardy used this odd word 'continuator' in the first version of 'The Pedigree' where he glumly concludes:

> 'I am mere continuator and counterfeit! –
> Though thinking, *I am I,*
> *And what I do I do myself alone.*'

His persona in 'Wessex Heights' also lacks free will and is enslaved by a mechanical and obsessive memory and conscience, by clanking 'mind-chains'. He cannot help remembering. The phantoms and ghosts that track him are the shadows of 'beings who fellowed with myself of earlier days' – they are eidetic memories which he is projecting outside his mind. The 'figure against the moon' and the 'profile against the pane' are both mnemonic silhouettes that obstinately remain in his 'long vision'. Like Luria's Mnemonist, Hardy did train his memory – the technique he developed for studying paintings in the National Gallery shows this, so does his method of isolating silhouettes and profiles, and so does his habit of marking his reading with dates and places-names. Like Christopher Julian in *The Hand of Ethelberta* he had a fixed habit of remembering, and in 'Wessex Heights' and 'In Front of the Landscape' he casts himself as someone trapped by his highly developed memory; someone who, like S. or the carefully named Bradley Headstone in *Our Mutual Friend,* has become the victim of what Sacks calls '*tabula congesta*'. His mind is a kind of rubbish heap of impressions (a 'junk heap of impressions' is the phrase used to describe S.'s memory in the introduction to *The Mind of a Mnemonist*). And in the first chapter I quoted Hobbes's definition of memory and imagination as 'decaying sense' and suggested that in 'In Front of the Landscape' Hardy tacitly compares his mind to a graveyard and a rubbish dump: 'robes, cheeks, eyes with the earth's crust/Now corporate.'

Like Bradley Headstone Hardy was largely self-taught. He had to be because he left school at sixteen and worked in an architect's office from which he could only snatch a brief twenty minutes studying in the National Gallery after lunch. This meant that he had to find a way of deriving the maximum benefit from such a short time. Circumstances forced him, as they must force anyone without a private income, to rationalise his study of paintings, to be severely practical and methodical about aesthetics. Obviously the results of his study were mainly highly beneficial, but his dedicated practice of self-help – those hours studying before and after work – did have some bad effects, and in these poems he is counting the cost not simply of this particular application of an essentially mechanical concept of mental processes, but of the whole empirical, utilitarian tradition of self-improvement in which he grew up.

Dickens also counts the cost of this early behaviourism in *Hard Times* and *Our Mutual Friend* where he describes Bradley Headstone's mental cemetery like this:

> He had acquired mechanically a great store of teacher's knowledge. He could do mental arithmetic mechanically, sing at sight mechanically, blow various wind instruments mechanically, even play the great church organ mechanically. From his early childhood up, his mind had been a place of mechanical stowage. The arrangement of his wholesale warehouse, so that it might be always ready to meet the demands of retail dealers – history here, geography there, astronomy to the right, political economy to the left – natural history, the physical sciences, figures, music, the lower mathematics, and what not all in their several places – this care had imparted to his countenance a look of care; while the habit of questioning and being questioned had given him a suspicious manner, or a manner that would be better described as one of lying in wait. There was a kind of settled trouble in the face.

Though it would be very unfair to compare Hardy directly to Bradley Headstone, he, like Dickens, is demonstrating the disturbing results of a commitment to Locke's concept of mind and of an obsessive practice of the mnemonic techniques it inspires. The combined Lockean picture gallery and graveyard in 'In a Former Resort after many Years' carries the same warning. His persona in 'Wessex Heights' and 'In Front of the Landscape' is, like S., a 'paradigm of polytechnical modern man who is bursting with unalive, mechanical possessions and power'. In 'Wessex Heights' his 'detective' vision and his accompanying powers of memory appear to have turned back on him and split his identity into a 'simple self that was' and a mechanical 'strange continuator', a sort of robot behaviourist. Sacks says that S.'s 'memory, his perceptions, become split off from his self: he becomes a prodigy, a phenomenon, a mnemotechnical monstrosity, increasingly cut off from the grounds of his being.' And though it would again be unfair to apply the term 'mnemotechnical monstrosity' to Hardy or his persona (there is almost always that slight, but significant split between his self and the voice of the poem), it does come close to describing the mental state he is presenting in these and other poems. The Dante-figure in 'Little Gidding' calls this state 'the rending pain of re-enactment/Of all that you have done and been', and for Eliot time, memory and history are servitude, a series of railway lines which we are carried helplessly along. For Eliot one way of escaping from this bondage – and it's partly the bondage of empirical philosophy and evolutionary theory – is through a series of intense images which are not sense impressions and which break across and redeem 'the waste sad time'. Incapable of Eliot's enormous negativity Hardy cannot take this route, and so in 'Wessex Heights' he escapes from his 'mind-chains', the clanking determinism and obsessive mental mechanisms that enslave him, by going to certain lonely hills which are outside society and which are what he calls in the *Life* places 'of no reminiscences'. What he discovers there is not total freedom but 'some liberty'. He finds a respite rather than a solution.

* * *

'The Phantom Horsewoman' is possibly more than one of memory's daughters:

I

Queer are the ways of a man I know:
He comes and stands
In a careworn craze,
And looks at the sands
And the seaward haze
With moveless hands
And face and gaze,
Then turns to go...
And what does he see when he gazes so?

II

They say he sees as an instant thing
More clear than to-day,
A sweet soft scene
That was once in play
By that briny green;
Yes, notes alway
Warm, real, and keen,
What his back years bring –
A phantom of his own figuring.

III

Of this vision of his they might say more:
Not only there
Does he see this sight,
But everywhere
In his brain – day, night,
As if on the air
It were drawn rose-bright –
Yea, far from that shore
Does he carry this vision of heretofore:

IV

A ghost-girl-rider. And though, toil-tried,
He withers daily,
Time touches her not,
But she still rides gaily
In his rapt thought
On that shagged and shaly
Atlantic spot,
And as when first eyed
Draws rein and sings to the swing of the tide.

This poem employs hypostatised vision in a complicated way. As Henry Gifford has shown, it was originally the final poem in the 1912–13 sequence where it must have formed an arresting and visionary conclusion, and, despite the inferior poems that now follow it, to a large extent it still does, as there is a blank space below it in the collected edition. The last line, which seems to surge forward beyond the bounds of the poem, completes the sequence on the highest possible note. The arrested movement of the horse, the woman, her song and the moving sea all combine to create this surging sense of a perpetual present. But – and it's a large but – the 'vision' which he sees is described as a 'phantom of his own figuring', as, in other words, a phantom well-beloved that is entirely subjective. It is a visionary image which is 'drawn' on the air just as the mental visions in 'After a Romantic Day' are also 'drawn' on the cutting. However, it's a decidedly better poem and this is partly because it tries to give the image more than a subjective existence.

In 'The Going', which begins the sequence, the dawn breaks like Tennyson's blank day and he watches 'morning harden upon the wall' – the grey light stiffens like a corpse or sets like concrete. There is an anticipation of 'The Phantom Horsewoman' in:

> You were she who abode
> By those red-veined rocks far West,
> You were the swan-necked one who rode
> Along the beetling Beeny Crest,
> And, reining nigh me,
> Would muse and eye me,
> While Life unrolled us its very best.

But there is a world of difference between the dead, grey world of 'The Going' and the rosy, living tissue which is the substance of the visionary image he sees in 'The Phantom Horsewoman'. The difference between the two poems is again one of reality and quality, and like Donald Davie I'm inclined to suspect that that reality is metaphysical rather than psychological.

Opinions vary as to who is speaking in 'The Phantom Horsewoman'. For Bailey the speaker in the first two stanzas is 'an observant gossip', for Hillis Miller Hardy is the speaker and is characteristically detached and self-observant; and for me the poem is a dialogue between Hardy and Emma: she speaks first, in the affectionate and mildly condescending tones of a woman teasing her lover for his slightly comic worship of her, as though, knowing that he stares raptly at her photograph in her absence, she is archly challenging him with his absurdity. This flirtatious relationship is like his earnest pursuit of the coyly superior woman in 'After a Journey':

> Hereto I come to view a voiceless ghost;
> Whither, O whither will its whim now draw me?
> Up the cliff, down, till I'm lonely, lost,
> And the unseen waters' ejaculations awe me.
> Where you will next be there's no knowing,
> Facing round about me everywhere,
> With your nut-coloured hair,
> And gray eyes, and rose-flush coming and going.

Here, his tone is intense, but in 'The Phantom Horsewoman' he replies to her ghost's coyly challenging opening with an adopted ingenuousness and coolly pretends not to know anything about the odd man with the 'careworn craze':

And what does he see when he gazes so?

In other words he also replies in an arch tone of voice, asking her a question to which they both know the answer. She gives that answer in the second stanza, though here, I'm bound to say, I begin to lose the sense of her talking – the last four lines, especially 'Warm, real, and keen', sound like a piece of dialogue that isn't quite working, as though the author hasn't fully detached himself from what the character is saying. This is a common fault in Hardy's dialogue – there is a particularly heavy moment in *Tess* when Felix tells Angel Clare to stop looking at the dancing girls because 'we must get through another chapter of *A Counterblast to Agnosticism* before we turn in'. Hardy is the speaker throughout the third and fourth stanzas, and he completely dominates the poem when he asserts his final vision of her immaculate image. The image becomes marvellously present but it does so at the expense of the dialogue. That it is meant to be a dialogue is shown by the development of the sequence from the wanly one-sided conversation which he is trying to change into a real dialogue in 'The Going'.

In 'Your Last Drive', which follows 'The Going', he addresses Emma again and writes in her reply:

You may miss me then. But I shall not know
How many times you visit me there,
Or what your thoughts are, or if you go
There never at all. And I shall not care.
Should you censure me I shall take no heed,
And even your praises no more shall need.

This is not a real dialogue because he is recognising that her indifference now will be the reflex of his indifference while she was alive. The listless, weary tone quickens when he says to her:

Dear ghost, in the past did you ever find
The thought 'What profit,' move me much?

However, his tone sinks back into a recognition that they can never communicate:

Yet abides the fact, indeed, the same, –
You are past love, praise, indifference, blame.

But she does speak in 'The Haunter', where she states her attitude to this situation in which neither of them is able to communicate:

He does not think that I haunt here nightly:
  How shall I let him know
That whither his fancy sets him wandering
  I, too, alertly go? –
Hover and hover a few feet from him
  Just as I used to do,
But cannot answer the words he lifts me –
  Only listen thereto!

Though 'The Haunter' is a much better poem than 'His Visitor', where she also speaks, it's perhaps rather conventional and fanciful:

Yes, I companion him to places
  Only dreamers know,
Where the shy hares print long paces,
  Where the night rooks go;
Into old aisles where the past is all to him,
  Close as his shade can do,
Always lacking the power to call to him,
  Near as I reach thereto!

And yet I think the gentle, appropriately feminine rhymes and the line about the 'shy hares' do lift the poem above such objections. She is as close to him as his 'shade' and we know that both that word and the word 'power' carry strong connotations of subjectivity, but the sense that she is actually speaking predominates, even though she lacks 'the power to call to him.'

Significantly, the rhyme 'all to him,' 'call to him' is carried over into the first stanza of the next poem:

Woman much missed, how you call to me, call to me,
Saying that now you are not as you were
When you had changed from the one who was all to me,
But as at first, when our day was fair.

'The Voice' is one of the best poems in the sequence – it opens with a marvellously sure, sweeping rhythm, the seeds of whose change are already apparent in the second stanza where Hardy's doubt is the appropriate result of his sign-seeker's wish to 'view' her. It's as though he has allowed a lack of trust to interfere with faith and love and, like Orpheus, turned his head:

Can it be you that I hear? Let me view you, then,
Standing as when I drew near to the town
Where you would wait for me: yes, as I knew you then,
Even to the original air-blue gown!

The rhythm changes into a bitter terseness in the last stanza and ends with a kind of compromise between the offered natural solution and her voice, between disenchantment and the old impulsive rhythm:

Thus I; faltering forward,
Leaves around me falling,
Wind oozing thin through the thorn from norward,
And the woman calling.

He is still doggedly searching.

He finds Emma in 'After a Journey' where he speaks to her intimately and lyrically:

Soon you will have, Dear, to vanish from me,

For the stars close their shutters and the dawn whitens hazily.

The scene is that of their courtship and the situation, naturally, is romantic and passionate. They're like Romeo and Juliet parting at dawn, though his tone doesn't belong to impulsive youth: it's the intimate accent of forty years of domestic familiarity. And it is this tone of familiarity which is gracefully and playfully present in 'The Phantom Horsewoman'. She adopts an archly ingenuous tone in:

Queer are the ways of a man I know,

while he, as though he doesn't know, playfully asks what the man sees. It's as though Hardy, with Emma, is looking down from a great height at himself, rather in the way that the speaker in 'Wessex Heights' looks down – though with very different feelings – at his older unhappy self being watched by his 'simple self that was'. They are looking back at their younger selves in the indulgent, slightly amused fashion of an older couple reminiscing about their youth and courtship.

The lushness of 'After a Journey' depends partly on his image of her face and her 'rose-flush coming and going', but in 'The Phantom Horsewoman' where that rosiness is the total image – his vision is 'drawn rose-bright' on the air – it's as though he has gone beyond images to a reality which is voiced but invisible. In the sequence he hears her faintly calling but can't 'view' her, then he comes to 'view a voiceless ghost', but he can never both see her and talk to her. In 'The Phantom Horsewoman' he appears to solve this problem by obliquely suggesting a conversation between Emma and himself where they talk to each other like a pair of gods looking down from Olympus at their mortal selves. Up there she is independent of the physical image which he has of her – which is like saying that she is a person in her own right no matter whether he idealises her or not. The metaphysical statement has its parallel on a human level just as at the beginning of the sequence their not talking in life is carried beyond life. And in the magnificent last couplet the language which until then had been soft and filmy tenses itself to bracingly recapture what she felt when on earth. It's as though Emma, participating fully in what she has so far watched with bemused detachment, is mastered by the remembered sensation of the horse-riding she loved. So one could say that although Hardy takes over in the third and fourth stanzas Emma comes very definitely back into the poem here.

These lines from the last stanza have a curious resonance:

> And though, toil-tried,
> He withers daily,
> Time touches her not.

In his account of the resurrection St Paul says: 'I protest by your rejoicing which I have in Christ Jesus our Lord, I die daily'; and it seems appropriate that Hardy should allude to his account of the times Christ was seen after his crucifixion, and to the ensuing discussion of the resurrection of man when 'Death is swallowed up in victory.' Chapter and verse are also echoed, as Pinion notes, in *The Well-Beloved* when Jocelyn Pierston says of his ideal phantom: 'As flesh she dies daily, like the Apostle's corporeal self; because when I grapple with the reality she's no longer in it, so that I cannot stick to one incarnation if I would.' Pierston's problem is that he's in love with an ideal phantom that takes up a temporary residence in practically every woman he meets. Each woman whom this 'elusive idealization' quits is, Pierston ruefully admits, 'a corpse, worse luck'. In the 'Poems of 1912–13' the woman is literally dead and her 'flitting' phantom – or is it just his idealization of her? – is pursued in 'After a Journey'. The problem for Hardy is that there's absolutely no problem if, as in 'The Shadow on the Stone', this 'thin ghost' which the seals and birds are ignorant of is simply an emanation of his own subjectivity – which makes what he sees pure fantasy and memory, like the lover's visions in 'After a Romantic Day'. The 'phantom of his own figuring' is projected onto the air and that's all. Everything is just shadows, mirrors, sophistry.

Against this Hardy sets the relationship and their communication within it which is implicit in the intimately familiar speech-tones he employs, and he also poses this voiced reality as an alternative to simple picture-thinking. I'm thinking of Shelley rather than Coleridge here and especially of Demogorgon's statement in *Prometheus Unbound* that 'the deep truth is imageless.' This ultimate truth exists, Shelley says, in a realm where 'the air is no prism', beyond the dead veil of refracted colours and sense perceptions 'which those who live call life.' Humean impressions become Platonic shadows and these necessarily imply the existence of a reality beyond them. The sound of intimate, musing speech in Hardy's poem and the speakers' detached contemplation of both the image and the 'man I know' who is gazing at the image, together with the biblical allusion which goes beyond its merely subjective application in *The Well-Beloved*, do suggest that Hardy is offering a metaphysical reality here, though it's entirely characteristic of him to end with a pictured sensation of intense vitality in this world. As he says in 'He Prefers her Earthly' he loves Emma as she was and not as a 'firmament-riding earthless essence'. Perhaps, then, the sense of victory in 'The Phantom Horsewoman' is simply an affirmation of life itself, a 'yes' perpetuated by the sea and carried into eternity as the song in 'In a Museum' blends into 'the full-fugued song of the universe unending'? However, 'In a Museum' and 'He Prefers her Earthly' are clearly inferior to 'The Phantom Horsewoman', so again there is that crucial difference of *quality*, of the force and authenticity of what is said.

Love is clearly an illusion in 'On the Way':

The trees fret fitfully and twist,
Shutters rattle and carpets heave,
Slime is the dust of yestereve,
  And in the streaming mist
Fishes might seem to fin a passage if they list.

But to his feet,
Drawing nigh and nigher
A hidden seat,
The fog is sweet
And the wind a lyre.

A vacant sameness grays the sky,
A moisture gathers on each knop
Of the bramble, rounding to a drop,
That greets the goer-by
With the cold listless lustre of a dead man's eye.

But to her sight,
Drawing nigh and nigher
Its deep delight,
The fog is bright
And the wind a lyre.

This is a mysteriously beautiful poem which echoes these lines from 'The Lover's Journey':

Love in minds his various changes makes,
And clothes each object with the change he takes;
His light and shade on every view he throws,
And on each object what he feels, bestows.

And in 'Epipsychidion' Shelley also describes a romantic love which is projected on to a barren world, though in these lines by the Beatrice-like beloved rather than – at least immediately – by her lover. His subjective vision of the woman is being given an apparently objective existence, as though the light falls from her, not him:

The glory of her being, issuing thence,
Stains the dead, blank, cold air with a warm shade
Of unentangled intermixture, made
By Love, of light and motion: one intense
Diffusion, one serene Omnipresence,
Whose flowing outlines mingle in their flowing,
Around her cheeks and utmost fingers glowing
With the unintermitted blood, which there
Quivers, (as in a fleece of snow-like air
The crimson pulse of living morning quiver,)
Continuously prolonged, and ending never.

Hardy echoes Shelley's crimson, blushing vision in the 'rose-flush' of 'After a Journey' and the 'rose-bright' of 'The Phantom Horsewoman' where he is also trying to give the vision an external, substantive existence and where there is the same problem of its subjectivity and objectivity. In 'On the Way' the desires of the converging lovers also stain the blank, cold air like Shelley's 'warm shade'. They make the fog sweet and bright and the wind more of a 'lyre' than they think. The lyre is again a Shelleyan symbol, like the vibrant, stringed instruments in 'In Front of the Landscape'. The lovers' idealising vision contrasts with the weirdly realistic description of the outer world in the first and third stanzas, a dangerous contrast that is also there in the eerily erotic sound of the poem.

Significantly, the word 'vacant' in the fine line: 'A vacant sameness grays the sky', is also used by Crabbe in 'The Lover's Journey' where he says that when our minds are self-absorbed the 'vacant eye on viewless matter glares' – it wanders over the outer world without seeing anything there. External reality either fades away or becomes a vacant screen whose blankness is coloured by its perceiver's state of mind. As a counter to this absent-minded, romantic solipsism Crabbe introduces a series of minute botanical descriptions, and Hardy's equivalent of these microscopic effects which he greatly admired is the accurate description of the rounding water drops. Like Crabbe, he is juxtaposing vague, idealistic vision and close, clear scrutiny. Both modes of perception come together in the line: 'With the cold listless lustre of a dead man's eye'. Like the moonlight in 'After a Romantic Day' this is a symbol of the pathetic fallacy, of the projection of subjectivity on to the outside world; but it also has a sinister accuracy. It's both a symbol and an observed fact. The eye is another 'vacant eye' because its surface is blank and because it's obviously blind. The implication is that the lovers, absorbed in their dreams of each other, are blind to the actuality of their surroundings, a blindness which the mist helps by screening them from reality and enveloping them in the subtle substance of their dreams. This is another visionary mist which blots out the real world, and by condensing on twigs and branches it makes that world into a dead eye, a series of blank mirrors that will reflect whatever the lovers want. For Hardy, as for both Crabbe and Shelley, the outside world is a dead and barren waste, a vast mirror into which we project our own shadows and sophistries.

When he describes the pond where Gabriel Oak's sheep drown, and says that it 'glittered like a dead man's eye', Hardy means that the hostility and cruelty of the pond are all in Oak's mind. They're a pathetic fallacy. Similarly, when Eustacia meets Clym by a pond which is like 'the white of an eye without its pupil', we're being told how their love affair on the dead heath will turn out. And again when Jude neglects his bible for Arabella and returns to see the capital letters on its title-page regard him 'with fixed reproach in the grey starlight, like the unclosed eyes of a dead man', his guilt is bouncing back at him from the vacant mirror of a dead eye. If the lovers in 'On the Way' are also projecting their feelings on to a blank screen, the sinister realism of the exactly detailed description of the water drop points to the enormous disparity between dream and reality and also suggests that the circumstances they think so sweetly bright are hostile and cruel – not indifferent, in fact.

In many respects 'A Wet August' is the companion-piece of 'On the Way':

> Nine drops of water bead the jessamine,
> And nine-and-ninety smear the stones and tiles:
> –'Twas not so in that August – full-rayed, fine –
> When we lived out-of-doors, sang songs, strode miles.
>
> Or was there then no noted radiancy
> Of summer? Were dun clouds, a dribbling bough,
> Gilt over by the light I bore in me,
> And was the waste world just the same as now?
>
> It can have been so: yea, that threatenings
> Of coming down-drip on the sunless gray,
> By the then golden chances seen in things
> Were wrought more bright than brightest skies to-day.

Clearly, this is inferior to 'On the Way'. It has the same combination of close scrutiny and minuteness of specification with radiantly transforming vision, but it has nothing of the other poem's intense atmosphere and sense of sexual fascination – the converging fascination of 'A Man was Drawing Near to Me'. The dull detail of the water drops is the equivalent of the 'peculiar tint of yellow-green' which is all Coleridge is left with in the Dejection Ode after vision has failed. They are just observed facts which the mind's light is powerless to transform.

In line with Crabbe and Shelley, Hardy goes on to wonder whether what he felt all those years ago was a subjective illusion: did the light of his own hopes merely gild the wet 'waste world'? And here, the source of this phrase is revealing. Hardy remembered it from a speech in *Prometheus Unbound* where Asia gazes into Panthea's eyes and sees Prometheus's smiles which promise that they will meet again: 'Within that bright pavilion which their beams/Shall build o'er the waste world.' As in 'A Wet August' a smiling light will make the gray world golden. But because Shelley has already formulated this idea Hardy is merely introducing it, ready-made, into three routine quatrains. They lack the subversive criticism of this kind of idealism which he implies in 'At Waking':

> When night was lifting,
> And dawn had crept under its shade,
> Amid cold clouds drifting
> Dead-white as a corpse outlaid,
> With a sudden scare
> I seemed to behold
> My Love in bare
> Hard lines unfold.
>
> Yea, in a moment,
> An insight that would not die
> Killed her old endowment
> Of charm that had capped all nigh,
> Which vanished to none
> Like the gilt of a cloud,
> And showed her but one
> Of the common crowd.

The idealised woman now seems 'but a sample/Of earth's poor average kind' and not particularly beautiful or gifted. However, the lover in this monologue doesn't exchange an idealistic illusion for a realistic truth: he merely exchanges one impression of the woman for another.

There is a similar moment in *Tess* when the disillusioned and fastidious Angel decides to leave the girl he had thought of as a 'visionary essence of woman':

> He thus beheld in the pale morning light the resolve to separate from her; not as a hot and indignant instinct, but denuded of the passionateness which had made it scorch and burn; standing in its bones; nothing but a skeleton, but none the less there.

In both cases the bare skeletal lines are reminiscent of the straight lines with which the architect disillusions the heiress: they represent the fixed tendencies of a certain type of male mind. They are the 'hard logical deposit' that is like a vein of metal embedded in the soft loam of Angel's nature. This is the kind of metallic, mechanical tendency which Hardy is dramatising in 'Wessex Heights' where his 'mind-chains', clamped tightly round the brain, are like railway lines running through a graveyard rather than a 'soft loam' (curiously, when he was a young architect Hardy actually helped to supervise a massive exhumation which allowed the Midland Railway to go through St Pancras Churchyard). Rochester's famous Hobbesian lines also describe this mixture of death and rigidity which is the mechanistic empiricist's mind:

> Huddled in dirt the reasoning engine lies,
> Who was so proud, so witty and so wise.

And 'At Waking', like 'Without, not Within Her' and 'The Chosen', is really about the man's sexist attitude towards the woman. His disillusion is the necessary condition of his tyrannically idealistic nature, and again and again Hardy identifies such a nature with cruelty and death.

The poem ends with the lover's horror at the loss of his vision and his dramatic refusal to believe that the 'prize' he drew can be 'a blank to me'. He means that he has drawn a blank lottery ticket and so feels cheated, but we know that the word 'blank', as in Shelley's 'dead, blank, cold air', means that his vision has been projected onto blankness like the youth's in 'After a Romantic Day'. And for Shelley, all reality is simply a projected 'vision':

> this Whole
> Of suns, and worlds, and men, and beasts, and flowers,
> With all the silent or tempestuous workings
> By which they have been, are, or cease to be,
> Is but a vision; – all that it inherits
> Are motes of a sick eye, bubbles and dreams;
> Thought is its cradle and its grave, nor less
> The Future and the Past are idle shadows
> Of thought's eternal flight – they have no being:
> Nought is but that which feels itself to be.

These lines are from *Hellas,* a poem Hardy told Florence Henniker he had read many times. He may well have recognised (since he followed Shelley's tracks so closely) that in stating here that reality is wholly dependent on our perceptions Shelley is echoing a passage in the *Treatise* where Hume argues that when we press one eye with a finger all the objects we see appear double: 'But as we do not attribute a continu'd existence to both these perceptions, and as they are both of the same nature, we clearly perceive that all our perceptions are dependent on our organs, and the disposition of our nerves and animal spirits.' This is confirmed, Hume says, by the way objects appear to increase and diminish according to their distance and by 'the changes in their colour and other qualities from our sickness and distempers'. In Shelley this becomes 'motes of a sick eye' and Hardy uses a similar comparison in 'At Day-Close in November':

> The ten hours' light is abating,
>   And a late bird wings across,
> Where the pines, like waltzers waiting,
>   Give their black heads a toss.
>
> Beech leaves, that yellow the noon-time,
>   Float past like specks in the eye;
> I set every tree in my June time,
>   And now they obscure the sky.
>
> And the children who ramble through here
>   Conceive that there never has been
> A time when no tall trees grew here,
>   That none will in time be seen.

In comparing the falling leaves to eye-motes he suggests that his sight is weakening with age, and he also, very significantly, compares a series of things which apparently exist externally and independently of his perception of them to floating specks which entirely depend on his sight. Truth here is dependent on perception – an idea that is developed in the last stanza, though its final line doesn't make grammatical sense.

Hardy is saying that the trees which he owns, has planted and brought into being, possess a series of personal associations stretching over a great many years, and for this reason, as well as the fact that their falling leaves seem like motes, they appear and feel part of himself. Yet they only seem to belong to him because really they will survive him, like the children. Their growth is actively shutting off the light from him now – there is a suggestion here of both the trees and the children growing beyond him and also of his being enclosed in what is apparently a perfectly insulated solipsism, the kind of 'self-contained position' which the idealistic and solipsistic Fitzpiers enjoys in his woodlands. Although he planted the trees, they are depriving him of what little light remains – a wintry, evening light that matches his old age. And just as their growth is independent of him so it's independent of the children, for whom they have a totally different meaning. The children, for whom the world is happily centred upon themselves, know only the present and so are unaware that some day the trees will decay and vanish from sight. In this way Hardy suggests that he is both inhabiting a solipsistic universe in which everything seems part of himself, dependent on his perception of it, and one which is completely outside himself and whose natural processes run blindly on, as indifferent to him as the wind that nonchalantly sways the pines. And this contrast between self-enclosure and indifferent actuality is also there in 'On the Way' and in 'After a Romantic Day', where the visionary motes in the youth's eye fall softly against that ominously 'bald' railway cutting.

7
The Cogency of Direct Vision

That natural processes are blind, chaotic and unjust is an attitude which underlies most of Hardy's poems. Sometimes he expresses it directly and when he does so the result is usually unsatisfactory. This is true of 'The Lacking Sense', where Time explains suffering, disease, life's imperfections, in terms of a blind nature which 'plods dead-reckoning on' through miserable darkness:

> –Ah! knowest thou not her secret yet, her vainly veiled deficience,
> Whence it comes that all unwittingly she wounds the lives she loves?
> That sightless are those orbs of hers? – which bar to her omniscience
> Brings those fearful unfulfilments, that red ravage through her zones
> Whereat all creation groans.

The word 'blind', which is the stale, traditional adjective we use to describe chance, is applied almost literally to nature in this poem and its associates: 'Nature's Questioning', 'Doom and She', 'To Outer Nature', 'A Philosophical Fantasy', 'God-Forgotten', 'Agnosto Theo'. These poems are offshoots of *The Dynasts* which Hardy was writing at the time he wrote most of them and they are the results of his need to endow a force behind circumstances with an anthropomorphic personality. Sometimes, as in the amusing 'Philosophical Fantasy' and in 'God-Forgotten' where God sounds like a pompously inefficient bureaucrat at the other end of a telephone, this is less a need than a means of satirising theology:

> –'The Earth, sayest thou? The Human race?
> By Me created? Sad its lot?
> Nay: I have no remembrance of such place:
> Such world I fashioned not.' –

This self-justifying God sounds like Milton's tetchy schoolmaster in book three of *Paradise Lost,* but unlike Milton in the great paragraph which opens that book Hardy is not working his way towards a theodicy. In a letter to Florence Henniker in 1893 he chides her in terms which make it clear that he doesn't believe there is any pattern of justification in suffering:

> What I meant about your unfaithfulness to the Shelley cult referred not to any lack of poetic emotion, but to your view of things: e.g., you are quite out of harmony with this line of his in Epipsychidion:
>
> 'The sightless tyrants of our fate'
>
> which beautifully expresses one's consciousness of blind circumstances beating upon one, without any feeling, for or against.

The reference to Shelley means that the tone of such poems must be one of plaintively falling upon life's thorns, rather than of stern justification, and the nearest Hardy approaches the kind of positive answers that a Christian might confidently affirm is in 'The Sleep-Worker' where he asks nature how she will react when she wakes up and sees the suffering she has caused:

> Wilt thou destroy, in one wild shock of shame,
> Thy whole high heaving firmamental frame,
> Or patiently adjust, amend, and heal?

As one of Hardy's notes shows, this is a development of the philosophies of Schopenhauer and von Hartmann:

> Only if the existence of the world was decided by the act of a *blind* will...only then is this existence comprehensible; only then is God as such not to be made responsible for the same....But why did not God when he became *seeing*, i.e. his all-wise intelligence entered into being, repair the error?...Here we are again aided by the inseparability of the idea from the will in the unconscious...the dependence of the idea on the will; (and) the whole world-process (i.e. throughout time) only serves the one purpose of emancipating the idea from the will by means of consciousness.

Hardy transcribed this passage from von Hartmann's *Philosophy of the Unconscious* into one of his commonplace books and it forms one element in the 'evolutionary meliorism' he rather unconvincingly professed. It's a clotted piece of jargon which surfaces in 'The Sleep-Worker' and the after scene of *The Dynasts*.

In 'The Lacking Sense' Hardy suggests, oddly, that just because nature is blind and making a mess of things, we shouldn't scorn her. Instead, we should pity her and give her a helping hand:

> 'Assist her where thy creaturely dependence can or may,
> For thou art of her clay.'

The effort, as at the end of *The Dynasts,* is to discover some positive principle, however tenuous or remote. This effort runs against the predominant tone of these poems which is reminiscent of a precociously miserable boy criticising his parents for bringing him into the world. And yet, poor as these poems are, to condemn this attitude as self-pitying and inadequate is to beg some of the largest questions. The attitude and its intuited objections are best summed up in Larkin's 'This Be the Verse', with its snarling mixture of contempt and self-contempt:

> They fuck you up, your mum and dad.
> They may not mean to, but they do.
> They fill you with the faults they had
> And add some extra, just for you.
>
> But they were fucked up in their turn
> By fools in old-style hats and coats,
> Who half the time were soppy-stern
> And half at one another's throats.
>
> Man hands on misery to man.
> It deepens like a coastal shelf.
> Get out as early as you can,
> And don't have any kids yourself.

Without remotely suggesting a positive attitude, this point of view is allowed to reveal its own querulous contradictions, its own sense that the unanswerable questions are somehow unaskable. Larkin's comment on life, or epitaph on a recognisable opinion of it, is also a comment on these poems of Hardy's, and yet if you listen to Benjamin Britten's setting of Hardy's 'Before Life and After' in his song-cycle, *Winter Words*, this sense of the cruelty of circumstances and the injustice of human sensitivity comes over with irrefutable power.

The opening paragraph of book three of *Paradise Lost*, which I mentioned earlier, is partly Milton's justification to himself of his blindness, and there is something of the note of reproach against God that predominates in Hardy's poems in these lines where he describes how his eyes

> roul in vain
> To find thy piercing ray, and find no dawn;
> So thick a drop serene hath quencht thir Orbs,
> Or dim suffusion veild.

Hardy of course knew these lines, and in one of his copies of Milton he read this detailed note on them:

> 'Drop serene', or gutta serena. It was formerly thought that that sort of blindness was an incurable extinction or quenching of sight by a transparent, watery, cold humour, distilling upon the optic nerve, though making very little change in the eye to appearance, if any; 'tis now known to be most commonly an obstruction in the capillary vessels of that nerve, and curable in some cases.

What makes it worth knowing that he read this is the fact that he uses the information as a metaphor for Bathsheba's state of mind immediately before Boldwood murders Troy:

> She was in a state of mental *gutta serena*; her mind was for the minute totally deprived of light at the same time that no obscuration was apparent from without.

Hardy is describing a state of acute mental suffering and he does so by referring indirectly to Milton's blindness, and though the conclusion of *Far from the Madding Crowd* – a winning-through against the odds – is essentially happy, he isn't suggesting that circumstances are fundamentally just. This is the belief Milton is working towards in the passage where he uses the phrase 'drop serene'. His effort to discover a justification for his blindness produces great poetry, both highly strenuous and melodic:

> Then feed on thoughts, that voluntarie move
> Harmonious numbers; as the wakeful Bird
> Sings darkling, and in shadiest Covert hid
> Tunes her nocturnal Note.

These lines on the nightingale and his own inspiration represent one stage in Milton's difficult, but eventually successful, development towards a resolution that is both an acceptance of his circumstances and a statement of resolve to 'see and tell/Of things invisible to mortal sight.' And just as his 'drop serene' is behind Hardy's description of Bathsheba's shocked misery, so the word 'darkling' and the context in which Milton uses it appear in 'The Darkling Thrush':

I leant upon a coppice gate
  When Frost was spectre-gray,
And Winter's dregs made desolate
  The weakening eye of day.
The tangled bine-stems scored the sky
  Like strings of broken lyres,
And all mankind that haunted nigh
  Had sought their household fires.

The land's sharp features seemed to be
  The Century's corpse outleant,
His crypt the cloudy canopy,
  The wind his death-lament.
The ancient pulse of germ and birth
  Was shrunken hard and dry,
And every spirit upon earth
  Seemed fervourless as I.

At once a voice arose among
  The bleak twigs overhead
In a full-hearted evensong
  Of joy illimited;
An aged thrush, frail, gaunt, and small,
  In blast-beruffled plume,
Had chosen thus to fling his soul
  Upon the growing gloom.

So little cause for carolings
  Of such ecstatic sound
Was written on terrestrial things
  Afar or nigh around,
That I could think there trembled through
  His happy good-night air
Some blessed Hope, whereof he knew
  And I was unaware.

31*st December* 1900.

As Bailey points out, Hardy knew that the tradition behind 'darkling' comprises Keats and Arnold as well as Milton. And the mood of 'The Darkling Thrush' is closer to Keats's 'The weariness, the fever and the fret/Here where men sit and hear each other groan' in 'Ode to a Nightingale', and to 'the turbid ebb and flow/Of human misery' in 'Dover Beach', than to Milton's winning-through from misery and darkness to light. Hardy's poem, in other words, is the work of an agnostic humanist, not a puritanical Christian, though in a very Miltonic way it is facing up to all that is dead, nasty and cruel: nature is a ruined church, so it and Christianity are both dead. Against this background which is steadily darkening under the day's 'weakening eye' – the idea of blind circumstances carries more conviction here – Hardy sets, in a sort of Miltonic upward movement out of darkness and hell, the sudden song of a battered thrush. The bird's joyous song is one of those freshnesses that suddenly spirit into a despairingly mechanical routine, a spontaneous joy like his own singing in 'The Something that Saved Him', but it represents an optimism about human possibilities for improvement in this world rather than a religious certainty that it will all come right in the next. The poem's darkling landscape is reminiscent of the leprous marsh in Browning's 'Childe Roland to the Dark Tower Came' where, like Hardy and Milton, he stares failure and deadness in the face and then also makes an affirmation:

> Dauntless the slug-horn to my lips I set,
> And blew. 'Childe Roland to the Dark Tower came.'

This is what the thrush's song means.

The thrush, as well as being a unique living creature, also represents humanity – man just coping and surviving like the ploughman and broken-down old horse in ' "In Time of the Breaking of Nations" '. At the beginning of *The Return of the Native* Hardy says that Egdon Heath is 'like man, slighted and enduring', and so is his frail thrush singing into the wind. He also says that Egdon 'had a lonely face, suggesting tragical possibilities', and the tragedy he's thinking of is *King Lear* which, like *Job* and *Paradise Lost*, discovers a principle of order and justice behind circumstantial and human cruelties – though it sounds false when this is put so baldy. As I suggested at the beginning of this chapter Hardy had no confidence in justifications of a metaphysical or divine principle behind circumstances, and, lacking that confidence, he wrote 'The Darkling Thrush' as a humanist's hymn that expresses a very tentative belief in progress. Its stern, wintry quality and its resolute power – it has all the melancholy of a hymn sung by a small congregation in a cold church as the light fades – has affinities with the growling sound of Milton's great lines:

> Thus with the Year
> Seasons return, but not to me returns
> Day, or the sweet approach of Ev'n or Morn,
> Or sight of vernal bloom, or Summer's Rose,
> Or flocks, or herds, or human face divine;
> But cloud in stead, and ever-during dark
> Surrounds me, from the cheerful ways of men
> Cut off, and for the Book of knowledge fair
> Presented with a Universal blanc –
> Of Natures works to mee expung'd and ras'd,
> And wisdom at one entrance quite shut out.

Milton is able to pull himself up out of this plunging despair with a characteristic recoiling qualification:

> So much the rather thou Celestial Light
> Shine inward,

but all Hardy offers is a Hope that he himself can only 'think' exists. It is the situation of 'The Impercipient': he is regretfully admitting his own scepticism about God and progress but at the same time wishing he could believe. Still, the thrush's song rather than his comment on it is an affirmation made in despite of deadness, blindness and despair. The darkling landscape is another Egdon Heath (curiously the thrush can also be like the spirit of human endurance which the heath resembles) and it is the visible equivalent of Milton's universal blankness. In the last light of the sun's weakening eye, it embodies a 'state of mental *gutta serena*' and signifies acute suffering. It is also the legacy of nineteenth century thought – nature bald and dead and still there as the world moved on into the twentieth century. For Hardy it's a corpse that shows every sign of staying that way, which means that the 'human tune' is the only value, the only beauty, that remains.

* * *

The injustice of circumstances and the sterility of the outer world make nature poetry largely impossible or irrelevant and religious poetry mainly a matter of rebuking a non-existent God for the mess he's made of things. The alternative is a humanist aesthetic, a belief that 'clouds, mists, and mountains are unimportant beside the wear on a threshold, or the print of a hand.' As in the Dutch paintings Hardy admired, nature becomes a background for human figures. In 'Drinking Song' he says:

> So here we are, in piteous case:
>   Like butterflies
>   Of many dyes
> Upon an Alpine glacier's face:
>   To fly and cower
>   In some warm bower
> Our chief concern in such a place.

There is no way of relating the grinding force of circumstances and the fragility of our lives, and because this is so our poems read like this:

> In the black winter morning
> No light will be struck near my eyes
> While the clock in the stairway is warning
> For five, when he used to rise.
>   Leave the door unbarred,
>   The clock unwound.
>   Make my lone bed hard –
>   Would 'twere underground!
>
> When the summer dawns clearly,
> And the appletree-tops seem alight,
> Who will undraw the curtain and cheerly
> Call out that the morning is bright?
>
> When I tarry at market
> No form will cross Durnover Lea
> In the gathering darkness, to hark at
> Grey's Bridge for the pit-pat o'me.
>
> When the supper crock's steaming,
> And the time is the time of his tread,
> I shall sit by the fire and wait dreaming
> In a silence as of the dead.

Leave the door unbarred,
The clock unwound,
Make my lone bed hard –
Would 'twere underground!

'Bereft' is a fine poem and it makes its point with great economy: the refrain carries all that the landscape in 'The Darkling Thrush' or the glacier in 'Drinking Song' or any of the other grey realities in the poems signify, while the other stanzas marvellously offer a unique sense of two shared lives and the good routines that patterned them. The couple's life together is visualised in a series of images which testify to a shared experience, a complete relationship: the first light of their mornings which he always gives, their evenings which her shopping and cooking identify her with, his going to meet her on the way back from market. This detailed ordinariness and its accompanying sense of a true reciprocity, of a full and happy relationship between man and wife, is extremely convincing.

In 'The Ballet' the rustling, fragile dancers, all of whom look alike in their 'tinsel livery':

muster, maybe,
As lives wide in irrelevance.

'Daughters, wives, mistresses', they are individuals with separate and concealed lives. Naturally, this fascination with other lives is to be expected in a novelist, and there is a passage in the *Life* where we can see him at work during a church service:

> Every woman then, even if she had forgotten it before, has a single thought to the folds of her clothes. They pray in the litany as if under enchantment. Their real life is spinning on beneath this apparent one of calm, like the District Railway-trains underground just by – throbbing, rushing, hot, concerned with next week, last week.... Could these true scenes in which this congregation is living be brought into church bodily with the personages, there would be a churchful of jostling phantasmagorias crowded like a heap of soap bubbles, infinitely intersecting, but each seeing only his own. That bald-headed man is surrounded by the interior of the Stock Exchange; that girl by the jeweller's shop in which she purchased yesterday. Through

> this bizarre world of thought circulates the recitative of the parson – a thin solitary note without cadence or change of intensity – and getting lost like a bee in the clerestory.

The hidden separateness of other people's lives fascinates him, and in many poems he compresses a story about them into just a few lines. In some poems – 'Tess's Lament', 'The Pine Planters', 'A Poor Man and a Lady', 'The Moth-Signal', 'Had You Wept', 'Midnight on the Great Western' – his own fictions become a kind of antecedent fact which these poems draw on. 'The Pine Planters' is a sad lyric-monologue spoken by Marty South about her love for Giles Winterbourne:

> We work here together
> In blast and breeze;
> He fills the earth in,
> I hold the trees.
> He does not notice
> That what I do
> Keeps me from moving
> And chills me through.

As they plant each tree,

> As if from fear
> Of Life unreckoned
> Beginning here,
> It starts a sighing
> Through day and night,
> Though while there lying
> 'Twas voiceless quite.

Even their work isn't justified because, to Marty, it seems as though they are merely perpetuating misery and giving birth to more and more sadness. Like Hardy's unsatisfactory 'Satires of Circumstance' sequence this poem is based on his conviction that circumstances are cruel and unjust – indeed it is this conviction which throws his imagination back upon (or out to) people and their lives. If he had been interested in what the parson was saying then it's unlikely that he would have been so fascinated by the mysterious, hidden lives of the congregation.

'The Pine Planters' has a chill misery which we can appreciate all the more when we know *The Woodlanders*. Similarly, we bring our knowledge of the novel to Tess's recollection of Angel's courtship:

'Twas there within the chimney-seat
He watched me to the clock's slow beat –
Loved me, and learnt to call me Sweet,
And whispered words to me.

These lines have a loving naivety and delicacy, and again the girl's character, the situation and relationship all come through – come through partly because we know the novel, though this doesn't mean that this poem and the others like it are just footnotes to the novels. Rather, the novels are footnotes to them, almost like cells that supply a basic charge. Hardy is not a novelist who wrote poems but a poet who wrote novels for a time, and these particular poems are ambitious works which belong to a poetic kind that hasn't yet been fully developed. The ambition was there right at the start of his career. The ashen landscape and parting couple in 'Neutral Tones' are a situation in a story and so, too, is the situation in 'Her Dilemma', a much less satisfactory early poem for which he drew a crude, but impressive illustration: the unhappy couple in a church, below them a layer of bones, skulls and lead-encased skeletons. *Wessex Poems* also contains four sonnets dated 1866 which are part of a larger number that Hardy lost or destroyed, and despite the obvious Shakespearean influences these 'She, to Him' sonnets have a tough power of their own:

I appear
Numb as a vane that cankers on its point,
True to the wind that kissed ere canker came:
Despised by souls of Now, who would disjoint
The mind from memory, making Life all aim.

As an insight into, and symbol of, her stagnant, frustrated fidelity to the man who has deserted her, this is thoroughly effective: her condition comes through with a sense of total rightness and accuracy in the presentation of her character – a presentation that is both sympathetic and critical.

Though Meredith had published his remarkable sonnet-cycle, *Modern Love*, four years before Hardy wrote these poems, it's doubtful whether it had any effect on them. Later poems like 'Once at Swanage' and 'To a Sea Cliff' do show residual traces of Meredith's ambitious poem which compresses the story of a breaking marriage into a sequence of fifty sixteen-line sonnets and presents subtle emotions and situations in ways we expect a novel, not a poem, to do. Just sometimes Meredith lets the real world in:

In our old shipwrecked days there was an hour,
When in the firelight steadily aglow,
Joined slackly, we beheld the red chasm grow
Among the clicking coals. Our library-bower
That eve was left to us: and hushed we sat
As lovers to whom Time is whispering.
From sudden-opened doors we heard them sing:
The nodding elders mixed good wine with chat.
Well knew we that Life's greatest treasure lay
With us, and of it was our talk. 'Ah, yes!
Love dies!' I said: I never thought it less.
She yearned to me that sentence to unsay.
Then when the fire domed blackening, I found
Her cheek was salt against my kiss, and swift
Up the sharp scale of sobs her breast did lift: –
Now am I haunted by that taste! that sound!

This is a scene from a novel and it feels indisputably real. The 'clicking coals', like Tess's slowly beating clock, are both accurately observed facts, totally convincing details, and part of a shared experience. They are authentically there.

Hardy's 'A January Night', which he said was set at the time his and Emma's 'troubles began', is also about a shared unhappiness and it makes circumstances a hostile force within their relationship:

The rain smites more and more,
The east wind snarls and sneezes;
Through the joints of the quivering door
  The water wheezes.

The tip of each ivy-shoot
Writhes on its neighbour's face;
There is some hid dread afoot
  That we cannot trace.

Is it the spirit astray
Of the man at the house below
Whose coffin they took in to-day?
  We do not know.

Despite its pathetic fallacies this has the texture of reality. The mental atmosphere is set within certain physical conditions as their shared, undefined anxiety attaches itself to the battering storm, the horrible detail of the leaves, a death in the street. And the uninsistent mention of the coffin's delivery is so particular and circumstantial that its validity underwrites the presentation of their feelings. Fact acts as a guarantor for both the emotion and the reality of the situation, while in a novel by Defoe (whom Hardy admired and whose 'affected simplicity' he imitated when he began writing novels) fact only guarantees the truth of the story. For Defoe, a bag never contains just peas – it contains half a bushel of white peas and because it does so its reality cannot be challenged. This kind of circumstantial realism is also there in 'A January Night' and in Meredith's sonnet where it ballasts the presentation of feeling.

In 'At a Seaside Town in 1869' the youth's narrative of fading love is touched into reality by these stanzas:

> The boats, the sands, the esplanade,
> The laughing crowd;
> Light-hearted, loud
> Greetings from some not ill-endowed;
>
> The evening sunlit cliffs, the talk,
> Hailings and halts,
> The keen sea-salts,
> The band, the Morgenblätter Waltz.

The waltz's name clinches it. Like the great last line of 'A Church Romance' – 'Bowing "New Sabbath" or "Mount Ephraim" ' – it's so utterly and surely right that Hardy appears to be triumphantly relishing actuality, to be amazed and delighted by its variousness. In 'A Conversation at Dawn' he describes an unhappy wife gazing into the red sunrise as her husband threatens her:

> She answered not, lying listlessly
> With her dark dry eyes on the coppery sea,
> That now and then
> Flung its lazy flounce at the neighbouring quay.

Again there is that indisputable sense of a scene being looked at and becoming part of an experience. This is another example of an 'involute' or 'perplexed combination of emotion and concrete objects', and Hardy's ability to fuse concrete objects and scenes with a human story is one of his great qualities. Usually – and here he differs from

Meredith – he doesn't treat subtle, complicated feelings as they are immediately shared by two people. A sense of happiness, almost always lost, or a sense of unhappiness are his two subjects, though 'In the Vaulted Way', one of a whole series of love stories given a separate section in *Time's Laughingstocks,* is a possible exception:

> In the vaulted way, where the passage turned
> To the shadowy corner that none could see,
> You paused for our parting, – plaintively;
> Though overnight had come words that burned
> My fond frail happiness out of me.
>
> And then I kissed you, – despite my thought
> That our spell must end when reflection came
> On what you had deemed me, whose one long aim
> Had been to serve you; that what I sought
> Lay not in a heart that could breathe such blame.
>
> But yet I kissed you; whereon you again
> As of old kissed me. Why, why was it so?
> Do you cleave to me after that light-tongued blow?
> If you scorned me at eventide, how love then?
> The thing is dark, Dear. I do not know.

The vaulted way and shadowy passage-corner are the only facts in the poem and they are not given any attention because the interest is directed at a difficult feeling the man has towards the woman – a queasy feeling he doesn't understand and is trying to make sense of. Hardy formulates this distinction between fact and feeling in an essay called 'The Science of Fiction' where he says that 'a blindness to material particulars often accompanies a quick perception of the more ethereal characteristics of humanity.' The science of fiction is not, he says, 'the paying of a great regard to adventitious externals to the neglect of vital qualities, not a precision about the outside of the platter and an obtuseness to the contents.' An example he would probably have disliked is the way external fact hazes into subtle feeling in a story by James. We don't go to James for the sounds and sights and flavours of reality just as we don't go to Hardy's novels for the delicate shades of feeling James's characters experience. A note of Hardy's on the subject shows why:

> Novel-writing as an art cannot go backward. Having reached the analytic stage it must transcend it by going still further in the

same direction. Why not by rendering as visible essences, spectres, etc., the abstract thoughts of the analytic school?

The positivist's strategy is to make emotion visible or, in Hardy's terms, to give 'ethereal characteristics' or 'abstract thoughts' a quasi-substantial existence. And often Hardy uses what he terms 'material particulars' rather than 'visible essences' to render emotion:

> The dreary, dreary train; the sun shining in moted beams upon the hot cushions; the dusty permanent way; the mean rows of wire – these things were her accompaniment: while out of the window the deep blue sea-levels disappeared from her gaze, and with them her poet's home. Heavy-hearted, she tried to read, and wept instead.

This is the best moment in 'An Imaginative Woman' and it works by expressing her emotions through the things she sees. As in 'her dark dry eyes on the coppery sea' we visualise both the scene and the woman's feelings. This is Hardy's characteristic technique of communicating emotion, though 'Her Confession', like 'In the Vaulted Way', is an exception:

> As some bland soul, to whom a debtor says
> 'I'll now repay the amount I owe to you,'
> In inward gladness feigns forgetfulness
> That such a payment ever was his due
>
> (His long thought notwithstanding), so did I
> At our last meeting waive your proffered kiss
> With quick divergent talk of scenery nigh,
> By such suspension to enhance my bliss.
>
> And as his looks in consternation fall
> When, gathering that the debt is lightly deemed,
> The debtor makes as not to pay at all,
> So faltered I, when your intention seemed
> Converted by my false uneagerness
> To putting off for ever the caress.

This is an early poem whose sonorities are Shakespearean, but its opening and developing comparison deftly captures the woman's complex coyness. The nearby scenery doesn't impinge as a visual detail and, instead, the conceit carries the feeling. Because the feeling is subtle and unstraightforward it can't be embodied as a 'visible essence', and the result is a neat, witty poem.

In just a few poems, Browning – who is much more influential than Meredith as far as Hardy is concerned – manages this most difficult combination of emotional subtlety with dollops of observed fact:

> I wonder do you feel today
> As I have felt since, hand in hand,
> We sat down on the grass, to stray
> In spirit better through the land,
> This morn of Rome and May?
>
> For me, I touched a thought, I know,
> Has tantalized me many times,
> (Like turns of thread the spiders throw
> Mocking across our path) for ryhmes
> To catch at and let go.
>
> Help me to hold it! First it left
> The yellowing fennel, run to seed
> There, branching from the brickwork's cleft,
> Some old tomb's ruin: yonder weed
> Took up the floating weft,
>
> Where one small orange cup amassed
> Five beetles, – blind and green they grope
> Among the honey-meal: and last,
> Everywhere on the grassy slope
> I traced it. Hold it fast!

'Two in the Campagna' is a monologue thought out silently to himself (rather than spoken to the woman) by a sensitive, self-conscious, rather pretentious young man who is trying to articulate his sense of unease in their relationship, his dissatisfaction at the rarity of their moments of complete identity with each other. Like Hardy, Browning seeks to give this intangible, tenuous emotion a visible existence by rather unfortunately comparing it to a spider's thread, but as the poem develops the feeling is communicated as an abstraction which is there to be analysed rather than seen.

Hardy follows his note on 'visible essences' with the remark that he put this idea into effect in *The Dynasts*:

> The human race to be shown as one great network or tissue

> which quivers in every part when one point is shaken, like a spider's web if touched. Abstract realisms to be in the form of Spirits, Spectral figures, etc.

Like Browning, he chooses a spider's web as a convenient visualisation of an abstraction. In Browning's poem the things that are incontrovertibly seen – the yellowing fennel, the green beetles in the orange cup – aren't symbols but ugly facts which have all the terrifying banality of actual things. They, too, carry an emotion though their main function is not to communicate a sense of boredom – they exist as real facts. Hardy valued fact as much as Browning and he also describes it for its own sake as well as using it to represent otherwise invisible emotions. The way he visualises the congregation's thoughts as a pattern of soap bubbles in the note I quoted earlier is one example. Another is this stanza from 'The Place on the Map':

> Weeks and weeks we had loved beneath that blazing blue,
> Which had lost the art of raining, as her eyes today had too,
> While she told what, as by sleight,
> Shot our firmament with rays of ruddy hue.

The 'blazing blue' is both a real blue sky and their intense passion. Notice, too, how his reaction to her dreadful news is likened to 'rays of ruddy hue', as though a sunset, like the sunrise in 'A Conversation at Dawn', has prematurely dyed their faces red. It casts a 'torrid tragic light'. This is a cinematic technique and one can imagine a sudden tremor in the music accompanying the ominous darkening of the image.

In 'Under the Waterfall' the woman says that the only 'real love-rhyme' she knows

> Is the purl of a little valley fall
> About three spans wide and two spans tall
> Over a table of solid rock,
> And into a scoop of the self-same block.

She and her lover, she remembers, walked under a blue sky 'with a leaf-wove awning of green.' The emotion is presented as an actual and visible fact with colour, sound and dimension. Its unique perfection is represented by a real object – the drinking-glass they lost in the stream:

> No lip has touched it since his and mine
> In turns therefrom sipped lovers' wine.

Hardy based this on an actual incident during his courtship of Emma and although the poem begins as a memory associated with the touch of cold water it soon gains such intense presence that it displaces reality rather like one of S.'s memories. Abstract feeling and material fact become one.

Meredith concludes *Modern Love* with an interesting visual image:

> Then each applied to each that fatal knife,
> Deep questioning, which probes to endless dole.
> Ah, what a dusty answer gets the soul
> When hot for certainties in this our life! –
> In tragic hints here see what evermore
> Moves dark as yonder midnight ocean's force,
> Thundering like ramping hosts of warrior horse,
> To throw that faint thin line upon the shore!

And in 'Once at Swanage' Hardy describes an actual scene which is reminiscent of what in Meredith's lines is not an observed scene but an image which the word 'yonder' gives a quick, tricky appearance of actuality to:

> The spray sprang up across the cusps of the moon,
> And all its light loomed green
> As a witch-flame's weirdsome sheen
> At the minute of an incantation scene;
> And it greened our gaze – that night at demilune.
>
> Roaring high and roaring low was the sea
> Behind the headland shores:
> It symboled the slamming of doors,
> Or a regiment hurrying over hollow floors....
> And there we two stood, hands clasped; I and she!

The comparisons are unsatisfactory and while their sinister, ominous qualities are meant to hint the lovers' destiny – the shadow of their future in the present moment – it's clear that what Hardy really values is the unusual visual effect of green moonlight through blown spray. The rest of the poem is an unconvincing gesture towards significance. In 'The Pine Planters' he successfully deploys an unusual effect – the way the young pines wail the moment they're planted – as part of Marty South's feelings, but the detail in this scene remains null. It doesn't fuse with feeling in the way that the scene in 'A Conversation at Dawn' or 'Neutral Tones' does.

This insistence upon observed fact was partly due to Leslie Stephen's influence. Hardy read an essay by him called 'The Moral Element in Literature' which appeared in *The Fortnightly Review* during 1881, and in it Stephen argues that an imaginative writer 'shows us certain facts as they appear to him' and if we are in sympathy with his presentation of them then they will have a truth whose proof 'has all the cogency of direct vision.' Consequently, our view of the world will be changed because 'the bare scaffolding of fact which we previously saw will now be seen in the light of keener perceptions than our own.' Stephen makes his point in a characteristically dreary fashion and he supports it with the positivist's belief that proof is a matter of actually seeing something, but his phrase 'the cogency of direct vision' is a good one and it clearly appealed to Hardy who slipped it into *A Laodicean* which he was writing at the time (he says that a trick photograph had 'all the cogency of direct vision'). The phrase is a positivist's credo: you look at bare facts with keen eyes and your observation of them is real knowledge, real truth. Hardy practised what he called 'the art of observation' and it's partly his direct, undeviating method of looking at things which accounts for the sense of reality we get from poems like 'Bereft'. The emotions of shared happiness in that poem are made visible through their presentation as visual images – images which the couple in the poem as much as Hardy himself visualise: the light is struck in the black morning very precisely 'near my eyes.' And this passage from *Far from the Madding Crowd* shows just how precise Hardy's observation was:

> The rain had quite ceased, and the sun was shining through the green, brown, and yellow leaves, now sparkling and varnished by the raindrops to the brightness of similar effects in the landscapes of Ruysdael and Hobbema, and full of all those infinite beauties that arise from the union of water and colour with high lights. The air was rendered so transparent by the heavy fall of rain that the autumn hues of the middle distance were as rich as those near at hand, and the remote fields intercepted by the angle of the tower appeared in the same plane as the tower itself.

Unfortunately, unlike the visual effects in 'Bereft' this has nothing to do with how a character is feeling, but it's a most acute piece of observation. The light effect here is not a stereotyped description; instead, it makes us realise how sunlight after rain crowds the middle distance closer and freshens colours so that the scene is flattened and brightened.

In '"I Am the One"' he describes the direct, keen quality of his sight:

> I hear above: 'We stars must lend
> No fierce regard
> To his gaze, so hard
> Bent on us thus, –
> Must scathe him not. He is one with us
> Beginning and end.'

This hard gaze, starry-eyed only in its cold detachment, is brought again and again to the hardness of facts. It's there in 'The Harbour Bridge' which ends with these lines:

> White stars ghost forth, that care not for men's wives,
> Or any other lives.

This is an excellent late poem which sets certain lives within a keenly observed reality. The exact visualisation is talked out gently:

> From here, the quay, one looks above to mark
> The bridge across the harbour, hanging dark
> Against the day's-end sky, fair-green in glow
> Over and under the middle archway's bow:
> It draws its skeleton where the sun has set,
> Yea, clear from cutwater to parapet;
> On which mild glow, too, lines of rope and spar
> Trace themselves black as char.

The green sky and the char-black outlines testify to the closeness of his observation, and he goes on to describe how the boats' painters 'shift' lazily against the bollards and how the citizens move quickly along the starkly outlined bridge like 'black-paper portraits'. This silhouette-effect was something he habitually noticed and valued. It's there in the thin, black beech-twigs in 'Lying Awake', and when he referred to his own poems as 'grave, positive, stark, delineations' he must have thought of them – and visualised them – as having the engraved starkness of bare twigs against a late or early sky. In 'The Harbour Bridge' he also notices the people in the scene – the 'dreamful girl', the 'practical woman' and the sailor who accidentally meets the wife he has deserted. She tries and fails to persuade him to come back to her:

> They go different ways.
> And the west dims, and yellow lamplights shine:
> And soon above, like lamps more opaline,

the ghostly stars come out. People, the changing quality of the light, the objects in the scene, are all observed with a clear, star-like detachment.

'On the Esplanade', another seaside poem, combines intense visualisation with the hushed sense of a story happening:

> The broad bald moon edged up where the sea was wide,
>   Mild, mellow-faced;
> Beneath, a tumbling twinkle of shines, like dyed,
>   A trackway traced
> To the shore, as of petals fallen from a rose to waste,
>   In its overblow,
> And fluttering afloat on inward heaves of the tide: –
> All this, so plain; yet the rest I did not know.

The visual effects are both lush and precise. The 'bald moon' has the same significance and precision as the water drops in 'On the Way', while the petalled lights are sweet, bright and artificial. They, too, are both observed facts and vehicles of significance. There is a mysteriousness in what cannot be seen:

> Inside a window, open, with undrawn blind,
>   There plays and sings
> A lady unseen a melody undefined.

This unusually balanced line prepares us for the undefined significance of: 'That, behind,/My Fate's masked face crept near me I did not know!' The speaker doesn't develop the story and this isn't important, partly because we can guess what's inevitable, partly because it leaves the situation open just as the story behind 'In the Vaulted Way' is left unresolved.

There is a similar combination of human interest and factual observation in 'An East End Curate', another of these quietly attractive late poems:

A small blind street off East Commercial Road;
Window, door; window, door;
Every house like the one before,
Is where the curate, Mr. Dowle, has found a pinched abode.
Spectacled, pale, moustache straw-coloured, and with a long thin face,
Day or dark his lodgings' narrow doorstep does he pace.

Faced with the inanimate coldness of this grey urban landscape Hardy chooses not to reject or run away from it but to discover value in the dogged, perhaps pointless, activity of another human being. The curate goes in and out of his neighbours' houses as though they're his own, hears the familiar sounds of a husband and wife arguing, and passes on:

Freely within his hearing the children skip and laugh and say:
'There's Mister Dow-well! There's Mister Dow-well!' in their play;
And the long, pallid, devoted face notes not,
But stoops along abstractedly, for good, or in vain, God wot!

In 'Beyond the Last Lamp', which I cited earlier as an example of the way Hardy infuses fact with emotion, he again faces the worst when he speculates about a sad couple trudging through the dark rain:

The pair seemed lovers, yet absorbed
In mental scenes no longer orbed
By love's young rays. Each countenance
As it slowly, as it sadly
Caught the lamplight's yellow glance,
Held in suspense a misery
At things which had been or might be.

The poem's ugly landscape is brutally real. Both it and what it contains – a man and a woman in a hopeless, undefined relationship – threaten a kind of terror which is kept at bay partly by the way the sheer dreariness of it all is formalised in the middle lines by the trochaic metre of *Hiawatha*. The couple here are sadly lost and this makes what he observes and describes almost unbearable. But in many other poems – 'An Autumn Rain-Scene', 'Ice on the Highway', 'Last Look round St. Martin's Fair' – he sets purposeful human activity against a blank backdrop. In 'An Autumn Rain-Scene' there are the diligent party-goer, the man hurrying to fetch 'the saving medicament', the herdsman, the postman and the coastguard to set against the unemployed labourer and the inevitable corpse in the last stanza. The refrain – 'On whom the rain comes down' – builds up a monotonous sense of pointlessness, a fundamental pointlessness that the labourer and the corpse are part of, but which doesn't quite outweigh the fact that people just get on with things despite it; for if Hardy starts in these poems with the assumption that reality is a dead blankness he then goes on to find meaning and value in the people who plod or sprint in front of it.

In 'No Buyers', another poem of direct observation, he describes a man and his wife hopelessly trying to sell brushes on a rainy day:

> A load of brushes and baskets and cradles and chairs
> Labours along the street in the rain:
> With it a man, a woman, a pony with whiteybrown hairs. –
> The man foots in front of the horse with a shambling sway
> At a slower tread than a funeral train,
> While to a dirge-like tune he chants his wares,
> Swinging a Turk's-head brush (in a drum-major's way
> When the bandsmen march and play).

Effort and purpose have become pointless here, and yet Hardy resolutely describes the exact kind of brush the couple are trying to sell and by noticing that the man swings his brush like a drum-major's baton while the woman carries hers 'more in nursing-wise' characterises them both. The effort is always to rescue a human value from the dreary facts that are the material of his observations.

Nature, being mechanical, is disenchantedly described as a purely industrial process in the opening lines of 'Last Look round St. Martin's Fair':

> The sun is like an open furnace door,
> Whose round revealed retort confines the roar
> Of fires beyond terrene;
> The moon presents the lustre-lacking face
> Of a brass dial gone green,
> Whose hours no eye can trace.
> The unsold heathcroppers are driven home
> To the shades of the Great Forest whence they come
> By men with long cord-waistcoats in brown monochrome.

The stars break out, and flicker in the breeze,
It seems, that twitches the trees. –
From its hot idol soon
The fickle unresting earth has turned to a fresh patroon –
The cold, now brighter, moon.
The woman in red, at the nut-stall with the gun,
Lights up, and still goes on:
She's redder in the flare-lamp than the sun
Showed it ere it was gone.
Her hands are black with loading all the day,
And yet she treats her labour as 'twere play,
Tosses her ear-rings, and talks ribaldry
To the young men around as natural gaiety,
And not a weary work she'd readily stay,
And never again nut-shooting see,
Though crying, 'Fire away!'

This is another quiet, marvellously skilful late poem which describes a scene closely and then sets a series of human activities within it. The slightly chilling atmosphere of early evening, the sense of enormous space above the fair as it closes down and the unsold horses are driven back to the shadowy, rather ominous 'Great Forest', are brilliantly established. The colours and light effects are scrupulously detailed and beneath the woman's routine 'Fire away!' a small affirmation is being made. Also, and this is part of the poem's visual cogency, it makes a distinct shape on the page. It, too, is starkly delineated like a silhouette.

* * *

In several of his best poems Hardy uses sight as a simple metaphor in the way we all do when we say 'I see' and mean that we understand. In 'Overlooking the River Stour' he sets a series of deliberate perceptions against the word 'see' in the last stanza where it represents all that can never be accurately observed and described:

The swallows flew in the curves of an eight
Above the river-gleam
In the wet June's last beam:
Like little crossbows animate
The swallows flew in the curves of an eight
Above the river-gleam.

Planing up shavings of crystal spray
  A moor-hen darted out
  From the bank thereabout,
And through the stream-shine ripped his way;
Planing up shavings of crystal spray
  A moor-hen darted out.

Closed were the kingcups; and the mead
  Dripped in monotonous green,
  Though the day's morning sheen
Had shown it golden and honeybee'd;
Closed were the kingcups; and the mead
  Dripped in monotonous green.

And never I turned my head, alack,
  While these things met my gaze
  Through the pane's drop-drenched glaze,
To see the more behind my back....
O never I turned, but let, alack,
  These less things hold my gaze!

The poem is set during what he termed 'the Stourminster Newton idyll' – the early years of his marriage – and is another backward look at a lost happiness. Each stanza rhymes in what seems to be a modification of a triolet and in doing so describes a monotonous arc like the swallows. This repetitive structure is designed to reinforce the way in which the 'less things' it contains 'hold' his gaze like the dingy facts in 'Shut out that Moon'. The last two lines of each stanza appear to reflect the first two like a mirror, as though far from looking through his rain-spotted window at what is outside he is really looking into it and seeing only himself. The words 'river-gleam', 'crystal', 'stream-shine' and 'sheen' all insist that the light is being reflected by a mirror that is natural but which feels artificial. The effect of the repeated stanza form is monotonous and constraining: it enacts the one-for-one transference from perceiver to object and object to perceiver. The swallows, the moorhen and the kingcups are conventional natural beauties, dead facts observed by the keen-sighted positivist. Like his architect the exercise of that rigidly mechanical 'measuring eye' makes him turn his back on life, on all that cannot be neatly measured and observed. This poem captures the sheer dreariness of always looking at and observing *things*, of being simply 'interested', drily and deadeningly, in visible facts. The closed stanza form encloses certain facts so efficiently within itself that it makes us feel there is something else which is missing. The scene itself is coldly repellent, part of its dreary chill stemming from the way Hardy compares the swallows to 'little crossbows animate' and the moorhen to the shoe of a plane which rips the water into crystal shavings. As Donald Davie notes Hardy likens them to machines, but he does so deliberately (Davie doesn't appear to realise this) in order to stress the sterility of his positivism. His comparisons are designed to make us draw back from their mechanical monotonies. It's as though he is freezing their living actions into the kind of banal unreality plastic gnomes occupy. His descriptions are synthetic and artificial intrusions into the natural scene, but then the natural scene itself is sterile and unrewarding in comparison with 'the more behind my back', the emotional life that cannot be precisely visualised.

'The Musical Box', which is this poem's companion-piece, again offers an opportunity outside the mechanism:

> Lifelong to be
> Seemed the fair colours of the time;
> That there was standing shadowed near
> A spirit who sang to the gentle chime
> Of the self-struck notes, I did not hear,
> I did not see.
>
> Thus did it sing
> To the mindless lyre that played indoors
> As she came to listen for me without:
> 'O value what the nonce outpours –
> This best of life – that shines about
> Your welcoming!'
>
> I had slowed along
> After the torrid hours were done,
> Though still the posts and walls and road
> Flung back their sense of the hot-faced sun,
> And had walked by Stourside Mill, where broad
> Stream-lilies throng.

> And I descried
> The dusky house that stood apart,
> And her, white-muslined, waiting there
> In the porch with high-expectant heart,
> While still the thin mechanic air
> Went on inside.
>
> At whiles would flit
> Swart bats, whose wings, be-webbed and tanned,
> Whirred like the wheels of ancient clocks:
> She laughed a hailing as she scanned
> Me in the gloom, the tuneful box
> Intoning it.
>
> Lifelong to be
> I thought it. That there watched hard by
> A spirit who sang to the indoor tune,
> 'O make the most of what is nigh!'
> I did not hear in my dull soul-swoon –
> I did not see.

William Barnes was born in the parish of Sturminster Newton and anyone who has read one of his finest poems – 'The Clote' – will recognise its golden drowse and rich happiness in Hardy's mention of the lilies on the river Stour:

> Oh! when thy brook-drinken flow'r's a-blowen,
> The burnen zummer's a-zetten in;
> The time o' greenness, the time o' mowen,
> When in the hay-vield, wi' zunburnt skin,
> The vo'k do drink, O,
> Upon the brink, O,
> Where thou dost float, goolden zummer clote!

This is the timeless, glowing warmth Hardy is describing throughout his poem. In 'Night in the Old Home' his ghostly ancestors advise him to 'Take of Life what it grants, without question', and the Spirit's imperative: 'O value what the nonce outpours' represents another and belated recognition of his failure to appreciate this only apparently timeless happiness. The clock-like bats flitting outside and the 'mindless lyre' tinkling inside powerfully identify nature, time and machines to disturb with the sense of a mechanical and deterministic process which is running on and down, which is indifferent and without value, and against which their missed, lost value is defined: the woman in cool, white muslin waiting to welcome him on their threshold and he in his intense self-absorption failing to recognize and so fully value such a moment of humanly graceful vision.

The poem's evening warmth which cocoons him in his 'dull soul-swoon', is a natural symbol which is used in several other poems. In 'The Revisitation', at the 'spirit-hour' of a warm July night, a soldier rests on a Sarsen stone where he used to meet a girl called Agnette twenty years before. This stone holds 'the heat of yester sun', some peewits rise against the clouds 'like a fitful phosphorescence', and then the figure of Agnette breaks the skyline and she comes to him. Another ghostly revisitation occurs in 'Friends Beyond' where the local worthies whisper to him 'at mothy curfew-tide,/And at midnight when the noon-heat breathes it back from walls and leads.' A similar symbolic use of the day's heat being reflected back in the evening is made in '"I Look into my Glass"' where Time 'shakes this fragile frame at eve/With throbbings of noontide', and in a less well-known poem called 'The Spellbound Palace' which begins:

On this kindly yellow day of mild low-travelling winter sun
  The stirless depths of the yews
  Are vague with misty blues:
Across the spacious pathways stretching spires of shadow run,
And the wind-gnawed walls of ancient brick are fired vermilion.

The setting is Hampton Court where there is a 'mindless fountain' which trickles on in the stillness like the equally mindless musical box. And this combination of the hidden, then 'now-visioned' fountain and the low sun on the ancient brick walls releases a vision of 'a straddling King' and his Minister who walks 'at a bold self-centred pace'. This is a subtle, good poem which, like the others, is about moments when the past comes to life in the present: Henry VIII and Wolsey mysteriously reappear. The sensory images of walls and stones which hold the heat of the day at twilight carry this significance. They are perfectly natural symbols of this process because they fuse both human sensations and things which, though they are outside those sensations, still appear to be in a kind of sympathetic communication with them. The warm walls and road in 'The Musical Box' actively fling back 'their sense' of the sun, and this drowsy, reflected heat represents a kind of eternity outside normal clockwork time, a dimension where past and present meet and join perfectly. The two time-schemes intersect and form a ghosting hour when time stands still. It's then that the dead or forgotten come back and 'murmur mildly' and a telepathic communication is opened with them. Hardy also uses this transfiguring effect in 'A Church Romance', 'Wives in the Sere' and 'Former Beauties', and in this line from 'Afterwards': 'If I pass during some nocturnal blackness mothy and warm'. Here, dying becomes the easiest of transitions into a warm, ghostly presence.

This reflected heat is altogether different from the reflected light in 'Overlooking the River Stour'. The things that he sees there give back only what he brings to them, while in 'The Musical Box' and the poems I've grouped with it certain physical things breathe back a stored warmth to him. In 'Honeymoon Time at an Inn' the reflected light is chill:

> While their large-pupilled vision swept the scene there,
> Nought seeming imminent,
> Something fell sheer, and crashed, and from the floor
> Lay glittering at the pair with a shattered gaze,
> While their large-pupilled vision swept the scene there,
> And the many-eyed thing outleant.
>
> With a start they saw that it was an old-time pier glass
> Which had stood on the mantel near,
> Its silvering blemished, – yes, as if worn away
> By the eyes of the countless dead who had smirked at it
> Ere these two ever knew that old-time pier-glass
> And its vague and vacant leer.

The stanza form, reminiscent of 'Overlooking the River Stour', is again designed to create a constrained, mirroring effect. The moon-struck sophism which the bride reads into the broken mirror – years of sorrow together – will come true not because this is an especially remarkable portent but simply because it 'fits all mortal mould'. The vision, or superstition, is the result of reflected moonlight here, but unlike 'The Musical Box' this is a cold poem which simply insists upon time running down to disillusion and death without asserting any contrary value – 'This best of life' – against it. The form of the poem, like the bride's reflex action in gathering up the broken glass as if she's 'an automaton', has a loom-like monotony.

Partly because it can't be seen, happiness is never caught at the time for Hardy. The rapt emotion in 'The Self-Unseeing' is only discovered fully when it's too late:

> Here is the ancient floor,
> Footworn and hollowed and thin,
> Here the former door
> Where the dead feet walked in.
>
> She sat here in her chair,
> Smiling into the fire;
> He who played stood there,
> Bowing it higher and higher.
>
> Childlike, I danced in a dream;
> Blessings emblazoned that day;
> Everything glowed with a gleam;
> Yet we were looking away!

The technique is deft and direct: we see the floor and its human associations, then the family group in the room. The end-stopped lines are wonderfully rapt and simple, and the last stanza with its short, sharp alliterations catches the intoxication of the music Hardy said he was 'extraordinarily sensitive to' as a child. The scene is a Dutch interior, but one whose beauty and happiness he has come to appreciate too late. And, looking back, he sees that even then they were 'looking away'. Each of them was self-absorbed and separate even though the feeling was one of shared euphoria: his mother was smiling, but she was half-absently looking into the fire as though not wholly content, his father was totally involved in the ecstatic violin-playing he preferred to his business, and he himself was absorbed in his solitary dancing, both the centre of attention and yet in a way ignored. None of them truly appreciated this intense, glowing happiness.

If happiness is only identified when it's too late to value it, unhappiness also shows itself to be part of a predetermined pattern which was never visible when it might have helped to know what was round the corner. Of course, this is impossible in terms of both logic and life. Still,

> Alien they seemed to be:
> No mortal eye could see
> The intimate welding of their later history.

The pattern is always there even though, as he says again in 'At the

Word "Farewell" ', it can't be perceived at the time. Hindsight imposes pattern and value, discovers a 'prelude' and a 'drama' and shapes experience into art. This means that the moment is never valued for itself – and here I think we've got to make a connection between this and the fact that Hardy was a professional writer for much of his life. Some of the notes in his journals are revealing: in 1890 he confesses that he is 'tired of investigating life at music-halls and police-courts', and in 1875 he felt that because he was 'committed by circumstances to novel-writing as a regular trade' he had to observe 'ordinary social and fashionable life' and reluctantly 'carry on his life not as an emotion but as a scientific game'. Even when he was able to give up writing novels for a living he still kept 'a record of his experiences in social life' just in case he might be driven to writing society novels. His habit of observation, precisely because it was a habit, never left him, and those small, dark, detective's eyes continued to stare directly at anything and everything. People, as much as the changing quality of light or the minute alterations of the seasons, were facts, the objects of his scientific interest. Throughout his life he was fascinated by what he termed 'human automatism' – *The Dynasts* is one of the products of this fascination – and his habit of observing things was a reflex action which he couldn't cure himself of, even if he'd really wanted to. The alternative to both his mechanically deliberate observations and to his equally mechanical pattern-making is affirmed by the spirit in 'The Musical Box': 'O value what the nonce outpours'. It's also expressed by Browning in 'By the Fire-Side', a poem which I've already suggested is behind 'At the Word "Farewell" ':

> How the world is made for each of us!
> How all we perceive and know in it
> Tends to some moment's product thus,
> When a soul declares itself – to wit,
> By its fruit, the thing it does!
>
> Be hate that fruit or love that fruit,
> It forwards the general deed of man,
> And each of the Many helps to recruit
> The life of the race by a general plan;
> Each living his own, to boot.

According to this existential ethic every deed has an absolute value for itself and is also part of a 'general plan' which doesn't prejudice its unique, free existence. But for Hardy, because time confers value and significance, there must be a plan, and in 'At the Word "Farewell" ' this 'Plan of the past' will ensure unhappiness beyond their present moment of intense happiness. And, significantly, 'He views himself as an automaton' was the original title of 'He Wonders about Himself':

> Part is mine of the general Will,
> Cannot my share in the sum of sources
> Bend a digit the poise of forces,
> And a fair desire fulfil?

The question is whether he can ever free himself from his own automatism, his subordination to a deterministic system, and value the spontaneous joy that 'the nonce outpours'. 'The Musical Box' is about his failure to appreciate the present moment – a failure which is partly the result, he implies, of his view of time as a clockwork mechanism running down to despair and death. For Hardy, contingency must always be given shape and pattern, which is why he comments on another farewell scene (in *The Hand of Ethelberta*) that the 'moment, upon the very face of it, was critical; and yet it was one of those which have to wait for a future before they acquire a definite character as good or bad'. Only time will tell, but when its verdict comes through the moment is long gone.

Hardy's difficulty is that for something to exist it must have a visible shape and it must be fixed as permanently as possible; but because an experience can only crystallise itself into a distinctive shape, a cameo-like silhouette, when it has become a memory, this means that the moment is never caught as it goes. The grandiose emotion of 'In Death Divided' springs from an agonised sense that their love will not have such a visible shape after their deaths. There will be no 'visible essence' and no positivist's resurrection. It's as though death will deprive them of their social existence as a pair of doomed platonic lovers:

> And in the monotonous moils of strained ,hard-run
> Humanity,
> The eternal tie which binds us twain in one
> No eye will see
> Stretching across the miles that sever you from me.

Taking this view that for something to exist – even an abstraction like their 'eternal tie' – it must be visible, what happens to love? Supposing, as in 'To Meet, or Otherwise', he were to go out and meet the girl of his dreams? The decision may seem a big one at the time:

Yet this same sun will slant its beams
At no far day
On our two mounds, and then what will the difference weigh?

On the other hand:

By briefest meeting something sure is won;
It will have been:
Nor God nor Demon can undo the done,
Unsight the seen.

Something once seen cannot be 'unsighted'. But there's a difficulty here in that he seems to be suggesting that what's over and done with and therefore incapable of being seen can in some way still be sighted. He overcomes this difficulty by changing the metaphor into a musical one in the remainder of the stanza and then developing it in the next along the lines of Wordsworth's 'still sad music':

So, to the one long-sweeping symphony
From times remote
Till now, of human tenderness, shall we
Supply one note,
Small and untraced, yet that will ever be
Somewhere afloat
Amid the spheres, as part of sick Life's antidote.

Partly because this is another poem in the grand style the struggled-for affirmation doesn't convince. Its cogency, after all, is not that of direct sight (or hearing), though it's difficult not to read 'mote' for 'note' and see the permanent significance of their rendezvous, their infinite moment, ascending into the heavens like a speck of dust.

Hardy is really more at home with a lost opportunity, especially if the situation can be visualised:

She wore a new 'terra-cotta' dress,
And we stayed, because of the pelting storm,
Within the hansom's dry recess,
Though the horse had stopped; yea, motionless
We sat on, snug and warm.

Then the downpour ceased, to my sharp sad pain
And the glass that had screened our forms before
Flew up, and out she sprang to her door:
I should have kissed her if the rain
Had lasted a minute more.

'A Thunderstorm in Town', like 'In Death Divided', stems from his platonic affair with Florence Henniker – she is probably the object of his 'fair desire' in 'He Wonders about Himself'. It beautifully captures a sudden atmosphere of warmth and intimacy, a critical moment when no one can see them – which is helpful since they're not married to each other and appear in society. But part of the point is that he was relieved when the rain stopped and allowed him to shrug the responsibility for a failed pass on to circumstances. He gladly colludes with what he calls 'the poise of forces' in 'He Wonders'.

A similar poem called 'Faintheart in a Railway Train' conceals the same equivocal attitude behind the apparently courageous certainty of its final exclamation:

> At nine in the morning there passed a church,
> At ten there passed me by the sea,
> At twelve a town of smoke and smirch,
> At two a forest of oak and birch,
>   And then, on a platform, she:
>
> A radiant stranger, who saw not me.
> I said, 'Get out to her do I dare?'
> But I kept my seat in my search for a plea,
> And the wheels moved on. O could it but be
>   That I had alighted there!

The wheels move on, the deterministic momentum of things carries him past her. And here we are back in the same territory as 'Bereft': a series of images and a story that's fused with them. Admittedly, the images aren't as clear and precise as they are in 'Bereft' – 'smoke and smirch' is over-casual and vague. But the fact that the first stanza consists of five picture postcards is significant because this technique of building a poem from a series of images is one that Hardy developed to the full in some of the best poems he ever wrote, poems which he grouped under the title *Moments of Vision*. There, the images disentangle themselves from the temporal mechanism, and the impressions recorded by direct, systematic observation are lifted above and beyond this kind of ultimately sterile positivism into a visionary dimension.

8

Moments of Vision

Though it has its 'miscellaneous verses' (as the full title of *Moments of Vision* honestly displays), many of the best poems in the volume are related, not always obviously, to the title-poem which introduces it:

> That mirror
> Which makes of men a transparency,
> Who holds that mirror
> And bids us such a breast-bare spectacle see
> Of you and me?
>
> That mirror
> Whose magic penetrates like a dart,
> Who lifts that mirror
> And throws our mind back on us, and our heart,
> Until we start?
>
> That mirror
> Works well in these night hours of ache;
> Why in that mirror
> Are tincts we never see ourselves once take
> When the world is awake?
>
> That mirror
> Can test each mortal when unaware;
> Yea, that strange mirror
> May catch his last thoughts, whole life foul or fair,
> Glassing it – where?

The gnomic interrogatives are challenging because they're as mysterious as the answers they seek. What does he mean by a 'transparency' or a 'breast-bare spectacle'? A passage in the fore scene of *The Dynasts* where the Spirit of the years demonstrates its 'gift to visualize the Mode' offers a possible answer:

> A new and penetrating light descends on the spectacle, enduing men and things with a seeming transparency, and exhibiting as one organism the anatomy of life and movement in all humanity and vitalized matter included in the display.

Notice how 'spectacle', 'transparency' and 'penetrating' are echoed in the poem. This is one of several scene directions in *The Dynasts* where the Spirit of the Years, who is the resolutely necessitarian incarnation of history, reveals a complex network of gossamer-like threads which connect each soldier in the fighting armies and show that human actions are not 'self-done'. These waving threads and coils resemble a vast brain or 'winds grown visible' and are Hardy's visual representation of the Immanent Will which is the real force behind historical events. Like human emotions, the historical process can be rendered as a 'visible essence' and in *The Dynasts* a kind of X-ray vision reveals its workings. This revelation is also a 'moment of vision'.

What Hardy appears to be saying in the first stanza of this poem is that someone has the power to make our motives transparent and then to offer them to us as an anatomizing 'spectacle'. In his preface he calls *The Dynasts* a 'Spectacle' and so the answer to the poem's first question would seem to be that the man who holds the mirror up to human nature is, naturally, the poet. But what *The Dynasts* shows is that Hardy would have us accept that there is a 'Prime mover of the gear', a Will which moves 'all humanity and vitalized matter'. So the answer which the first question implies may be inadequate because there is the problem of free will: does the poet hold the mirror freely or does this deterministic force merely impel him to do so? The human actions he shows in his work are predetermined and automatic, so isn't his writing equally a function of fate? Isn't he just another Bradley Headstone who has absolutely no imagination and freedom, but possesses a highly developed artificial memory? Isn't everything he writes simply dictated and conditioned by his memories, by decaying sense impressions? This is a notion which Coleridge indulges in order to destroy when he pursues Hartley's theory of association to its logical conclusion in the assumption that 'all acts of thought and attention' are the parts and products of a 'blind mechanism' and that therefore the page of *Biographia Literaria* on which he's scribbling this idea is 'the mere motion of my muscles and nerves' and these are 'set in motion from external causes equally passive'. But because he belongs unenthusiastically to the same empirical tradition as Hartley,

Hardy is unable to approach this problem with Coleridge's certainty that it's utter nonsense. All he can offer is the mysteriousness of an open question.

The next question concerns the mirror's penetrating, dart-like magic and this inevitably suggests falling in love: is that, too, merely a matter of mirrors? There's ample evidence in the novels and poems that Hardy thought it was. Edred Fitzpiers defines love as a 'subjective emotion' and when he sees Grace in a mirror believes she has appeared to him in a 'vision', though she's actually there in the room with him – the vision isn't real and neither is his love for her. This is the question the poem asks: is love meaningless, like art and action, because it's subjective? because it's predetermined like the iceberg and maiden ship in 'The Convergence of the Twain'? And the word 'start' suggests a horrified recognition – not a vision – of a truth which is forced upon us by someone else. Again, this could be the writer offering an unflattering mirror.

Bailey says the third stanza 'seems to symbolize memory, introspection, and conscience penetrating the gloss of everyday self-justification and revealing the "tincts" (stains) of the soul'. This is a Wemmick-like separation of business efficiency and imaginative privacy – the kind of separation between 'visioning powers' and the 'material screen' that Hardy is obliquely suggesting in 'The House of Silence', a poem he also, significantly, included in this volume. The taut, nagging, insistent tone of 'Moments of Vision' makes the 'night hours of ache' feel very real, and so the suggestion here doesn't seem to be that guilt is also another illusion, the last relic of a dead faith. Instead, the question is aimed more at why the conscience's incisive clarities have so little effect on our waking existence. The last mirror can 'test each mortal when unaware' – a strenuous idea this, and one which is simply asserted as being true, though it begs a number of questions: is there a tester? a figure like the Duke in *Measure for Measure*? a force which sets up tricky situations like apple-trees in gardens and watches to see what we make of them? which is watching and recording our actions when we are behaving normally and unthinkingly – mechanically, in fact? It's as though we, and not some puppet-master, are responsible for our routine actions – actions which aren't predetermined by that external force and which we are yet responsible for to something or someone else. Finally, this 'strange mirror' can catch our dying thoughts, our whole life – but where? The question suggests that they ought to have a spatial location, though the idea itself is the familiar one of the dying, especially the drowning, man seeing his whole life flash past him. For example, in his 'Confessions of an English Opium-Eater' De Quincey describes how his mother, after she had been rescued from drowning, 'saw in a moment her whole life, clotted in its forgotten incidents, arranged before her as in a mirror, not successively, but simultaneously'. For De Quincey the human brain is what he terms 'a mighty palimpsest' on which everlasting 'layers of ideas, images, feelings' have fallen 'softly as light'. And the mind's organising principles will not, he says, permit its 'ultimate repose to be troubled in the retrospect from dying moments, or from other great convulsions.' His certainty that the human mind is 'heaven-created' is implicit in this concept of mind as a deep palimpsest, but Hardy's final question – 'where?' – is scarcely a nod of agreement, however much De Quincey's 'retrospect from dying moments' resembles his own 'last thoughts, whole life foul or fair'.

When William Archer suggested to him that many of the love letters he used to transcribe as a boy for the girls from his village 'remained written in your mind in sympathetic ink, only waiting for the heat of creation to bring them out', Hardy was understandably reluctant to accept Archer's reduction of his imagination to mere mechanical memory. His reply, which glances at De Quincey, was fair but unenthusiastic: 'Possibly, in a sub-conscious way. The human mind is a sort of palimpsest, I suppose; and it's hard to say what records may not lurk in it.' And in the last stanza of 'Moments of Vision' he appears to imply that all these records can be caught in one moment, like a breath misting a mirror.

These, as I try to understand the poem, are some of the issues it raises. Shelley's moon-struck sophist who sees his own shadow projected onto the world's 'vast mirror' doesn't offer an adequate identification because the reiterated question nags at the idea that there is some non-human cause behind the impressions and perceptions such a mirror would reflect, a kind of thing-in-itself which is screened by the surface phenomena it upholds or causes.

When Hardy speaks of the mirror's magic he's referring to a 'magic mirror' in which one is traditionally supposed to see the future. And this is partly what he means by 'the running of Time's far glass' in 'Near Lanivet, 1872', a poem that describes a sudden vision of the future and which he placed near the beginning of *Moments of Vision*. It tells how Emma, tired by their walk, leant against a 'stunted handpost' on the crest of a hill. She had laid her arms on the post's arms, her open palms 'stretched out to each end of them' and her 'sad face sideways thrown':

> Her white-clothed form at this dim-lit cease of day
> Made her look as one crucified
> In my gaze at her from the midst of the dusty way,
> And hurriedly 'Don't', I cried.

The atmosphere of this poem – the murky twilight, dusty road, their fatigue – feels electrically charged, like the atmosphere in 'The Musical Box' and 'The Revisitation', and Hardy associated such close, static warmth with telepathic communications with the past or future. Here, he shows how he and Emma gave an ominous significance to a present incident and, aware of each other's thoughts, tried to ignore it by staying silent. Eventually she admits her fears and he 'lightly' reassures her. His reassurance sounds hollow, like the husband's in 'Honeymoon Time at an Inn' where a broken mirror releases another moment of premonitory vision. She replies that she's thinking of a spiritual crucifixion and it's then that they both share the vision they've been trying to shun:

> And we dragged on and on, while we seemed to see
> In the running of Time's far glass
> Her crucified, as she had wondered if she might be
> Some day. – Alas, alas!

Like the rest of the poem this last stanza is slack and too prosaic, but as this is another of those ambitious poems about human relationships it ought to be respected. It establishes the atmosphere and setting of a particular moment in time as it was shared by two lovers. The actual scene seems proleptically to mirror not just their mood at the time but all that their marriage later became. They are seen to have 'dragged on and on' in the kind of 'atmosphere of stale familiarity' that Henchard and his wife ploddingly endure in the opening pages of *The Mayor of Casterbridge*.

A different kind of vision occurs in 'The Pedigree':

> I bent in the deep of night
> Over a pedigree the chronicler gave
> As mine; and as I bent there, half-unrobed,
> The uncurtained panes of my window-square let in the watery
> light

Of the moon in its old age:
And green-rheumed clouds were hurrying past where mute and cold it globed
Like a drifting dolphin's eye seen through a lapping wave.

This is the setting for the vision, carefully established as in 'Near Lanivet'. Because the clouds are called 'green-rheumed' and the moon is compared to a dolphin's eye (it was a 'dying dolphin' in the first edition) a natural symbolism is again being used. The moon-eye and the clouds are not just pathetic fallacies – they represent and symbolise the pathetic fallacy, and this prepares us for the way the tangled branches of his family tree change into a 'seared and cynic face' which tips him a wink and a nod towards the window 'like a Mage/Enchanting me to gaze again thereat.' He now sees into the window, not through it:

It was a mirrow now,
And in it a long perspective I could trace
Of my begetters, dwindling backward each past each
All with the kindred look,
Whose names had since been inked down in their place
On the recorder's book,
Generation and generation of my mien, and build, and brow.

An infinitely receding series of family faces – the visualisation of the names on the page in front of him – is reflected on a window which has become a magician's mirror. Like the magic mirror in 'Moments of Vision' it works in the night hours when it throws his mind back on him, in the atavistic sense of 'throw back', and reveals that his actions are not prompted by his free will. His every move, thought and word is shown in the glass as 'long forestalled by their so making it.' This is the vision of necessity in *The Dynasts* where 'Earth's jackaclocks' are 'fugled by one will' just as his actions here are paced by his ancestral 'fuglemen'. And this is his conclusion:

Said I then, sunk in tone,
'I am merest mimicker and counterfeit! –
Though thinking, *I am I,*
And what I do I do myself alone.'
– The cynic twist of the page thereat unknit
Back to its normal figure, having wrought its purport wry,
The Mage's mirror left the window-square,
And the stained moon and drift retook their places there.

He sounds like Richard III facing up to the mechanism of retribution which he thought he had complete control over; but the deterministic conclusion is made trickier by the fact that what he sees is quite clearly projected by himself, and so the mirror-vision is a moon-struck sophism. The branches of his family tree are like a Rohrschach-blot into which he projects a visual shape and an intellectual value. He is the cynical magician. As I mentioned in Chapter 5 'mimicker' was originally 'continuator', a word he uses in 'Wessex Heights', so he is asking himself whether his art is a forgery in the sense of being dictated by fate and memory, by the kind of deterministic process that the 'strange continuator' of 'Wessex Heights' is enslaved by. However, his conclusion that it's a counterfeit is only a provisional, fugitive impression, a reflection of himself. Like the dead God in 'God's Funeral' it is 'man-projected'. But for all this the poem is somehow dissatisfying – its elaborate form seems to mask a lack of real involvement with the idea it's exploring. There is none of the terrifying, constrained pressure that there is in 'Wessex Heights'.

Its backward-dwindling generations reappear later in *Moments of Vision:*

I see the hands of the generations
  That owned each shiny familiar thing
In play on its knobs and indentations,
  And with its ancient fashioning
    Still dallying:

Hands behind hands, growing paler and paler,
  As in a mirror a candle-flame
Shows images of itself, each frailer
  As it recedes, though the eye may frame
    Its shape the same.

The next three stanzas of 'Old Furniture' beautifully detail a series of events which are both routine and mysterious, domestic and visionary:

On the clock's dull dial a foggy finger,
  Moving to set the minutes right
With tentative touches that lift and linger
  In the wont of a moth on a summer night,
    Creeps to my sight.

On this old viol, too, fingers are dancing –
As whilom – just over the strings by the nut,
The tip of a bow receding, advancing
In airy quivers, as if it would cut
The plaintive gut.

And I see a face by that box for tinder,
Glowing forth in fits from the dark,
And fading again, as the linten cinder
Kindles red at the flinty spark,
Or goes out stark.

The pieces of glossy furniture are more than solid facts because their patina and their ancestral associations spiritualise them. Hardy describes a similar effect near the end of *Far from the Madding Crowd* when Gabriel Oak and Bathsheba sit down together in his cottage,

> the fire dancing in their faces, and upon the old furniture,
> all a-sheenen
> Wi' long years o' handlen,
> that formed Oak's array of household possessions, which sent back a dancing reflection in reply.

This offers more than just the obvious prose-parallel. The lines Hardy quotes are from Barnes's 'Woak Hill' and one of the most striking features of Barnes's poetry is just this quality of warm, reflected light. The 'sheen' of things fascinates him:

As I went eastward, while the zun did zet,
His yollow light on bough by bough did sheen.

An' there, among the gil'cups by the knap,
Below the elems, cow by cow did sheen.

The 'sheen' in 'Lowshot Light' and a whole host of similar light effects in Barnes's poems are neatly introduced into 'The Last Signal', Hardy's tribute to his friend:

Silently I footed by an uphill road
That led from my abode to a spot yew-boughed;
Yellowly the sun sloped low down to westward,
And dark was the east with cloud.

Then, amid the shadow of that livid sad east,
Where the light was least, and a gate stood wide,
Something flashed the fire of the sun that was facing it,
Like a brief blaze on that side.

Looking hard and harder I knew what it meant –
The sudden shine sent from the livid east scene;
It meant the west mirrored by the coffin of my friend there,
Turning to the road from his green,

To take his last journey forth – he who in his prime
Trudged so many a time from that gate athwart the land!
Thus a farewell to me he signalled on his grave-way,
As with a wave of his hand.

This fine poem is also in *Moments of Vision* and it, too, sparks a vision. Again, it's a very human vision: the 'sudden shine' is like a 'wave of his hand'. It is entirely apt.

There is a most beautiful vision in Barnes's 'The Wold Clock' where the speaker remembers the family's clock and fondly wonders:

Who now do wind his chaïn, a-twin'd
As he do run his hours,
Or meäke a gloss to sheen across
His door, wi' goolden flow'rs,
Since he've a-sounded out the last
Still hours our dear good mother pass'd?

These lines are really marvellous. They're both Dutch and visionary. Barnes transforms the ordinary action of carrying a bowl of flowers past the polished clock and their sudden, passing 'sheen' into something quite extraordinary. Together, the glossy light, the woman behind it and the golden flowers make a factual vision, and Hardy clearly admired this effect for he's deploying it in 'Old Furniture'. What he admires is not just the rubbed smoothness and glossy depths of the furniture but a mysterious sense of human presence which inheres there. His ancestors' routine actions come back strangely and tentatively, like ghostly moths trying to get in from outside. These lives return as they were and do something quite ordinary like light the fire or set the clock, and here the comparison of their lifting, lingering fingers to the way a moth taps and stops and taps again further along a lighted window is beautifully accurate and at the same time mysterious. It has the same significance as the 'mothy and warm' night of dying in 'Afterwards' or the 'mothy curfew-tide' when the dead start whispering through the summer darkness in 'Friends Beyond'. It means that they are trying to get through to the living, that they are already there in the sheen of dark, polished wood.

* * *

'Moments of Vision' is the only symbolist poem Hardy ever wrote: it isolates a symbolic, magic mirror which is then applied in poems like 'Old Furniture', 'The Pedigree', 'Honeymoon Time at an Inn', 'Near Lanivet' and 'The Last Signal'. But the significance of this symbol isn't exhausted with these poems, for it has another meaning – the 'magic mirror' is also a 'magic lantern'. During the Victorian period magic lanterns were very popular family toys and they consist, a contemporary encyclopaedia explains, of 'a lantern body to contain the source of light and the reflectors, an optical system and a slot to accommodate the slide-frame.' So they also make use of light reflected in a mirror. Like our modern slide-projectors they illuminate a single 'transparency', a 'photograph or picture on glass or other transparent substance, intended to be seen by transmitted light', and this is the meaning of the word in: 'That mirror/Which makes of men a transparency.' As in the passage I quoted earlier from *The Dynasts* 'transparency' may suggest X-rays, and although they had been discovered in 1895, nine years before Hardy published the first part of his epic drama, he had already described an X-ray effect long before when Diggory Venn, in *The Return of the Native,* holds an ordinary oil lantern up to Thomasin's face and

> her several thoughts and fractions of thoughts, as signalled by the changes on her face, were exhibited by the light to the utmost nicety. An ingenuous, transparent life was disclosed; as if the flow of her existence could be seen passing within her.

Here, thought and emotion are again revealed as a visible essence. This transparent effect seems to have appealed to Hardy because he describes it again in the passage at the beginning of *The Mayor of Casterbridge* where Michael and Susan Henchard are drearily trailing along a dusty road, bored with each other. She has a plain face, but when she looks down at her baby she becomes pretty, partly because she glows with love for the child, but particularly because in the action of looking down 'her features caught slantwise the rays of the strongly-coloured sun, which made transparencies of her eyelids and nostrils and set fire on her lips.' In both cases this irradiating and transfiguring effect is being compared to an illuminated slide in a magic lantern. As I suggested in the last chapter such an effect is similar to the moments when time appears to stand still on warm summer nights. It's described again in 'Wives in the Sere':

I

Never a careworn wife but shows,
  If a joy suffuse her,
Something beautiful to those
  Patient to peruse her,
Some one charm the world unknows
  Precious to a muser,
Haply what, ere years were foes,
  Moved her mate to choose her.

II

But, be it a hint of rose
  That an instant hues her,
Or some early light or pose
  Wherewith thought renews her –
Seen by him at full, ere woes
  Practised to abuse her –
Sparely comes it, swiftly goes,
  Time again subdues her.

This isn't an especially important poem, though the repeated feminine rhymes and the trochaic metre help to suffuse it with the softly blushing warmth it's describing.

Hardy again describes this effect of light beaming from the face in *Jude* where he's echoing Shelley's lamp of the soul:

> Through the intervening fortnight he ran about and smiled outwardly at his inward thoughts, as if they were people meeting and nodding to him – smiled with that singularly beautiful irradiation which is seen to spread on young faces at the inception of some glorious idea, as if a supernatural lamp were held inside their transparent natures, giving rise to the flattering fancy that heaven lies about them then.

Hardy's self-portrait in ' "In the Seventies" ' parallels this:

In the seventies I was bearing in my breast,
Penned tight,
Certain starry thoughts that threw a magic light
On the worktimes and the soundless hours of rest
In the seventies; aye, I bore them in my breast
Penned tight.

This in its turn is very close to another description of Jude who, just before Arabella tosses a pig's pizzle at him, is similarly locked up in his own dreams of future success:

> In his deep concentration on these transactions of the future Jude's walk had slackened, and he was now standing quite still, looking at the ground as though the future were thrown thereon by a magic lantern. On a sudden something smacked him sharply in the ear, and he became aware that a soft cold substance had been flung at him, and had fallen at his feet.

The 'supernatural lamp' of the earlier passage is characteristically naturalised as a magic lantern. And the magic vision which it projects on to reality abruptly disappears when a 'soft cold substance' smacks Jude on the ear. The body's desires and the mind's ideals are hostile, separate and, even as the man and the woman converge, totally divergent. In *Jude* Arabella, pig-flesh, sex and circumstances are all one, and they are stronger than Jude's vision; but in ' "In the Seventies" ' the raw coldness of circumstances, like a freezing night fog, is kept at bay by his magic vision:

In the seventies those who met me did not know
Of the vision
That immuned me from the chillings of misprision
And the damps that choked my goings to and fro
In the seventies; yea, those nodders did not know
Of the vision.

In the seventies nought could darken or destroy it,
Locked in me,
Though as delicate as lamp-worm's lucency;
Neither mist nor murk could weaken or alloy it
In the seventies! – could not darken or destroy it,
Locked in me.

The vision's delicate texture is compared, in a kind of pun, to a 'lamp-worm's lucency': it is partly the light of a glow worm, partly the light of a magic lantern or 'supernatural lamp'. This is the mind's own light. For Coleridge this 'light, this glory, this fair luminous mist' is the soul, his 'shaping spirit of Imagination' which transforms the 'inanimate cold world', and though he adopts Coleridge's terms, Hardy lacks this kind of mystical confidence in the structure and powers of the mind, while at the same time valuing a transcendental radiance in it. And this valuation is there in 'The Youth who Carried a Light' which is also in *Moments of Vision* and which again shows the mind's power to drive the cold darkness back:

I saw him pass as the new day dawned,
Murmuring some musical phrase;
Horses were drinking and floundering in the pond,
And the tired stars thinned their gaze;
Yet these were not the spectacles at all that he conned,
But an inner one, giving out rays.

Such was the thing in his eye, walking there,
The very and visible thing,
A close light, displacing the gray of the morning air,
And the tokens that the dark was taking wing;
And was it not the radiance of a purpose rare
That might ripe to its accomplishing?

The 'close light' here and the visionary radiance in the other poems are most emphatically not the same as the 'visions' which the youth in 'After a Romantic Day' projects on to the blank railway cutting. We must distinguish between real vision and fantasy even though their results are identical: fantasy involves a separation between what the mind sees and the environment that serves as a projection screen for it, but vision, in certain cases, possesses an active power to transform fact.

In 'First Sight of Her and After', which is the equivalent of 'After a Romantic Day' in *Moments of Vision,* the lover's slight smugness in the last two lines is a delicate joke at this distinction between fact and fantasy:

A day is drawing to its fall
I had not dreamed to see;
The first of many to enthrall

My spirit, will it be?
Or is this eve the end of all
Such new delight for me?

I journey home: the pattern grows
Of moonshades on the way:
'Soon the first quarter, I suppose,'
Sky-glancing travellers say;
I realize that it, for those,
Has been a common day.

This is a gently perfect little poem. The stolid, slightly wistful sobriety of the other travellers' practical remarks on the new moon plays beautifully against the youth's superior consciousness. And this begs a large question: is there any way of connecting his moon-struck idealism with their utilitarianism? Can fact and fantasy combine and co-operate to produce vision? In many respects Hardy's answer would seem to be that they can't. In 'God's Funeral' and 'A Plaint to Man' God is a 'projected' lantern-slide, and so is the Muse in 'Rome: The Vatican'. Love, religion and literature are all subjective, he appears to be saying.

In his essay on 'The Profitable Reading of Fiction' Hardy again uses the magic lantern as an implicit metaphor for creativity. He says that a reader should inquire whether a novel is 'based on faithful imagination, less the transcript than the similitude of material fact', and he goes on to say that the really 'perspicacious reader will do more than this':

> He will see what his author is aiming at, and by affording full scope to his own insight, catch the vision which the writer has in his eye, and is endeavouring to project upon the paper, even while it half eludes him.

It's as though he wears his imagination like a miner's helmet. However, in comparing it to a projector Hardy is really doing little more than modernise Locke's comparison of the mind to a *camera obscura*, except – and this is an important qualification – he's giving it an active quality which Locke denied it. Again, we come up against his compromise between a passive empiricism and an active idealism. I've called the magic lantern a symbol, but it's a particularly physical symbol of the mind which makes it into a piece of rather old-fashioned furniture which is nowadays to be found gathering dust in attics and junk shops.

The imagination, though it transforms and 'translates' fact, has become a fact itself.

In this note from the *Life* Hardy formulates the relationship between fact and imagination:

> So, then, if Nature's defects must be looked in the face and transcribed, whence arises the *art* in poetry and novel-writing? which must certainly show art, or it becomes merely mechanical reporting. I think the art lies in making these defects the basis of a hitherto unperceived beauty, by irradiating them with 'the light that never was' on their surface, but is seen to be latent in them by the spiritual eye.

This seems to me to differ from the simple projection of imaginative shadows on to sterile face which occurs in 'After a Romantic Day' where the huge disparity between the mental vision and its environment points to the flimsiness of the one and the inimical ugliness of the other. Here, it seems that there must be a co-operation between fact and imagination in the idea that a latent light is elicited from outside ugliness by the 'spiritual eye'. The 'light that never was' is a Wordsworthian phrase and though it's misapplied in the way Wordsworth invites, these lines from 'Tintern Abbey':

> all the mighty world
> Of eye, and ear, – both what they half create,
> And what perceive,

elaborate a similar combination. They, too, make a compromise between observed fact and imaginative vision. But, to alter the terms slightly, for Hardy this would mean a happy marriage between his utilitarian architect and his romantic heiress, and this seems totally impossible. For Hardy, circumstantial fact encroaches on and destroys imaginative freedom. Even the great Napoleon is:

> Moved like a figure on a lantern-slide.
> Which, much amazing uninitiate eyes,
> The all-compelling crystal pane but drags
> Whither the showman wills.

The Will is like the 'deft manipulator' of the slides in a 'phantasmagoric show', except that it can't laugh at its own work. It is the 'Great Unshaken'.

This is very similar to a passage I quoted earlier from *The World as*

Will and Idea where Schopenhauer says that the immovable Will manifests itself as the visibility of all phenomena just as 'the magic-lantern shows many different pictures.' For Schopenhauer, as for Hardy, there are moments when the mind can cast off 'those mechanical instincts which are guided by no motive or knowledge' – routine, reflex actions – and attain an imaginative freedom. Then 'the light of knowledge penetrates into the workshop of the blindly active will, and illuminates the vegetative functions of the human organism.' This, says Schopenhauer, is 'clairvoyance', and the scenes in *The Dynasts* where light penetrates visibility and transparently reveals the workings of the Will are based on this idea. Similarly, the clairvoyant moments in 'Near Lanivet, 1872' and 'Honeymoon Time at an Inn' are also insights into the 'blindly active will'. But they are not true freedoms, for they only reveal a total subordination to necessity, like the seeming vision in 'The Pedigree'. Louis MacNeice puts this idea best in this comment on 'the paradox of the Will':

> One supposes the Will to be the great instrument of individuality, of freedom, and one lets it rip, then cannot put the drag on, the Will runs away with the lot of us, we have no more choice in the matter than a falling stone. Hence Schopenhauer's view of the Will as determinist tyranny and his opposition to it of *Vorstellung,* the freedom which is freedom from the Will and from narrow personality, the presentation to the mind's eye in a crystal of entities which are not subordinate to any practical purpose, the death that remains visible and is not, as life is, the death of shape or pattern.

For Schopenhauer, the artist cuts free of the Will and his own desires and discovers a state of 'pure perception', a 'clear vision of the world'. Eliot calls this the release from the 'practical desire', while MacNeice sees it as the understanding which is beyond 'any practical purpose'.

In 'The Thing Unplanned' Hardy shows how a sudden moment of impulsive freedom can triumph over all the ingrained monotonies of narrow, fixed personality:

> The white winter sun struck its stroke on the bridge,
> The meadow-rills rippled and gleamed
> As I left the thatched post-office, just by the ridge,
> And dropped in my pocket her long tender letter,
> With: 'This must be snapped! it is more than it seemed;
> And now is the opportune time!'

But against what I willed worked the surging sublime
Of the thing that I did – the thing better!

This is a moment of ecstasy and freedom which is won by going against the grain and contradicting a cautiously deliberate reflex action. It is an intense valuation of 'what the nonce outpours'. Unfortunately, the phrase 'surging sublime', though it's impulsive, isn't as fresh as it could be, and this is also a problem in 'Midnight on the Great Western' where the possibility of a transcending vision and freedom is given a stale expression:

Knows your soul a sphere, O journeying boy,
Our rude realms far above,
Whence with spacious vision you mark and mete
This region of sin that you find you in,
But are not of?

Like Schopenhauer's state of 'pure perception' – a state of perfect detachment which transcends the Will's deterministic tyranny – the boy's 'spacious vision' lifts him above the train's monotonously practical rhythms and severely dreary interior. But the language – 'rude realms', 'spacious vision', 'mark and mete', 'region of sin' – lacks clarity, sounds inflated, and is imprecise. Hardy works much better with the concrete details at the beginning of the poem:

In the third-class seat sat the journeying boy,
And the roof-lamp's oily flame
Played down on his listless form and face,
Bewrapt past knowing to what he was going,
Or whence he came.

In the band of his hat the journeying boy
Had a ticket stuck; and a string
Around his neck bore the key of his box,
That twinkled gleams of the lamp's sad beams
Like a living thing.

Again, reflected light symbolises a vision, but a vision which exists in time and not above it, for it hints the future the boy is travelling towards. The only 'key' to life which he will discover is to put a rope round his neck and hang himself. He carries both this noosed key and his coffin with him.

The earlier 'A Commonplace Day' has something of the same concentration upon the inescapably and deadeningly factual:

I part the fire-gnawed logs,
Rake forth the embers, spoil the busy flames, and lay the ends
Upon the shining dogs;
Further and further from the nooks the twilight's stride extends,
And beamless black impends.

He has utterly wasted the day; outside, the rain is sliding down the windows – it's a situation of Baudelairean spleen, a mixture of despair at himself, at his parsimonious routine, and at the dreary ugliness of things. Out of it Hardy tries to rescue a sense of worthwhileness, an 'enkindling ardency' which is the opposite of 'beamless black', like the 'close light' of ambition in 'The Youth who Carried a Light'. It's an idealistic impulse like 'the thing better' which, he suggests, can eventually transform reality. This is what the thrush throwing its song against the wind and darkening landscape stands for. Again, the difficulty is that because the language – 'ardency', 'maturer glows' – is overblown and jaded, it carries no conviction, while the description of his careful dousing of the fire is close and accurate. Here, he's convicting himself of negation, identifying himself with a mean-spirited, dampening hostility to kindling idealisms, and at the same time showing how, because of this attitude, he just plods on with his daily routine of tidying the hearth and carefully saving some wood for next day. He knows that time and again his cautious, mean practicality will 'spoil the busy flames' – a process he describes factually and accurately. This total separation between fact and imagination has bad effects, resulting in empty verbosities and plangent sonorities, and a mixture of fact and translatese:

Wanly upon the panes
The rain slides, as have slid since morn my colourless thoughts.

And even his factual description contains grandiose phrases like 'beamless black impends'. Really, the problem is whether Hardy can unite observed fact with free, active imagination.

He points the way to such a unity in 'The Clock of the Years' where a 'Spirit' makes time's clock run backwards:

He answered, 'Peace';
And called her up – as last before me;
Then younger, younger she freshed, to the year
I first had known
Her woman-grown,
And I cried, 'Cease!' –

Against the ticking mechanism the lovely verb 'freshed' moves like a sudden transcendence, but the Spirit refuses to stop the clock:

> And she waned child-fair,
> And to babyhood.

And then 'smalled till she was nought at all'. He is worse off than when he started because his memories of her have totally disappeared. These memories are represented, rather than actually visualised, as a rapid succession of images which are like the frames of a film being run backwards. The momentum of these images can't be halted; they are fixed like the Will's 'fixed foresightless dream' in *The Dynasts*. Significantly, the poem's epigraph – 'A spirit passed before my face; the hair of my flesh stood up' – also refers to a dream. This is the nightmarish vision which Eliphaz describes in *Job*:

> Now a thing was secretly brought to me, and mine ear received a little thereof.
> In thoughts from the visions of the night, when deep sleep falleth on men,
> Fear came upon me, and trembling, which made all my bones to shake.
> Then a spirit passed before my face; the hair of my flesh stood up:
> It stood still, but I could not discern the form thereof: an image was before mine eyes, there was silence, and I heard a voice saying,
> Shall mortal man be more just than God? shall a man be more pure than his maker?

These verses are intensely dramatic and by quoting from them Hardy means that the terror they communicate was his when he had his nightmare or saw his vision. Eliphaz is describing a fearful theophany, but Hardy is describing fear of an utter oblivion where all memories disappear, the 'second death' that so perturbed him. Possessing all his memories of his wife visually like a pile of transparencies or photographs it's as though he can flick through them and give her a jerky life which in facts kills her off, for the memories are fixed in the Spirit's 'checkless griff', a kind of deterministic tyranny which runs down into a void. It's as though he is identifying the act of remembering with this tyranny. Memory has become a terrifying mechanism and this is a variation on the experience of being in bondage to it which he describes in 'Wessex Heights'. And so this poem, referring as it does to a further nightmare vision, is another 'Lockean nightmare' as Oliver Sacks calls *The Mind of a Mnemonist*.

However, in 'A Procession of Dead Days' there is no sense of the terrors of total visual recall:

> I see the ghost of a perished day;
> I know his face, and the feel of his dawn:
> 'Twas he who took me far away
>   To a spot strange and gray:
> Look at me, Day, and then pass on,
> But come again: yes, come anon!
>
> Enters another into view;
> His features are not cold or white,
> But rosy as a vein seen through:
>   Too soon he smiles adieu.
> Adieu, O ghost-day of delight;
> But come and grace my dying sight.

In this poem the act of remembering is very definitely like operating a projector. Hardy introduces the slides like this:

> Enters another into view.
>
> Enters the day that brought the kiss.
>
> Ah, this one. Yes, I know his name.
>
> The next stands forth in his morning clothes.

And he comments on the visualised image in each stanza. In the first he's showing a photograph of the day when he left for Cornwall where he first met his wife, in the next three stanzas he describes three scenes during their courtship, the fifth is a wedding photograph of 'misty blue' morning clothes, and the next seems to refer to some terrible misery that can't be evaded or forgotten: 'I close my eyes; yet still is he/In front there, looking mastery.' Then the last stanzas describe the day of his wife's death. Again, there is that effect of reflected light in the shrewd detail of the dawning light catching the fringe of ivy leaves on the sill of his bedroom window:

> I did not know what better or worse
>   Chancings might bless or curse
> When his original glossed the thrums
> Of ivy, bringing that which numbs.

This is the same daylight that hardens on the wall in 'The Going'.

The repeated word 'day' has a Tennysonian reference which shows just how much Hardy's imagination is working with memories in 'A Procession of Dead Days'. He made this note in his journal when he was staying in Cornwall in 1870, the time he's referring to in the early stanzas of the poem:

> Went with E.L.G. to Beeny Cliff. She on horse-back....On the cliff....'The tender grace of a day,' etc. The run down to the edge. The coming home.

The line he quotes is from Tennyson's elegy on Hallam, 'Break, Break, Break', which he remembered partly, I would think, because of the similarity of the cliff-top settings as much as for his own sense of being parted from the woman he was in love with. Fifty years later, he draws upon a combination of personal recollection and literary reminscence – the two seem inextricably fused – in a poem where the emotion of loss is altogether stronger because now they've been parted finally by death, not evening. Tennyson's lines: 'But the tender grace of aday that is dead/Will never come back to me' supply the 'dead days' of Hardy's title – days that come back to him as ghostly memories. The second day is emphatically distinguished as not having a ghostly or cadaverous pallor: it is 'rosy as a vein seen through'. And this transparent effect means (though this poem is from *Late Lyrics and Earlier*) that we are in the same territory as some of the poems in *Moments of Vision*. What Hardy means by this line is best shown by this passage from *The Return of the Native*:

> Litters of young rabbits came out from their forms to sun themselves upon hillocks, the hot beams blazing through the delicate tissue of each thin-fleshed ear, and firing it to a blood-red transparency in which the veins could be seen.

This is clearly similar to the transparent effect in *The Mayor of Casterbridge* which I quoted earlier, and it's also close to the smiling, instant 'hint of rose' in 'Wives in the Sere'. So the day he is describing is suffused and irradiated with joy, with a sunny feeling of intense life. It has a transcendental, visionary quality, an absolute presence and permanence.

He describes a similar effect in a curious poem called 'She who Saw Not' which is also in *Late Lyrics and Earlier*. In it a woman says she can't see something in a house that endows the 'common scene' with an unforgettably 'richened impress'. The 'Sage' tells her to look again:

> '– Go anew, Lady, – in by the right....
> Well: why does your face not shine like the face of Moses?'
> '– I found no moving thing there save the light
> And shadow flung on the wall by the outside roses.'

She looks again and sees an utterly average man looking at the sun:

> 'As the rays reach in through the open door,
> And he looks at his hand, and the sun glows through his fingers,
> While he's thinking thoughts whose tenour is no more
> To me than the swaying rose-tree shade that lingers.'

However, years later in a dank foggy time when 'the form in the flesh had gone' she saw: 'As a vision what she had missed when the real beholding.' This is a poor poem which reads like a rewrite of 'The House of Silence' with its fable of materialistic ordinariness and 'vision ing powers', but its combination of roses, sunlight through living flesh, and vision is revealingly close to both 'rosy as a vein seen through' and the other transparent effects I've mentioned. The clumsy reference to Moses, partly because it is so clumsy, adds to the meaning.

In *Exodus* Moses has a vision of God – 'the sight of the glory of the Lord was like devouring fire on the top of the mount in the eyes of the children of Israel' – and when he returns from Sinai with the tablets of stone, 'the skin of his face shone'. Hardy refers to Moses's visionary smile several times in his work, and he was probably interested in it because it gives a glowing visibility to a spiritual vision. It's also very similar to the 'supernatural lamp' which seems to be held inside Jude's transparent face when he gives one of his intensely idealistic smiles. Hardy obviously associated light shining through living flesh with vision and here he is again naturalising the supernatural because he presents the spiritual vision in biological terms. It exists physically as blood, veins, tissue and light. In 'The Phantom Horsewoman' the 'vision of heretofore' is drawn 'rose-bright' – again we have a transcending vision which is also physical. The bright rose is both love and pink flesh. In 'The Fallow Deer at the Lonely House' the couple are lit by the deer's eyes which are called 'lamps of rosy dyes', so its eyes which beam with light are both natural and supernatural lamps. This vision – and it's a delicately beautiful one – irradiates the couple's domestic routine.

Sometimes these transparencies have a kind of permanent existence, unlike the memories in 'The Clock of the Years'. In 'The Absolute Explains' the Absolute shows that Time is an illusion because everything that seems to have died or disappeared still exists:

There fadeless, fixed, were dust-dead flowers
Remaining still in blow;
Elsewhere, wild love-making in bowers;
Hard by, that irised bow
Of years ago.

There were my ever memorable
Glad days of pilgrimage,
Coiled like a precious parchment fell,
Illumined page by page,
Unhurt by age.

Hardy was horrified that anyone or anything can simply disappear into oblivion and that memory, which was his way of preserving existence, is also perishable. In 'His Immortality' a dead man is gradually forgotten by the people who knew him, until he becomes a 'spectral mannikin':

Lastly I ask – now old and chill –
If aught of him remain unperished still;
And find, in me alone, a feeble spark,
Dying amid the dark.

In the *Biographia* Coleridge speculates that 'all thoughts are in themselves imperishable', not perishable as they are in 'His Immortality'

> and, that if the intelligent faculty should be rendered more comprehensive, it would require only a different and apportioned organization, – *the body celestial* instead of *the body terrestrial*, – to bring before every human soul the collective experience of its whole past existence. And this, this, perchance, is the dread book of judgement, in the mysterious hieroglyphics of which every idle word is recorded! Yea, in the very nature of a living spirit, it may be more possible that heaven and earth should pass away, than that a single act, a single thought, should be loosened or lost from that living chain of causes, with all the links of which, conscious or unconscious, the free-will, our only absolute Self, is co-extensive and co-present.

This is similar to both 'The Absolute Explains' and De Quincey's palimpsest, and in his very last poem Hardy says:

> Let Time roll backward if it will;
> (Magians who drive the midnight quill
> With brain aglow
> Can see it so,)
> What I have learnt no man shall know.
>
> And if my vision range beyond
> The blinkered sight of souls in bond,
> – By truth made free –
> I'll let all be,
> And show to no man what I see.

Like Coleridge he appears to consider that there may be a 'dread book of judgement' in which every event, thought and word is recorded, a kind of absolute memory even more detailed and retentive than that of Luria's mnemonist. However, the combination of 'brain' and 'aglow', 'sight' and 'vision', insists on that familiar combination of physicality and spirituality. The vision in 'The Phantom Horsewoman' is also seen 'in his brain' and this suggests a physical concept of mind as an electro-chemical organism, rather than a transcendental unity. And when Hardy tries to lift memory above our temporal and spatial dimensions in 'The Absolute Explains' his success is limited because the memories are not particularised or visualised. The poem doesn't persuade us of the reality of the moons, flowers and rainbow it lists, and after so much visibility one is conditioned to operate the sign-seeker's criterion of proof, to ask not just 'where?' as Hardy himself does in 'Moments of Vision' but to demand to see them.

'The Interloper', which is in *Moments of Vision*, is much more satisfactory because its memories are particularised and given that sense of permanent presence which is only stated in 'The Absolute Explains':

> There are three folk driving in a quaint old chaise,
> And the cliff-side track looks green and fair;
> I view them talking in quiet glee
> As they drop down towards the puffin's lair
> By the roughest of ways;
> But another with the three rides on, I see,
> Whom I like not to be there!

Like the invisible spirit in 'The Musical Box' or the ghosts that mingle with the officers at the Duchess of Richmond's ball in *The Dynasts*, the interloper is a future shadow threatening a happy present. It is 'that under which best lives corrode'. The poem keeps its images moving with a fluid mixture of ambs and anapaests:

> Next
> A dwelling appears by a slow sweet stream
> Where two sit happy and half in the dark:
> They read, helped out by a frail-wick'd gleam,
> Some rhythmic text.

And as in 'A Procession of Dead Days' a spoken commentary plays over these images of threatened happiness:

> Ah,
> Yet a goodlier scene than that succeeds;
> People on a lawn – quite a crowd of them. Yes,
> And they chatter and ramble as fancy leads.

This commentary appears to be spontaneously provoked by the images, as if they're gradually clearing into sharp focus, and there is the same sense of absolute visual presence that there is in *The Dynasts*. The voice stops and starts as the eye moves over the remembered scene: 'People on a lawn – quite a crowd of them. Yes.' And this sheer cinematic presence is there again in:

> In a tedious trampling crowd yet later –
> Who shall bare the years, the years! –
> In a tedious trampling crowd yet later,
> When silvery singings were dumb;
> In a crowd uncaring what time might fate her,
> Mid murks of night I stood to await her,
> And the twanging of iron wheels gave out the signal that she was come.
>
> She said with a travel-tired smile –
> Who shall lift the years O! –
> She said with a travel-tired smile,
> Half scared by scene so strange;
> She said, outworn by mile on mile,
> The blurred lamps wanning her face the while,
> 'O Love, I am here; I am with you!'... Ah, that there should have come a change!

'The Change' is composed of a series of such radiant images barred over by repetition and the refrain. These two stanzas, brilliantly arranged and compressed, are like a scene from one of the novels presented in a few lines of verse – two lovers meeting secretly, his intensely idealistic love, her uncertainty, and the whole development of the story implied in the refrain. The murky night, the crowd, the 'twanging of iron wheels' are part both of the vision itself and of all that's hostile to it, like the raw darkness in ' "In the Seventies" '. The poem is filled with a strange light, the 'purple zone' of love, and at the same time insists on the metallic harshness of external things which have nothing to do with love or happiness. The 'blurred lamps' which make her face wan are utilitarian objects, not supernatural lamps, though at the time their light and the light of his vision may have seemed one. The vision here is trembling between the idealistic 'magic' in the first stanza and the reality of a tired and nervous woman arriving at a railway station, uncertain, her face pale instead of radiantly shining. These stanzas carry a complexity of emotional response which give them the depth and substance of a lengthy story, and like many of the poems I discussed in the last chapter they compress a narrative into a very short space. The images are so strangely placeless, so much like a shadowy meeting somewhere in last-century Russia, in some anonymous central European city.

But 'The Change' reads like the first draft of the best poem in *Moments of Vision* and one of the best poems of this century – 'During Wind and Rain'. This time the lamps are candles:

> They sing their dearest songs –
> He, she, all of them – yea,
> Treble and tenor and bass,
>   And one to play;
> With candles mooning each face....
>   Ah, no; the years O!
> How the sick leaves reel down in throngs!

The beautiful image of the candles 'mooning each face' is both real and visionary, while the blurred lamps in 'The Change' point only to a separation between hard facts and imagination, not a co-operation between them. This is a central moment of vision and it's a perfectly natural and human one – a moment of domestic perfection with the family gathered round the piano at night, singing, intensely happy. Like Barnes's 'The Wold Clock', but even more so, this scene is both

Dutch and visionary. It's factual and human and yet spiritualised.

The next scene is also one of family harmony:

> They clear the creeping moss –
> Elders and juniors – aye,
> Making the pathways neat
> And the garden gay;
> And they build a shady seat....
> Ah, no; the years, the years;
> See, the white storm-birds wing across!

As Thom Gunn says, their tidying the moss is 'a quiet clearing of space in nature so as to make room for human assertions'. There may be a threat in the 'creeping moss' but they are pushing it firmly back in the way that the 'close light' in ' "In the Seventies" ' keeps the cold darkness back. What these lines communicate is a fundamental sense of worthwhileness: we know from the refrains and the countless other poems that, yes, the 'shady seat' will rot and weeds and moss will cover paths and garden, but that kind of knowledge is left outside and somewhere else because it has nothing to do with the sheer, ordinary perfection of their gardening or their singing. They are all together in the natural setting as they are again in:

> They are blithely breakfasting all –
> Men and maidens – yea,
> Under the summer tree,
> With a glimpse of the bay,
> While pet fowl come to the knee....
> Ah, no; the years O!
> And the rotten rose is ript from the wall.

The unexpected uniqueness of that detail of the pet fowl is marvellous, and in a perfectly natural way this also shows how successfully they have tamed and domesticated nature. They can breakfast outside, under 'the summer tree', and like gods looking down have 'a glimpse of the bay' – it's the perfection of this life. There is something both biblical and Victorian about this scene of 'men and maidens' breakfasting outside. It feels both timeless and a period-piece, and Hardy's point is that in this particular moment – as in the others – they are in contact with a fundamental, timeless worthwhileness. And breakfast, especially outside in the sunshine, on Sunday or a holiday, can have this sacramental quality more than any other meal.

Each moment in the poem seems both uniquely itself and one of many similar ones. They are doing something which they often do together as a complete, happy family. But in the last stanza they do something unusual, though with the same rapt blitheness:

> They change to a high new house,
> He, she, all of them – aye,
> Clocks and carpets and chairs
> On the lawn all day,
> And brightest things that are theirs....
> Ah, no; the years, the years;
> Down their carved names the rain-drop ploughs.

The 'high new house' and the 'brightest things that are theirs' represent all those perfectly natural feelings which everyone has about owning property and things, an instinctive materialism. Again, these are visionary objects like the furniture in 'Old Furniture' or 'The Wold Clock'. They have their ancestral associations and they are also 'brightest' – a rather worn adjective perhaps, like 'dearest' and 'blithely', but one which Hardy has chosen carefully because it's instinct with their valuation of things, the glow they put into them. Like 'dearest songs' and 'blithely breakfasting' the phrase is rubbed with the personality of a happy, confident family. It's as if Hardy has introduced a word like 'super' without either sneering at it or letting it sound like a vapid cliché, and yet has done so in order to place and class the type of person who uses it without in any way patronising them. He has deliberately selected good, solid superlatives that will never quite become obsolete.

However, as Thom Gunn points out, there is something odd and disconcerting in this picture of interior things outside on a lawn, and with so much wind and rain in the poem one can't help worrying that a sudden thunderstorm will rust the clocks and soak the carpets. Inside a house one credits the solid certainties of ornaments and furniture, but place them outside and the flimsy arbitrariness of the domestic order is exposed. And yet the rapid, confident movement of the lines has the same verve as the other stanzas and this prevents all the hesitations and anxieties that belong to the word 'change' from making themselves felt. 'The Change' is about a terrible transformation from ecstatic happiness to despair and death, but this change is a simple removal to a 'high new house'. The family is prospering, moving up in the world, acquiring more property. Their new house is an achieved ideal; it reaches up into the sky. Again, the furniture outside during their removal can, and does, have all the freshness of a spring clean – windows and doors open, carpets outside – the domestic order is being renewed out in the air and sunshine. So this is another example of a sudden freshness blowing into a fixed routine, like the fallow deer peeping through the window or the wind on the stair. These pictures of family life have the same qualities of warm closeness and convinced joy that we find in Tolstoy's descriptions of those family expeditions to the birch woods to gather mushrooms and wild strawberries.

However, each of the four images falls just short of perfection. Each tails off in a series of dots as though torn at the edge, and then the last two lines violate the integrity of what should be a pure, single, perfect image. Alternatively, one could argue that the dots simply suggest the utter disparity and total lack of continuity between each moment of happiness and the corroding time beyond it. They make a division between one reality of timeless vision and another reality of ordinary, destructive time, of waste, dead matter. We know – and this is both a help and a hindrance – that these images didn't just appear out of nowhere, because the text of an account of her childhood which Hardy's wife wrote survives and has been published. Many of the details in the poem are there in Emma Hardy's *Some Recollections* – the singing, the summer tree, their garden, those unique pet fowl, the move to another house. But there they are just so many rather fascinating facts, and it would be both terribly wrong and reductively Hobbesian to make Hardy's imagination wholly dependent on them, for, naturally, his imagination transformed them, rather in the way that the abbey mason transmuted the frozen rain on his sketch, the given facts, into a work of the highest imagination. And in this poem, 'The Abbey Mason' and 'The Figure in the Scene' the temporal rain makes imaginative value. But it isn't wholly responsible for that value: there is also the poet's imagination which co-operates with both fact and memory and totally transforms them.

In her freshly ingenuous account of her childhood Emma Hardy mentions how their house had

> a singular water-purifier in the large court. It was a stone pedestal of enormous size, with four huge columns of stone supporting a huge stone basin, 'a dripstone', and under which a bucket

received the water drop by drop purified – a monster drop long a-coming, and long delaying its fall.

With childlike delight she presents this as something quaint and interesting, while Hardy seizes her recollection and transforms it into a violent symbol of time's erosion of the memories of the dead: 'Down their carved names the raindrop ploughs.' He seems to crush her delighted description, as if rubbing time's message home like the architect to the heiress. There is a parallel with the violation of this image in 'The Convergence of the Twain':

> Over the mirrors meant
> To glass the opulent
> The sea-worm crawls – grotesque, slimed, dumb, indifferent.

Here, the hostility of experience and both human and non-human nature ravish the proud, bridal beauty of the maiden ship, just as each image in 'During Wind and Rain' is torn by the hostilities of sick leaves, white storm-birds, rotten roses and the ploughing rain-drops. These are inescapable realities and their natural cruelty shouldn't be palliated, but Hardy is also, to an extent, identifying himself with them, just as he identifies the iceberg and the sea-worm with the bridegroom. They are instances of what he means by the architect's 'facile foresight', though that in no way diminishes their brutal truth and reality.

What is crucial here is the sense we get of all that the major images represent – the joy of life – surviving in despite of these corroding refrains. They are not like the heiress's pretentiously romantic optimism and nor are they an opulent showiness overwhelmed by icy water and smeared by the sea worm. Instead, they testify to a fundamental worthwhileness and assert the joy and grace of life, not a minimal endurance like the ploughman and horse in '"In Time of the Breaking of Nations"'. They represent the highest possible valuation of the here-and-now and they are each victories over all the interloping hostilities that will sooner or later taint, not them but the family we see so perfectly assured of their happiness going on forever. If this family's concerted gardening is a doomed effort to reduce nature to a tame domestic order, to keep ugliness and untidiness at bay, they are still doing something which is natural and instinctive. And if their harmony with each other and nature will eventually be destroyed, it would be wrong to allow a sense of this to drag down their affirmations, because the 'yes' they are saying to life transcends the grinding inevitabilities of change.

As I've said before the separation between fact and vision in 'After a Romantic Day' makes the external world terrifyingly dead and threatening and imagination just a flimsy fantasy. However, this is not what happens in 'During Wind and Rain', because the images there are visionary transparencies which are not projected onto dead fact – they have transcendental capabilities that float them above the ruck of wind, weather and disappointment. These images are packed with facts which have been totally transformed by the imagination and they exist in the kind of timeless reality which is unconvincingly elaborated in 'The Absolute Explains'. They are so beautifully and freshly present, are so uniquely human in their details and visionary in their total composition, that it would be quite wrong to place 'During Wind and Rain' with poems like 'The Five Students', 'Heiress and Architect', 'The Convergence of the Twain' – poems which detail an inevitable progress from confident illusion to cruel disappointment. These images belong with the youth's 'magic light' that is 'as delicate as lamp-worm's lucency'. They're illuminated transparencies, but this does not mean that they are just subjective illusions flickering on an empty, cold screen. They are true visions and they are somewhere else.

Conclusion

Though I began by citing Hardy's statement that the 'poetry of a scene varies with the minds of the perceivers', and though much of what I've said has been an attempt to show how firmly his work is tied to the positivism and sceptical empiricism implicit in that statement, I'm aware that there are areas of my discussion – particularly in the last chapter – which suggest that his imagination wasn't wholly governed by a despotic eye, that he wasn't the absolute prisoner of his sense impressions. For me there are times when he breaks out of Hume's imaginative universe and achieves a visionary freedom. This is what happens in 'During Wind and Rain', where each of the four major images is a vision that transcends the injustices of time. In arguing this, I've deliberately left the last sentence of the final chapter open – open not so much as a question but as an unsubstantiated assertion – and in doing so I'm aware that some of Hardy's readers may well object that such moments of vision can't possibly be reconciled with the 'full look at the worst' which he takes in those pitiless and terrible refrains. Here, I would simply argue that such a reconciliation is impossible: there can be no connection between the truth of the refrains and the truth of the images, and Hardy doesn't attempt to make one. Each truth is uncompromising and, in its own terms, final.

The other objection is the familiar objection to Hardy's 'pessimism'. We think of him primarily as a writer who found life cruel and unjust and said so, and it is this which has recently led Geoffrey Grigson – one of his most actively sympathetic readers and followers – to argue that in saying so Hardy tended to give life rather less than its due. For Grigson, Hardy has not enough 'relish' to offer and so, finally, we must turn away from him. Such a dismissal cannot be very compelling – the diffident, quiet authority of Hardy's poetic achievement is too strong for it. And in any case part of that achievement is located in those moments when he contradicts both his own pessimism and positivism and also – it has to be said – Grigson's long-considered, but ultimately shallow, reading of his work. Here, 'During Wind and Rain' is the crucial poem. Though it holds both death and living vision, both grace and time, it is possible to read it as a poem which simply sets a number of short-lived happinesses against a ruthless background of obliteration; and for some readers this may be too pessimistic. The mistake is understandable, for between the constrained mitigations of small mercies and the total freedom of grace there is the thinnest and most absolute of distinctions. But it is a distinction which Hardy makes.

Notes

INTRODUCTION

page

2 'Rationalists . . . Revelationists': Florence Emily Hardy, *The Life of Thomas Hardy* (1970), p. 332.

2 'material world . . . so uninteresting': William Archer, *Real Conversations* (1904), p. 45.

2–3 'despotism of the eye': Samuel Taylor Coleridge, *Biographia Literaria* (1906 edition), p. 56.

3 'We have but faith': Tennyson, prologue to *In Memoriam*.

6 'inert observation': Donald Davie, *Thomas Hardy and British Poetry* (1973), p. 48.

6 'instead of transforming': Davie, p. 62.

6 'Hardly Anything Bears Watching': Davie, p. 67, quoted from the *Spectator*, 16 August 1965.

7 Colin Falck, 'The Poetry of Ordinariness', *The New Review*, April 1974.

7 'Neither in Hardy nor in Auden': *Thomas Hardy and British Poetry*, p. 118.

7 'An object or mark': *The Life of Thomas Hardy*, p. 116.

7 'Let others – Dylan Thomas': Calvin Bedient, 'On the Poetry of Charles Tomlinson', *British Poetry Since 1960*, ed. Michael Schmidt and Grevel Lindop (1972), p. 175.

10 'without meaning to': Davie, p. 78.

CHAPTER 1

13 Hardy's account of his life. As R. L. Purdy shows in *Thomas Hardy: A Bibliographical Study* (1954), the first volume of this biography – *The Early Life of Thomas Hardy* – though it was published under Florence Hardy's name in 1928 is 'in reality an autobiography . . . the writing is throughout Hardy's own'. The second volume, *The Later Years of Thomas Hardy* (1930), was 'largely written by Hardy himself'. The last four chapters were written by Florence Hardy. All references are to the one-volume edition, *The Life of Thomas Hardy* (Macmillan, 1962, last reprinted 1975).

15 'Change dissolves the landscapes': 'In the Mind's Eye', *The Collected Poems of Thomas Hardy* (1930), p. 210.

15 'but what a rough unsightly Sketch': Addison, *Spectator*, no. 413, quoted by Marjorie Nicolson in *Newton Demands the Muse: Newton's* Opticks *and the Eighteenth-Century Poets* (Princeton, 1966), p. 149.

16 'sensible qualities': George Berkeley, *Three Dialogues between Hylas and Philonus* (1713). See *Berkeley's Philosophical Writings*, ed. David M. Armstrong (New York, 1965), p. 623.

16 'would cease to exist': Bertrand Russell, *The History of Western Philosophy* (1969), p. 623.

17 'Each one of us': *The History of Western Philosophy*, p. 591.

17 Hume's *Treatise*: the auction catalogue of Hardy's library lists Green and Grose's edition of the *Treatise* (1874). J. I. M. Stewart quotes this sentence from a letter Hardy wrote in 1911: 'My pages show harmony of view with Darwin,

page

Huxley, Spencer, Hume, Mill, and others, all of whom I used to read more than Schopenhauer' (*Thomas Hardy: A Critical Biography* (1971)), p. 31.

18 Ruskin's *Modern Painters*: Hardy's letter is printed in the *Life*, p. 38.

18 'The Pathetic Fallacy': R. L. Purdy, *Thomas Hardy: A Bibliographical Study*, p. 115.

19 Crabbe's influence: Hardy owned an 1861 edition of Crabbe's *Life and Poetical Works.*

20 'the mind in apprehending': A. N. Whitehead, *Science and the Modern World* (New York, 1964), p. 55, quoted by Marjorie Nicolson in *Newton Demands the Muse*, p. 147.

21 'The method of Boldini': *Life*, pp. 120–1.

22 'With respect to the view': Charles Darwin, *The Origin of Species*, 4th ed. (1866), pp. 238–9. Darwin added this passage to the 1866 edition and though it influenced Hardy's 'Let Me Enjoy' it can't have influenced his 1865 note.

23 'The intensest feeling': John Stuart Mill, *Autobiography* (1873), p. 152.

25 'constant conjunction': *A Treatise on Human Nature*, ed. Green and Grose (1874), I, 466.

25 'the effect of repeated perceptions': *Treatise*, I, 487.

25 Hume defines an impression. David Hume, *An Enquiry Concerning Human Understanding*, Part I, Section II. See *Enquiries*, ed. L. A. Selby-Bigge (1962), p. 16.

27 'one of the few people': Alastair Smart, 'Pictorial Imagery in the novels of Thomas Hardy', *Review of English Studies* (1961), p. 275.

27 'In her present beholder's mind': *The Woodlanders* (chap. 2).

27 'the subjective act': Arnold Hauser, *The History of Western Art* (1962), III, 159.

28 'Every woman': *A Pair of Blue Eyes* (chap. 3).

29 'Recollection of what had passed': *Desperate Remedies* (I, 3).

29 'The Affliction of Childhood': *The Collected Writings of Thomas De Quincey*, ed. David Masson (1889), I, quoted in *The English Mind: Studies in the English Moralists Presented to Basil Willey*, ed. Hugh Sykes Davies and George Watson (1964).

32 'This *decaying sense*': Thomas Hobbes, *Leviathan*, ed. Michael Oakeshott (1946), p. 10. R. L. Brett quoted this passage in his essay on Hobbes in *The English Mind.*

33 Locke's comparison: John Locke, *An Essay Concerning Human Understanding*, ed. A. S. Pringle-Pattison (1924), p. 42.

35 'The Profitable Reading of Fiction': reprinted in *Thomas Hardy's Personal Writings*, ed. Harold Orel (1967).

35 *The French Revolution*: Thomas Carlyle, *The French Revolution* (1896), p. 5.

35 'works actively': Basil Willey, *Nineteenth-Century Studies* (1969), p. 22.

35 'were dark': *The Woodlanders* (chap. 14).

36 'observed facts': *The Positive Philosophy of Auguste Comte*, freely translated by Harriet Matineau, with an introduction by Frederic Harrison (1896), I, 3.

36 Bentham and Coleridge: see *Mill on Bentham and Coleridge*, ed. F. R. Leavis (1950).

38 'A novel, good': *Life*, p. 284.

39 Darwin admits: *The Origin of Species* (1860), pp. 186–9.

39 Paley. William Paley, *Natural Theology*, ed. Frederick Ferré (New York, 1963), p. 13.

39 'Theism': John Stuart Mill, *Three Essays on Religion* (1874), p. 174. For Hardy's reading of Mill's essays see W. R. Rutland, *Thomas Hardy: A Study of his Writings and their Background* (1938), p. 67.

40 'The eye and ear': Leslie Stephen, *Essays on Freethinking and Plainspeaking* (1873), p. 27.

40 'Newman's Theory of Belief': Leslie Stephen, *An Agnostic's Apology* (1893), pp. 168–241.

40 *A Grammar of Assent*: Hardy's copy is in the Dorset County Museum.

page

40 'This perception of individual things': John Henry (Cardinal) Newman, *An Essay in Aid of a Grammar of Assent*, ed. Charles Frederick Harold (1947), p. 84.
41 'about a day old': *Far from the Madding Crowd* (chap. 2).
41 'As the magic-lantern': Arthur Schopenhauer, *The World as Will and Idea*, trans. R. B. Haldane and J. Kemp (1883), I 199–200. For Hardy's reading of Schopenhauer see Rutland, *Thomas Hardy: A Study of his Writings and their Background*, p. 93.

CHAPTER 2

45 the margins of the Shelley volume: see Phyllis Bartlett, 'Hardy's Shelley', *Keats-Shelley Journal*, IV (1955) 16.
45 'not two-score years': *Life*, p. 17.
45 Buxton Forman's 1882 edition: *The Poetical Works of Percy B. Shelley*, ed. H. Buxton Forman (1882). Hardy owned this edition and an 1865 edition of Shelley.
46 1 Kings 19, 12: see Kenneth Phelps, *Annotations by Thomas Hardy in his Bibles and Prayer-Book*, Toucan Press Monograph no. 32 (St Peter Port, 1966).
48 'Clifford's Theory of the Intellectual Growth of Mankind': Hardy transcribed this passage from the introduction to Clifford's *Lectures and Essays* into his 'Commonplace Book I'.
48 'atoms and ether': *Lectures and Essays by the late William Kingdom Clifford*, ed. Leslie Stephen and Frederick Pollock (1879), II 67.
49 'the great mistake': Clifford, *Lectures and Essays*, I 251.
51 'Relativity': *Life*, p. 419.
52 'One shape of many names': *The Revolt of Islam*, VIII, 9. For Hardy's underlining of the phrase see Phyllis Bartlett, ' "Seraph of Heaven": A Shelleyan Dream in Hardy's Fiction', *PMLA*, 70 (1955) 628.
53 'God is not': J. Hillis Miller, *Thomas Hardy: Distance and Desire* (1970), p. 150.
54 'I have no philosophy': *Life*, p. 410.
54 'what we call a mind': *A Treatise on Human Nature*, ed. Green and Grose, I 495.
55 'a subjective thing': *The Woodlanders* (chap. 16).
55 'the theory of the transmigration': *Life*, p. 286.
57 'less Byronic': *Tess of the D'Urbervilles* (chap. 31).
57 'a visionary essence': *Tess* (chap. 36).
57 'hard logical deposit': *Tess* (chap. 36).
58 'Tess stole a glance': *Tess* (chap. 36).
58 'serve': *Tess* (chap. 47).
62 'natural solution': Hardy took this phrase from Hume's essay 'Of Miracles and used it in *The Mayor of Casterbridge*, chap. 41.
62 'The season developed': *Tess* (chap. 20).

CHAPTER 3

73 'elaborately cunning metre': Donald Davie, 'Hardy's Virgilian Purples', *Agenda: Thomas Hardy Special Issue*, ed. Donald Davie (1972), p. 139.
77 reading that Dylan Thomas gives: record no. TCE 109.
81 'Years earlier': *Life*, p. 301.
83 Giles Winterbourne: *The Woodlanders* (chap. 28).
84 'sentence-sound': see *Modern Poets on Poetry*, ed. James Scully (1966), pp. 48–57.
85 'absolute fidelity': *Letters from Edward Thomas to Gordon Bottomley*, ed. R. George Thomas (1968), pp. 250–1, quoted in *Edward Thomas: Poems and Last Poems*, ed. Edna Longley (1973), p. 396.
85 'Speech was shapen': quoted in *Selected Poems of William Barnes*, ed. Geoffrey Grigson (1950), p. 38.

CHAPTER 4

91 'the greatest thing': *The Works of John Ruskin*, ed. E. T. Cook and Alexander Wedderburn (1904), v 333.
91 'Saw Gladstone': *Life*, p. 178.
92 'Cold weather': *Life*, p. 177.
94 'They show the ultra-structure': Arthur Koestler, *The Act of Creation* (1966), p. 392.
94 'Waterfalls not only skeined': *Poems and Prose of Gerard Manley Hopkins*, ed. W. H. Gardner (1954), p. 116.
95 'continued existence': *Treatise*, I 485.
95 'from any other principle': *Treatise*, I 404.
95 'constant conjunction': *Treatise*, I 466.
101 'remarked on the expression': quoted by Cosmo Hamilton in *People Worth Talking About* (1934), p. 47.
103 'Though they be mad': Dylan Thomas, 'And Death Shall Have no Dominion'.
105–6 'the errors of systematic materialism': Thomas Henry Huxley, *Lectures and Essays* (1902), p. 57.
106 'sentimental materialist': Edward Wright, 'The Novels of Thomas Hardy', reprinted in *Thomas Hardy: The Critical Heritage*, ed. R. G. Cox (1970), p. 365.

CHAPTER 5

107 'love of fact': *The Works of John Ruskin*, ed. Cook and Wedderburn, x 232.
107 'the fresh originality': Preface to 'Wessex Tales' in *The Short Stories of Thomas Hardy* (1928), p. 4.
107 'pure crude fact': Robert Browning, *The Ring and the Book*, I 35
108 'The "simply natural" ': *Life*, p. 185.
109 'The longer I live': quoted by Betty Miller in *Robert Browning: A Portrait* (1954), p. 164.
109 'He was not simple': quoted in *The Life of Thomas Hardy*, p. 403.
111 'that pattern': *Life*, p. 153.
111 'his plodding steed': *The Woodlanders* (chap. 28).
111 'distinctly visible now': *A Laodicean* (chap. 3).
111 'distinctly visible': 'The Honourable Laura', *The Short Stories of Thomas Hardy*, p. 694.
111 repudiation of Hillis Miller: *Agenda: Thomas Hardy Special Issue*, p. 154.
112 'He stood bareheaded': *Life*, p. 330.
113 'In all my poor historical . . .': Thomas Carlyle, *Critical and Miscellaneous Essays* (1898), IV 406. Hardy's preface to *Wessex Worthies* is reprinted in *Thomas Hardy's Personal Writings*, ed. Orel.
113 'Was struck by the profile': *Life*, p. 128.
114 'A chilly but rainless afternoon': *The Dynasts*, I 4 v.
114 Dick Dewy: *Under the Greenwood Tree* (chap. 1).
114 'His interest in painting': *Life*, p. 52.
115 'unique sensitivity to shape': Alastair Smart, 'Pictorial Imagery in the Novels of Thomas Hardy', *Review of English Studies* (1961), p. 264.
117 'Memories of Church Restoration': reprinted in *Thomas Hardy's Personal Writings*.
119 'Berkeley established': Hardy transcribed this passage from a review of Clifford's *Lectures and Essays* which appeared in the *Edinburgh Review*, CLI (April 1880) 474–511.

CHAPTER 6

121 'eidetic': Arthur Koestler, *The Act of Creation*, pp. 535–6.
123 'The word fell': *A Pair of Blue Eyes* (chap. 34).

page
123 'He was a man': *The Hand of Ethelberta* (chap. 2).
125 'a struggle against images': A. R. Luria, *The Mind of a Mnemonist*, translated by Lyn Solotaroff, with a foreword by Jerome S. Bruner (1969), p. 113.
125 'no real border-line': *The Mind of a Mnemonist*, p. 77.
125 *The Man with a Shattered World*: Oliver Sacks's review of this book, 'The Mind of A. R. Luria', appeared in *The Listener*, 28 June 1973.
126 correspondence: Sacks's closing letter appeared in *The Listener*, 1 November 1973.
130 'He had acquired mechanically': Charles Dickens, *Our Mutual Friend*, ed. Stephen Gill (1971), pp. 266–7.
130 'a paradigm': Oliver Sacks, *The Listener*, 28 June 1973.
137 'As flesh she dies daily': *The Well-Beloved* (chap. 9).
138 'The deep truth': *Prometheus Unbound*, Act II, scene iv, 116.
141 'Within that bright pavilion': *Prometheus Unbound*, Act II, scene i, 119–31.
142 'He thus beheld': *Tess* (chap. 37).
143 'this Whole': *Hellas*, 776–85.
143 Hardy told Florence Henniker . . .: *One Rare Fair Woman: Thomas Hardy's Letters to Florence Henniker, 1893–1922*, ed. Evelyn Hardy and F. B. Pinion (1972), p. 63.
143 'But as we do not attribute': *Treatise on Human Nature*, I 498.

CHAPTER 7

147 letter to Florence Henniker: *One Rare Fair Woman: Thomas Hardy's Letters to Florence Henniker, 1893–1922*, ed. Evelyn Hardy and F. B. Pinion (1972), p. 17.
147 'Only if the existence of the world': Eduard von Hartmann, *The Philosophy of the Unconscious*, trans. William C. Coupland (1884), II 273–4.
149 'Drop serene': *The Poetical Works of John Milton: A new edition from the text of Thomas Newton D.D.* (1864), p. 65. Hardy's copy of this edition is in the Dorset County Museum.
149 'She was in a state': *Far from the Madding Crowd* (chap. 43).
152 'Human tune': 'To the Moon', *Collected Poems*, pp. 410–11.
154 'Every woman': *Life*, p. 210.
155 'Had You Wept': This is a monologue spoken to Eustacia by Clym Yeobright.
157 'In our old shipwrecked days': *Modern Love*, XVI.
157 'troubles began': *Life*, p. 124.
159 'The Science of Fiction': reprinted in *Personal Writings*.
159 'Novel-writing': *Life*, p. 177.
160 'The dreary, dreary train': *The Short Stories*, p. 271.
164 'The Moral Element in Literature': Leslie Stephen, *The Cornhill Magazine*, XLIII (January 1881).
164 a trick photograph: *A Laodicean* (V 4).
164 'The rain had quite ceased': *Far from the Madding Crowd* (chap. 46).
171 Hardy compares them to machines: Donald Davie, *Thomas Hardy and British Poetry*, p. 23.
175 extraordinarily sensitive': *Life*, p. 15.
176 'tired of investigating life': *Life*, p. 227.
176 'committed by circumstances': *Life*, p. 104.
177 'moment, upon the very face': *The Hand of Ethelberta* (chap. 1).

CHAPTER 8

181 'all acts of thought and attention': *Biographia Literaria*, p. 61.
183 'saw in a moment': *The Collected Writings of Thomas De Quincey*, ed. David Masson (1897), III 435.

page

183 'a mighty palimpsest': *The Collected Writings*, ed. Masson (1890), XIII 346–7.
183 'remained written in your mind': William Archer, *Real Conversations*, p. 32.
187 'the fire dancing': *Far from the Madding Crowd* (chap. 46).
189 'her several thoughts': *The Return of the Native* (I 4).
190 'Through the intervening fortnight': *Jude* (I 4).
191 'In his deep concentration': *Jude* (I 6).
193 'He will see what his author': *Thomas Hardy's Personal Writings*, pp. 116–17.
194 'So, then, if Nature's defects . . .': *Life*, p. 114.
194 'light that never was': Wordsworth, 'Elegiac Stanzas upon a Picture of Peele Castle'.
195 'those mechanical instincts': *The World as Will and Idea*, II 197.
195 'One supposes the Will': Louis MacNeice, *The Strings Are False*, ed. E. R. Dodds (1965), p. 32.
195 'practical desire': 'Burnt Norton', II.
200 'Went with E.L.G.': *Life*, p. 75.
200 'Litters of young rabbits': *The Return of the Native* (IV 2).
202 Coleridge speculates: *Biographia Literaria*, p. 60.
206 'a quiet clearing of space': Thom Gunn, 'Hardy and the Ballads', *Agenda*, ed. Davie, p. 30.
208 'a singular water-purifier': *Some Recollections by Emma Hardy*, ed. Evelyn Hardy and Robert Gittings (1961), pp. 67–8.

Select Bibliography

Archer, William, Real Conversations, 1904.
Auden, W. H., *Letters from Iceland*, 1937.
—— *Collected Shorter Poems*, 1966.
—— *City Without Walls*, 1969.
Bagehot, Walter, *Estimates of Some Englishmen and Scotsmen*, 1858.
Bailey, J. O., *The Poetry of Thomas Hardy: A Handbook and Commentary* (Chapel Hill, 1970).
—— *Thomas Hardy and the Cosmic Mind: A New Reading of* The Dynasts (Chapel Hill, 1956).
Barnes, William, *Selected Poems of William Barnes*, ed. Geoffrey Grigson, 1950.
—— *William Barnes: A Selection of his Poems*, ed. Robert Nye, 1972.
Barrie, J. M., 'Barrie Reviews Hardy', *The Literary Digest*, C (February, 1929), 22.
Bartlett, Phyllis, 'Hardy's Shelley', *The Keats-Shelley Journal*, IV (1955), 15–29.
—— ' "Seraph of Heaven": A Shelleyan Dream in Hardy's Fiction', *PMLA*, 70(2) (1955), 624–35.
Bedient, Calvin, 'On the Poetry of Charles Tomlinson', in *British Poetry Since 1960*, ed. Michael Schmidt and Grevel Lindop, 1972.
Berkeley, George, *Berkeley's Philosophical Writings*, ed. David M. Armstrong (New York, 1965).
Bond, Donald F., ed. in *The Spectator*, 1965.
Brett, R. L., 'Thomas Hobbes', in *The English Mind: Studies in the English Moralists Presented to Basil Willey*, ed. Hugh Sykes Davies and George Watson, 1964.
Carlyle, Thomas, *The French Revolution*, 1896.
—— *Sartor Resartus*, 1896.
—— *Past and Present*, 1897.
—— *Critical and Miscellaneous Essays*, 1898.
Clifford, W. K., 'The late Professor Clifford's Essays', anon. review in *The Edinburgh Review*, CLI (April, 1880), 474–511.
—— *Lectures and Essays by the late William Kingdom Clifford*, ed. Leslie Stephen and Frederick Pollock.
Coleridge, Samuel Taylor, *The Poetical Works of Samuel Taylor Coleridge*, ed. James Dykes Campbell, 1893.
—— *Biographia Literaria*, 1906.
Comte, Auguste, *The Positive Philosophy of Auguste Comte*, trans. Harriet Martineau, intro. Frederic Harrison, 1896.
Cox, C. B., and Dyson, A. E., *The Practical Criticism of Poetry: A Textbook*, 1966.
Crabbe, George, *The Poetical Works of George Crabbe*, 1863.
—— *A Selection from George Crabbe*, ed. John Lucas, 1967.
Darwin, Charles, *The Origin of Species*, 2nd ed., 1860.
—— *The Origin of Species*, 4th ed., 1866.
Davie, Donald (ed.) *Agenda: Thomas Hardy Special Issue* (spring–summer 1972).
—— *Thomas Hardy and British Poetry*, 1973.
—— 'Hardy and the Avant-Garde', *New Statesman* (October, 1961).
Davies, Hugh Sykes, 'Wordsworth and the Empirical Philosophers', in *The English Mind: Studies in the English Moralists Presented to Basil Willey*, ed. Hugh Sykes Davies and George Watson, 1964.

Deacon, Lois, and Coleman, Terry, *Providence and Mr. Hardy*, 1966.
Dickens, Charles, *Our Mutual Friend*, ed. Stephen Gill, 1971.
Donne, John, *John Donne: The Complete Poems*, ed. A. J. Smith, 1971.
Dunn, Douglas, *Terry Street*, 1969.
—— *The Happier Life*, 1972.
—— *Love or Nothing*, 1974.
Eliot, T. S., *Four Quarters*, 1964.
Falck, Colin, 'The Poetry of Ordinariness', *The New Review* (April 1974).
Firor, Ruth A., *Folkways in Thomas Hardy* (New York, 1962).
Gray, Thomas, *The Poems of Gray and Collins*, ed. Austin Lane Poole, 1961.
Gunn, Thom., 'Hardy and the Ballads', in *Agenda: Thomas Hardy Special Issue*, ed. Donald Davie (spring–summer 1972).
Grigson, Geoffrey, *A Skull in Salop*, 1967.
—— *An Ingestion of Ice-Cream*, 1969.
—— *Discoveries of Bones and Stones*, 1971.
—— *Sad Grave of an Imperial Mongoose*, 1973.
—— *Angles and Circles*, 1974.
—— *The Contrary View*, 1974.
Hamilton, Cosmo, *People Worth Talking About*, 1934.
Hardy, Evelyn, and Robert Gittings (eds), *Some Recollections by Emma Hardy*, 1961.
Hardy, Evelyn, and Pinion, F.B. (eds), *One Rare Fair Woman: Thomas Hardy's Letters to Florence Henniker, 1893–1922*, 1972.
Hardy, Florence Emily, *The Life of Thomas Hardy*, 1970.
Hardy, Thomas, *The Collected Poems of Thomas Hardy*, 1930.
—— *The Dynasts: An Epic-Drama of the War with Napoleon*, ed. John Wain, 1968.
—— The Novels.
—— *The Short Stories of Thomas Hardy*, 1928.
—— 'Commonplace Book I' (in the Dorset County Museum).
—— 'Literary Notes II' (in the Dorset County Museum).
Hartmann, Eduard von, *Philosophy of the Unconscious*, trans. William C. Coupland, 1884.
Hauser, Arnold, *The Social History of Art*, 1962.
Hobbes, Thomas, *Leviathan*, ed. Michael Oakeshott, 1946.
Holland, Clive, *Thomas Hardy O.M.*, 1933.
Hopkins, Gerard Manley, *Poems and Prose of Gerard Manley Hopkins*, ed. W. H. Gardner, 1954.
Hume, David, *A Treatise on Human Nature*, ed. T. H. Green and T. H. Grose, 1874.
—— *Enquiries*, ed. L. A. Selby-Bigge, 1962.
Huxley, Thomas, *Lectures and Essays*, 1902.
Hynes, Samuel, *The Pattern of Hardy's Poetry*, 1961.
Koestler, Arthur, *The Act of Creation*, 1966.
Larkin, Philip, *The Whitsun Weddings*, 1964.
—— *High Windows*, 1974.
—— 'Wanted: Good Hardy Critic', *The Critical Quarterly* (summer 1966).
Locke, John, *An Essay Concerning Human Understanding*, ed. A. S. Pringle-Pattison, 1924.
Luria, A. R., *The Mind of a Mnemonist*, trans. Lyn Solotaroff, with a foreword by Jerome S. Bruner, 1969.
MacNeice, Louis, *The Strings Are False*, ed. E. R. Dodds, 1965.
Marsden, Kenneth, *The Poems of Thomas Hardy: A Critical Introduction*, 1969.
Mill, John Stuart, *Three Essays on Religion*, 1874.
—— *Autobiography*, 1873
—— *Mill on Bentham and Coleridge*, ed. F. R. Leavis, 1950.
Miller, Betty, *Robert Browning: A Portrait*, 1954.

Miller, J. Hillis, *Thomas Hardy: Distance and Desire*, 1970.
Milton, John, *Milton's Poems*, ed. B. A. Wright, 1963.
—— *The Poetical Works of J. Milton: A new edition from the text of Thomas Newton D.D.*, 1864.
Nevinson, Henry W., *Thomas Hardy*, 1941.
Newman, John Henry, *An Essay in Aid of a Grammar of Assent*, ed. Charles Frederick Harold, 1947.
Nicolson, Marjorie Hope, *Newton Demands the Muse: Newton's* Opticks *and the Eighteenth-Century Poets* (Princeton, 1966).
Paley, William, *Natural Theology*, ed. Frederick Ferré (New York, 1963).
Phelps, Kenneth, *Annotations by Thomas Hardy in his Bibles and Prayer-Book*, Toucan Press Monograph 32, St Peter Port, 1966.
Pinion, F. B., *A Hardy Companion*, 1968.
Pound, Ezra, *Literary Essays of Ezra Pound*, ed. and intro. by T. S. Eliot, 1968.
Purdy, R. L., *Thomas Hardy: A Bibliographical Study*, 1954.
De Quincey, Thomas, *The Collected Writings of Thomas De Quincey*, ed. David Masson, 1889.
Ruskin, John, *The Works of John Ruskin*, ed. E. T. Cook and Alexander Wedderburn, 1904.
Russell, Bertrand, *History of Western Philosophy*, 1961.
Rutland, W. R., *Thomas Hardy: A Study of his Writings and their Background*, 1938.
Sacks, Oliver, 'The Mind of A. R. Luria', in *The Listener* (28 June 1973).
—— 'Alexander Luria', letter in *The Listener* (1 November 1973).
—— *Awakenings*, 1973.
Schopenhauer, Arthur, *The World as Will and Idea*, trans. R. B. Haldane and J. Kemp, 1883.
Shelley, Percy Bysshe, *The Poetical Works of Percy B. Shelley*, ed. H. Buxton Forman, 1882.
—— *The Complete Works of Percy Bysshe Shelley*, ed. Roger Ingpen and Walter E. Peck, 1930.
—— *The Complete Poetical Works of Percy Bysshe Shelley*, ed. Thomas Hutchinson, 1952.
Siegel, Paul N., 'Hardy's "Convergence of the Twain" ', *Explicator*, XI (1952).
Smart, Alastair, 'Pictorial Imagery in the Novels of Thomas Hardy', *Review of English Studies*, 12 (1961).
Stephen, Leslie, *Essays on Freethinking and Plainspeaking*, 1873.
—— *An Agnostic's Apology*, 1893.
—— 'The Moral Element in Literature', *The Cornhill Magazine*, XLIII (January 1881).
Stevenson, Lionel, *Darwin Among the Poets*, Chicago, 1932.
Stewart, J. I. M., *Eight Modern Writers*, 1963.
—— *Thomas Hardy: A Critical Biography*, 1971.
Tennyson, Alfred, *The Poems of Tennyson*, ed. Christopher Ricks, 1969.
Thomas, Edward, *Edward Thomas: Poems and Last Poems*, ed. Edna Longley, 1973.
Tomlinson, Charles, *Seeing Is Believing*, 1960.
—— *A Peopled Landscape*, 1963.
—— *American Scenes*, 1966.
—— *The Way of a World*, 1969.
—— *Written on Water*, 1972.
—— *The Way In*, 1974.
Virgil, *Aeneid*, trans. John Dryden, in *The Poems of John Dryden*, ed. James Kinsley, 1958.
Whitehead, A. N., *Science and the Modern World* (New York, 1964).
Willey, Basil, *Nineteenth-Century Studies*, 1969.
Wordsworth, William, *The Prelude* (1805), ed. Ernest de Selincourt, 1932.
—— *The Poetical Works of William Wordsworth*, ed. Thomas Hutchinson, 1966.

Wright, Edward, 'The Novels of Thomas Hardy', in *Thomas Hardy: The Critical Heritage*, ed. R. G. Cox, 1970.

Yeats, W. B., *Collected Poems of W. B. Yeats*, 1969.

Zietlow, Paul, *Moments of Vision: The Poetry of Thomas Hardy* (Harvard University Press, 1974).

Index